Published in 2025 by Provoco Publishing who own the publishing rights.

ISBN: 978-1-9192637-0-0

Cover Design and Artwork - © Inés and reproduced under licence
Logo Design - © MJC at Martyn Carson Creative
Edited by Jane Murray

The Unwrapping

Nicholas Vaughan

Chapter One

In a stifling room, within a hot and dusty back street of Cairo, during the reign of the King's Imperial men in nineteen hundred, a small crowd had gathered. Nitocris Symonds, Ramses and Cleopatra Cholmondeley were staring at a mummy.

Nitocris gave a shriek of delight, "He's alive!"

And he was. The People's Pharoah gave a yawn while he gasped for air. It was difficult to tell if he was genuinely struggling to breathe, or if it was just a side effect of the virus that had struck him down so long ago. As cobwebs fell from his wrinkly face, a puffy countenance appeared; ruddy with good health but looking a bit old and long in the tooth. Beneath the puffiness, his cheeks were gaunt after many years in a sarcophagus. As he was being brushed free from mud and caked on sand, his features began to undergo a transformation, and soon he appeared to display a rosy complexion, which would have been envied by many.

Ramses replied to Nitocris's shriek. 'Well, he's taken his time to arrive back!'

"Back from where?" asked Cleopatra.

"Well, he's been gone for so many years, you probably wouldn't have noticed, dear. But I suspect he's still not as old as you."

Cleopatra, who lied about her age, spluttered and huffed in disgust. "That's no answer," she told Ramses. "Where's he been, I want to know!"

Ramses answered. "According to public myth he evaporated in an explosion of dust and cholera particles many years ago, and he's not been seen since. He had cholera, suffering greatly, but is now well again. He obviously didn't explode. Here he is!"

As Augustuskamoun, the People's Pharaoh, came to, he gave a snort of derision meant for the audience that he had left behind many generations before. He was re-emerging in a new world, one where the next wave of the pandemic hadn't reached yet, but now there was every danger of it being transported by his portly self. With each person who left the room, they could be transporting traces of that fifth killer cholera epidemic across the city.

Ramses looked across at Nitocris, Ladyship Symonds who, as she could see Augustuskamoun being materialized back, was obviously thinking what a damn good partner the awakening Pharoah might make. She was middle-aged with white skin, verging on transparent.

He gave a polite cough in her direction and stuttered, "Get that idea out of your head. Your jewellery all looks fake, precious stones spilling over your flabby upper arms, and of poor imitation Egyptian quality."

Nitocris guffawed. "Thanks for the compliment, darling," she replied, playfully, one eye on Lady Cholmondeley for a reaction.

Cleopatra Cholmondeley looked the other way. She had been listening with a smile which grew at the thought of somebody else's misery. Namely, Ladyship Symonds'. "What do you reckon the size of the dowry is then, Twosret?"

Twosret Seymour was married to Pepi Seymour and therefore part of the little group who purported to be the inner circle, the ones who would be closest to the awakening Augustuskamoun. She wriggled her thumb to indicate Nitocris was under it, meaning a partner, then went on to reel off her calculations. "She's probably got less to her name than either of the pair of us."

They both shrieked with laughter at this. Twosret was in her fifties and dressed in an off-brown ribbed cloak, with long flowing arms that dangled elegantly down, thus covering any telltale flabby arms that bore more than a passing resemble to Nitocris's arms.

Cleopatra said, "You'd never marry under your status, would you?"

Twosret answered. "I would never risk jeopardizing my future by marrying under my wealth."

Cleopatra elbowed her and the two cackled in a bullying and matronly way. "She'll learn the lie of the land as she gets older," she smiled, rather cattily towards Ladyship Symonds, who remained where she was, trying not to look discomfited.

Deciding their own dowries were comparable to hers, they both gave a bemused giggle, proceeding to taunt, bug, and poke the reawakening form of Augustuskamoun himself.

As Augustuskamoun came around, he ordered a suckling pig to satiate the hunger of his guests, and a handful of partridges for himself. He was middle-aged and wore a blue war crown, linen skirt, and arm bracelets, with a feather fan laid across his chest.

Ramses said, "Papyrus scrolls at his feet show he is a learned man."

Cleopatra cried, "It shows he's good at getting laid more like. Each one should have a list of women he's entertained over the years."

There was an offended silence from Nitocris, and Twosret raised a finger to her lips to nip it in the bud.

After much pomp and ceremony, the servants brought in the feast from the kitchen, but to Augustuskamoun's horror, in front of him sat a camel, a jackal, and a crocodile, each neatly served on a bed of bulrushes.

"I can't eat this!" Augustuskamoun exclaimed. "I need fine English gamekeeper's fare, rich and juicy. This desert food is far too dry."

After another short while, food appealing to the awakened Pharaoh was brought in, which seemed to calm him.

Cleopatra called out, "Cooks!" and the two responsible for the preparation and cooking of the feast ambled through the door. "You haven't got a brain cell between the pair of you, and for ruining the master's first proper meal back on this planet, you're both sacked."

Cleopatra dismissed the pair with a wave of her hand. One was heard to mutter something about poison, in the context of wishing he had doused the feast with it, but sadly, at least for him, he hadn't thought of it until now.

As Augustuskamoun's lifeforce and will to live were slowly rekindled with his intake of food, his memories of what he just left and thoughts of what he was coming back to, began to form in his mind. The last plague was awful. Millions died everyday globally. For so many years, nobody was able to pinpoint what they were fighting against. Augustuskamoun's party had been in control back then, and he had been taking advice from his governing partners as to the best way for the plague to be managed. Their efforts had still gone wildly amiss, and their judgments about what was best for the country were publicly ignored.

As those that gathered around the room began to disperse, they took off in various directions across the city. Some headed for the old town, the religious quarter and shanty district; others lived out near the new necropolis that had been built on the outskirts of the more traditional areas.

One of those shuffling away towards the old town, Ammon said, "The Pharaoh was brought back to life; didn't you see that today?"

Femi nodded. "Yes, it was just another way to combat the virus, by bringing another form of rebirth back into play."

"It's better to see it that way." Ammon replied. "Currently we need all the help we can get! What I saw earlier on had me quaking with fear. I have no knowledge of Egyptian kings, or their dynasties either, so to see a man materialize out of another time and bring with him a deadly organism in hot pursuit, I was riveted."

"That was incredible," another called Keket piped up. "But I know a thing or two about our history, and how fraught with curses and superstitions it is. The way he suddenly came alive from beneath those yellowing bandages, with glowing eyes, and that musty stench was from hell to be sure."

"It scared the living daylights out of me, too." Femi exclaimed.

But even by putting their heads together they couldn't come up with a suitable answer as to the origins of the Pharaoh, and why he appeared to them that day.

Kissa, a researcher, had spent many years studying the culture, and she offered her opinion on the whole event. What she knew about the reasons a king might give for this journey from the afterlife.

She said, "He has probably acted wrongly and is trying to cover his path quickly, usually this is the case. Doing this is just a quick escape to a new beginning, where he can erase his past, and his ill reputation, and move onto better things again. You must imagine that this man has come from a time before us, this is like entering a world of corpses for him. All the people he knew are long since gone, he looks around and all he sees are dead faces that cannot comment on his bad actions. Of course, he would want to come here and restart his life, though most likely he will be eternal now. You know how these elite people can be, they don't always care about the wellbeing of the ordinary people, they're more likely to be caught up in their own affairs and importance."

As they arrived home to their various quarters of the city, they began to spread the word of what they saw that afternoon. Ammon related the tale to his family, most were horrified, some blamed it on the English.

"The colonialists are always looking for solutions to manage the country more effectively. Solutions that suit their own needs better than the indigenous people," his father Husain said.

Ammon said, "Are they really that bad?"

Husain, choked with emotion, stuttered out, "Yes, they are terrible." Recovering himself, he said, "It occurred to me that the English are looking for a way to hide something. During the unravelling, a myriad of germs made its escape, they are now filtering through the back streets of the old town, and soon they will reach us. I have a friend, Karim, who can help us, though."

Ammon looked worried. "That sounds awful, are we at peril?"

Husain replied, "If the last time is anything to go by, I'd say yes."

Ammon gulped.

Husain said, "Karim works at the society of pests and diseases, and has faithfully passed it on, that a huge cloud of cholera has been seen gravitating slowly towards the centre of Cairo."

Ammon asked, "How could you tell?"

Husain replied, "You can tell by its colour, purply silver tinges and hues, bright blue molecular spheres with blood red tendrils, billowing out. You can't argue with that!"

"Tell me a story," Ammon said.

Husain began. "My grandparents were here last time; they were really badly hit before."

Ammon replied, "I've heard about this from other family members, saying how badly they were treated by the English, they gave them no mercy. They were even setting up quarantine bases in other countries, so people could be deported easier."

Husain nodded. "That's exactly what happened, we lost hundreds of thousands. If you were inflicted with it, you came a cropper within weeks. The medicine was ill-suited and there wasn't enough of it around. The pharaohs were making all sorts of outrageous deals with the English to bring over more suitable drugs. But anything that came over went towards the upkeep of their own friends and family's health. The advice they were handing out was abominable. But they had to dish out advice so that people could see they were trying to get the death rate down, so it would look good on them in the future."

Meanwhile, a newly invigorated Augustuskamoun had

a plan for the repurposing of older buildings, structures like pyramids, sphinx, temples, and mosques. He decided they should be used as giant hospitals for the leprous sick, or for plague victims to be disposed of in purpose-built cremation facilities, as this is deemed the most humane, speedy, and hygienic way of dealing with the problem a cholera outbreak would present.

Augustuskamoun also figured that back in the thirteenth century, halting the spread of the bubonic plague, by setting the place on fire had worked for London. That was the birth of the modern city. But could Augustuskamoun convince the citizens of Cairo that their beloved home will be better off being burnt to the ground, purely to cleanse the place of an infection? He doubted it.

He was so ruthless, he was willing to try anything and summoned his two Pharoah's in Waiting to attend. Ramses Cholmondeley and Pepi Seymour, who wore sandals, necklace, regal headdress, and a waistcoat adorned with resplendent rare and bedazzling stones. He had been trained as a member of royalty to always have his spear by his side.

"Go forth and inform the Egyptians their fate lies in their own hands," Augustuskamoun told them. "I'm giving them two options; they can either come peacefully and work for the English, in which case we will take their belongings and make use of their businesses to store medical supplies in, their houses will be commandeered and used as testing centres. Or, if they want to look after themselves, we will leave them to their own devices, then begin copying their tactics when they are getting the upper hand."

Pepi and Ramses rushed out as they had been bid by

Augustuskamoun. They entered the nearest square and waited for a sizeable crowd to build, then they gave their speech. Ammon, Femi, and Keket, were stood nearby listening diligently to the address, and now deliberated the best way to approach the situation.

Ammon said, "Should we defect to the Pharaohs? Go over to their side and give full access to our properties and possessions? Or risk it all for what we know about the virus, which is next to nothing, in the hope that we can make some headway against it. But without any effective tools or a strategy."

Femi considered the options and said, "We will be far better off deviating to the opposition, even though I know how untrustworthy they can be."

Keket disagreed. "We have a lot more chance to save our skins if we fight our own battles. I refuse to move from my parents' home, and I'm fully prepared to defend their position. The government is wrong in trying to prise us from our home, what little else do we have?"

Ammon was so afraid; his legs became jellified on the spot. "Perhaps a better way to fight this invisible enemy would be to leave ourselves to its mercy," he said.

The other two looked at him incredulously as they tried to comprehend his defeatist attitude.

When he heard his sons crushing approach, Husain was in shock. He decided to go and find him, pull him out into the street for all to see. He wanted to shame him in front of the whole neighbourhood, to show that he had been so frightened in the first place.

At that moment Karim came around the corner; he had just finished his shift, it appeared. He spent the day with his face glued to a microscope, analysing petri dishes, trying to work out if there was a different approach that could be used. That way, they could have one up on the pharaohs. Karim had been experimenting with cholera samples the whole day, tipping them from one test tube to another in the vain hope they will react. Adding various elements to each to see what their reaction was, then determining his response from there.

As soon as Augustuskamoun received word from his cronies that the public were willing to give themselves up for their own good, for the benefit of the ruling classes, they were overjoyed, but little grateful. He knew the 'unwrapping' had been a great way to cause terror to be sent out amongst them. Half of them already believed he was a deity from another era. The rest would just fall into line because they always did.

"We must press on with our plans," Augustuskamoun roared. "Now is the perfect time to catch them unawares. From early tomorrow morning, we begin pushing out across the city and its districts. Every owner of property who has deigned to fall into line with our new tactics will be a target. Every building, in every ghetto and shanty town. Even traditional forms such as those that are built into the rockface will be sequestered. The residents will be kicked out and left to fend for themselves."

Nitocris, Cleopatra, and Twosret, were informed before retiring for the night, that they can make themselves useful by providing breakfast. They had nothing planned apart from shopping, drinking coffee, and gossiping, so were quite happy to have this low level of input to the activity. They felt that if the place was going to be crawling with foot soldiers who were displacing people from their homes and livelihoods, perhaps shopping might not provide the spoils they wished for, anyway. They would be far safer and probably gain more themselves by staying close to the Pharoah.

Pepi and Ramses spent the night out by the coast, close to a vineyard where fine wines were assured, and the company of felines guaranteed. They headed back early to the place where Augustuskamoun had called for them to meet. His stately villa, so well preserved in his absence, you'd almost think they knew he was going to return! As they hurried back, they ran into the ladies along the way, heading for the villa for the purpose of preparing a suitable breakfast for the Pharoah. The building they were headed for had been erected in the fourth century with a central avenue that was lined with huge sandstone columns. The palace was high on a precipice, had fine views over the city, and was wildly flourished with decorative columns. A great authority was brought to the building by its subsequent architecture.

As the ladies headed for the kitchen, Pepi and Ramses gathered in the central court; they were brought weapons and other necessities for their day of visitations, to convert the lower orders' houses into test centres. There was a whole legion of chariots and warriors, with winged wheels on their carts. Each spoke and other minute detail had been beautifully carved from rare woods, such as mahogany and cedar. As they took instructions as to the best way to go about their task, they made notes. Cleopatra and Twosret ambled over lazily, with huge steaming urns of sweet, sugary tea.

Pepi cursed. "Now we won't be able to leave for

hours."

Nitocris caught up with them. She had just finished preparing breakfast and was carrying it for the men on a gilt tray. She was used to putting herself in second place when it came to the basic rights in life, such as eating, sleeping, resting, and other considerations. Hurrying away before they could become embroiled with Nitocris and the breakfast party, Pepi and Ramses took flight with their entourage of vehicles; they sped through streets that were silent and had been cleared of human traffic for many hours.

A sandstorm was beginning to blow. It was distributing large quantities of sand up against buildings, partially burying them and making them more difficult to distinguish. Subsequently, the chariots lost their bearings, being unable to recognise the houses and buildings because of the sand. Pepi had been navigating these conditions for many years now, crossing the dunes on camelback, and was in his element. He stopped at nothing, forging ahead with their mission. He threw a left, then a right, then rushed forwards with arcs of sand being thrown from his wheels.

All the soldiers that Augustuskamoun bequeathed to him were charging after him in hot pursuit. The soldiers rallied to Pepi's call. He pulled up at the first address, reading the decree out loud from a parched scroll of papyrus.

Number ten, Sunshine Scrapers was a residential block where an oasis was also found. This was a place of bountiful life and vegetation. The fighters were roused by the thought of its life-giving waters, and its ability to quench their thirst. As they fell into its glassy depths, they were submerged for several minutes, before coming gurgling back up.

Razor blades of sunlight pierced the oasis' impenetrable bottom. As the tempest of dust began to ease above, Ramses rapped at the rocky doorway with his knuckles, as loud as he could, in the hope that somebody would come running. A protocol had been agreed with the men, so they knew exactly what hand signal he would give to instruct them to forge forward and fall upon the house and its occupants.

The dwelling was stormed in record time. All the family members were immediately put under house arrest, before being brought to the front of the building, under the watchful eye of the invaders. Pepi marched around to check if they were being treated with as little amount of respect as they deserved. He caught the faces of Husain and Ammon under the desert boot of a soldier in his military greatcoat. The rest of the family, children, and grandparents had already been seen to, and were not given the chance to squeal. He described what would happen to their home after they left, and that they were now considered homeless.

"There's a department for the likes of your sort, where you might be able to scrape together a few measly pounds," Pepi smugly remarked, watching Husain and Ammon rushing away, presumably in the direction of the social security palace, an unfortunate choice of words considering it offered no security whatsoever.

Karim's residence was next on the list, but by the time the soldiers arrived, he was nowhere to be seen.

"He's defected", Ramses cried. "He's obviously abandoned his place because he heard we are coming, and thought *if I scarper, I'll be free*. We can set up a testing unit in his laboratory as he has this built into his basement already. He has microscopes, test tubes and their holders, huge glass funnels, and conical shaped containers. These can be used to mix, distil, and decant all the necessary substances we need for us to develop our own superior formula in the war on cholera. We must have a highly sophisticated and technological location for us to work from."

Pepi replied, "Let's make this our headquarters from now on. I'll send out several soldiers on a reconnaissance of the land, and the constructions that make up its plot, to see if there is anything else worth picking up."

One of the men came upstairs after scouring one of the adjoining rooms of the cellar, claiming he had found evidence of experiments. Ramses took them to one side and laid them out carefully, then pulled out some equipment from his private stash. He began to set out the various things that he needed to gauge what had been carried out there.

Ramses said, "Someone is trying to work through something with their continual examinations. You can see they are rigorous and dogged in their pursuit of the truth, for the most effective formula that can be used to combat the virus. The one that gives the best chance of making headway against this beast."

Meanwhile, Karim had spent the day stealing through the metropolis, to a backdrop of ancient and wizened lion faces. Etched from the sand like gigantic sculptures, these were the sphinx. Oblivious to the events that occurred whilst his back was turned, Karim made the decision to parade the tree lined arcades that surrounded one of the major pyramids. Here he can find all manner of like-minded souls, people who he could argue, debate, and find solace with.

As Karim gazed up into the moonless, pitch-black sky, he realized that the tar beneath his feet had been slowly melting all day. He tried to extricate himself but with difficulty, going further was not an option, anymore. The immense triangular creation above him had been put up with much effort and labour, many aeons before. Numbers and formulas were streaming through his mind as if on a giant abacus, laws of probability, resulting calculations that brought him ever closer to an equation.

By chance, Kissa was quietly making her way in the opposite direction, pursuing her own thoughts, and reasoning whether what she has revealed makes much sense or not.

She mulled over her next move. "If only I could form an alliance with somebody, then we could work together," she decided.

At that, and as if by some divine coincidence, they both stumbled back into one another. Each broke the others fall as they dropped to the ground. Kissa forced Karim into the nearest bench and parked herself beside him, so they were in a more pleasant position to talk. Gushing with words, they both soon realised they were on an equal footing, having respect for one another's political stance, as well as recognition of the world of academia to solve many of society's ills. Karim elucidated his own personal challenge, in being able to fabricate another medicine suitable for the current onslaught of cholera.

Kissa listened with wide eyes and a look of patience on her face, then she said, "This is the perfect occasion to collaborate, I'd be more than welcome to assist in your plight."

Chapter Two

On the opposite side of the city, a dig was taking place. It had been attracting archaeologists from all over the globe, but also many English colonialists, as there was such a community of them around there. These were people with a passion for collecting, devoted to acquiring new treasures, fossils, and finds. Many working-class citizens of Cairo built their lives around this whole operation, so much infrastructure had gone into it already: Temporary accommodation for the workers, places for them to eat, relax, carry out leisure activities, buy equipment, or to clean their finds.

The list went on. Plus, if you needed work, chances were it would revolve around this huge and industrious site on the fringes of the desert, with quick and easy access to the tunnels, mines, and quarries below.

Nour and Tarek were married and worked together in the bakery.

Nour, who was only small but perfectly capable of punching above her weight, shouted over, "Bring me up another sack of flour!"

Tarek looked across and saw her pull a rolling pin out of her frock pocket, and wave it threateningly over her head.

Tarek said, "The bread's been in the oven far too long and must be burnt."

Nour replied, "Go and pull it out, then, stupid! I've got to go and attend to the volunteers; they've been stepping out of line again."

Tarek said, "Have you seen Nephi the cat?"

"I haven't seen her the whole day, but she's been following us around for many years now, she'll know where to come. She knows our nomadic ways."

Tarek said, "Maybe it's time to rethink our strategy, how about it?"

"We've been doing alright so far, why change? For me, the bakery - it works fine. When my customers peeter out, pass on, or stop buying bread, then it's time to move on."

"It works well for you, but I never get the chance to work up any decent relationships with clients," Tarek whined.

Fed up with his incessant moaning, Nour shouted over, "Another delivery has arrived, can you go over and attend?"

There was a reluctant scowl from Tarek, for whom the bakery did not work fine. He would much rather be doing something else, such as selling the trinkets he made as an artist, mostly imitations of pyramids, sphinx, and other popular symbols of the culture. As well as doing occasional commissions, he had to help Nour because he couldn't survive otherwise, so he spent most of his time in the centre because there was more opportunity for business around there. He would hawk his wares from a blanket at the market, in the shadow of an ancient mosque, where the occasional tourists were to be found. They sometimes took the locomotive up to the site once a week on the old railway line that ran out from the centre.

Also, with the tourists came fresh supplies, yeast, flour, salt, and fresh water, as any found on the site was rancid. Every morning at six, Nour had her ovens firing, producing a wide range of locally produced loaves, such as flatbreads, Shamsi, and Baladi, which the tourists would also sometimes purchase.

Tarek helped Nour out during busy times, but when

he wasn't being her own personal slave, he went back to the daily grind of painting and drawing portraits for generals, officials, colonels, great traders, and any English who wanted a keepsake of their travels to that far-flung part of Africa. Tarek usually travelled to the places where these rich types lived, and was put up for a few days, becoming part of the furniture. They liked having him around longer as then he became more inconspicuous, and observational.

Some offered to become his patron, something Tarek always angled after, as he was assured a more pleasant and easy life, where he could get on with his trade and be respected for what he did, instead of helping to burn bread. The shambolic and noisy lifestyle of the site was far behind him in those instances, and he could escape the constant banging of a shovel and a pick against rock and solidified sand and became accustomed to the noble life of dining on cucumber sandwiches for lunch, instead. How very genteel.

Tarek usually arose at 7am., put on his best outfit and went in the search of quick cash. He wasn't too fussy what he ended up doing, whether it was art based, or some other form of temporary labour. There was a vacant lot on one of the boulevards, and if you arrived by a certain time every day, then people came along and took you away for a day of toil. Usually out on their plantations, or other large estates, mostly owned by rich Egyptians, or English colonialists. In this way, Tarek had done his time in many pharaohs' palaces, too, working in the kitchens, skinning and preparing animals, sweeping sand in the courtyards, humping sacks of flour in the mill, or any number of other menial tasks that were available.

Tarek mentioned it to Nour sometimes, but she was too proud to go and work for somebody else, saying she'd rather earn a living for herself. The day he burnt the bread, Tarek was lucky; instead of Nour's wrath, he was picked up immediately and thrown with force into the back of somebody's horse and cart. He was bewildered and disoriented and didn't have any idea where he was, when they tipped him from the back of the wagon. He only heard the distant cantering of hooves, as they made off, before he blacked out. Tarek was then left for several hours, until the new owners came along.

He felt a boot in his side, and somebody shouting. "Oi you, wake up, sunshine, you've got work to do!"

As he came around, he got his first glance of who appeared to be in charge. Tarek was at the villa of Augustuskamoun, and two cooks were taking delivery of a new kitchen hand. As they put their new charge to work, they were chatting away merrily, one to the other.

"With this reprobate giving us a hand, we will never be in for another beating from the pharaohs again."

By eight o'clock, he had his nose to the grindstone for the royals. No breaks were allowed. Well, not for him, anyway, the two cooks took plenty, while Tarek sweated blood and tears.

Nour didn't even notice he was missing, apart from when she realised he wasn't around to help lumber fresh bags of flour back into the bakery, and the bread was burnt. Taking stock of the situation, Nour backtracked through the events of the day, and worked out when she last saw him. From her memory and by consulting Nephi, she convinced herself he had been lost in action. Then suddenly, Nour remembered Tarek told her he was going out to search for work that day, once he'd made a start on the bread.

Early the next morning, two new faces were at Nour's front door. They seemed friendly rather than nosey, so she let them in, and they introduced themselves as Femi and Keket.

Femi said, "The pharaohs are giving people the choice to clear out their residences, haven't you heard about this yet?"

Nour hadn't heard, and replied, "No, this sounds serious."

She offered to walk them around the dig, as they hadn't been there before, and they set off past the bakery, where she did her milling, past the old well. Before they arrived at the site, which was a huge rift in the valley with all its sides plastered in polythene, scaffolding, and countless sets of ladders. Men ran up and down them, two to the dozen, transporting all manner of goods that were needed by the archaeologists below. Most of the time they just brought up tonnes of brickwork, sandstone, smashed up bits of earthenware, and jugs with chipped handles, porcelain pots with broken spouts, and jewellery; most of it in smithereens.

It took many days and weeks to excavate certain objects. When one was found that was deemed to be of major importance, there would be great excitement that soared through the dig, in an infectious way, so all men working were alight with an intense burst of energy.

Nour said, "The discovery of the late King Tutankhamun's tomb has provided a lot of work for all concerned, up on top, and down below in the ground."

"For people like you, this can be a saviour, those who have suffered hard times," Keket replied.

"The surge in interest means that I have cashed in on it through an increased consumption of bread," Nour told her with satisfaction.

"So, things are getting better?"

"No, I'm still struggling!" Nour told her, with emphasis.

Femi said, "Had you ever thought to see if you needed a curse removing?"

Nour looked at her thoughtfully. "Not really. Why, what does that entail?"

"You can find out whether you need to have a hex removed, or not."

"I think my business might do well from some spiritual intervention. And if the hex is removed, it could only improve my luck." Nour was weighing up the pros and cons.

"The psychic has been out and about again, giving warnings about the king's tomb." Femi told her.

Nour made her decision. "Can you pass on my details. What are the warnings about?"

"They are about a curse that has escaped from King Tutankhamun's tomb."

"I can't see how it's got anything to do with me. This psychic sounds like he could have a positive impact on my life, though."

"Yes, I'll let him know about you," Femi said.

Once they got back from the dig, Nour made them Egyptian tea. She offered a basket of loaves, that she had prepared earlier. Femi and Keket fell upon the food because they were ravenous.

Nour said, "My bakery is suffering so badly!"

"Well, the last thing you want to do is to accept support from the pharaohs," Keket told her, waving a piece of bread around. "Mm, this is delicious!"

"Despite what my colleague here says, I believe you can get help by going to speak to the pharaohs, to resolve your problem." Femi gave Keket a glare and finished the last of the bread before Keket could take it.

They conversed for a while about what the best approach for Nour would be; around lunchtime they collected their belongings and prepared to leave. They agreed with Nour that she will escort them back into the centre, then they would attempt to track down Karim and Kissa.

The journey back into the centre was arduous, dusty, and hot. They climbed aboard a steam engine as it pulled close to the outskirts of the dig, hoping to claim a free ride back. They had no other option. It was crammed with intrepid explorers, many of whom had made great finds that day, and were heading home for the evening. Some were adventurers in hats with strings of bullets slung across their chests. Others wore leather trousers and shirts with open necks. One carried a gun draped over his treasure. It was a coffin made of copper and other fine and precious metals. It had inlays of brass, palladium, bronze, and platinum, with lead casing beneath, through which you could just see the head of a bandaged mummy peeking out. Its pattern and distinctive striped cowl were reminiscent of the god of Resurrection, Osiris.

"Has this been taken from King Tutankhamun's tomb?" Nour muttered to herself. "Because if so, this is the curse before my very eyes."

As she peered closer, without wanting to get too close, she could see a pair of tiny, wrinkled eyes, a nose that barely had one nostril, and a mouth that was being pulled so tight by the surrounding skin, it made it difficult to distinguish if it was smiling or pulling a frown. She gasped and jumped back, saying, "Here is clearly a god in displeasure."

The engine was pulling into the shadow of a temple, where enormous cats, monkeys, crocodiles, scarab beetles, and falcons sat atop giant columns, each preserved in resin. Keket and Femi, who were sitting in another part of the train, were completely unaware of what had just happened. So, when Nour came running in blind fear and pulled them violently off at the next stop, they didn't know what to say.

"I just saw the curse!" Nour screamed.

They began shaking her because they could see a crazy look in her eye.

Keket said, "We must head towards the main square and pyramid. Once there, we can attempt to track down Karim and Kissa. They are doing wonderful things to improve our chances in the fight against the next cruel and evil pandemic that may inflict us. Beneath the pyramid there are rows and rows of catacombs, and these can be accessed easily enough via the numerous drains that populate the streets above. In the eventuality of the virus striking, or the pharaoh's making us homeless, we run for the crypts below. This is the best place for us to take cover; we can be concealed for weeks underground. There are places for the storage of fresh food and weapons."

Femi nodded in agreement. "We will take you to find Kissa and Karim, you haven't met them yet, but they are an entrepreneurial minded couple. You may learn a lot from them with regards to your business."

The passages and lanes of the pyramid district were

tight, and many had dead ends. There were structures that came through the wall of one building and interconnected with another. Some streets were on stilts that weaved between roads, houses, and buildings, eventually leading into the pyramid itself. The stench and the heat were unbearable at this hour of the day.

The interior of the pyramid was almost visible, and sand stalactites could be seen dripping from the ceiling, stalagmites emerging from the ground. They pushed on until they found the tree lined avenues where Karim and Kissa had made their acquaintance the night before.

It was late afternoon, and the heat began to abate. Suddenly, as they turned a corner, a pungent aroma hit them in the back of their nasal passages, their senses were overcome, and they nearly fell to the floor, trying to recover from the assault. Instead, they rushed past, giving a hurried glance at the cause, which was the combined odour of wilting flowers, seeds, bullrushes, and grasses, as well as the half rotten corpse of a mummified dog. Now, as it broke down quickly in the heat of the day, an array of insects, and other organisms were keen to make a meal of it. Somebody had offered it as a gift to Osiris, a bribe to get themselves into the afterlife pretty damn quick, but judging by its smell, it must have been turned down. Only a half-witted god would take something so deadly and risk the heavens having to be fumigated.

The next turn was more fruitful and led them straight into the paths of the eloping couple, they were making haste after so many hours in each other's company.

Formal introductions were made by Femi who said, "This is Nour, we met her at the archaeological dig today where she lives with her husband. They are from an impoverished bracket in society, and they badly need help. She has this vague idea that she could improve her finances by contacting a psychic, though it's more likely that a hex has been put upon her in the past, and this just needs removing."

Keket interposed. "Yesterday, she lost her husband, Tarek, she knows not where he is or even if he is still alive! This is a woman living on the edge. She slept barely an hour because the cat wanders continuously, and when she's not chasing it down, she worries incessantly about money, whether they can make it from one week to the next. If we can return her life to some semblance of normality, by bringing either the cat or the man back, let's do it."

At this, Nour launched into a new tirade of how close to the edge her life was. How living at the dig had taken it out of their marriage.

She told them, "We barely see each other anymore, one comes home from one job, the other leaves to theirs. On a good day I'll see Tarek for a handful of hours, usually when he comes home and offered to assist with cleaning the bakery. Then one of us must cook which usually kills the last grains of passion, before having to go to bed. Not much energy left for anything else after that! This lifestyle is wiping us out, but it's due to the pharaoh's negligence, and it's not just us as a couple, but millions more like us."

As Nour fell silent, you could hear a pin drop around her.

Karim and Kissa had the sense not to make a comment, but Keket couldn't resist the chance to put the oar in.

She bleated, "All they do is make our lives infinitely more tiresome and complex. It's bad enough that we don't have any time to see one another, let alone for our loved ones and family. The pharaohs are responsible for a lot."

Her words echoed in the silence, each of them concerned about whether what they had revealed was something they were allowed to say. Nowadays, you just never knew!

Tarek remained with the cooks for several days, and they transported him from one job to another. Carrying in the pharaoh's dinner became his latest job and required dragging an immense wooden cart behind him, laden with their choices of aperitifs, starters, mains, desserts, sweetmeats, and digestifs. Each needed to be unloaded as carefully as it had been brought in, then the crockery from the remaining meal removed and taken away.

No room for error was allowed for, and if they caught him trying to secure or steal any scraps, the strictest admonishment was paid. Snaffling away even a modest amount for himself, was regarded as stealing from the royal table, and an archaic set of rules and laws were issued to ensure that it never happened again. The cooks barely even saw him, but when they did, they bellowed.

"Shift your skinny butt!"

The royals sat about as if in a daze, waiting for the next assault of food to come their way. When it did, they usually grumbled about how poorly it had been prepared. Never a single word of consideration for their own cooks, let alone Tarek for carting it in. He couldn't do much about this, as he had no rights at all, let alone access to books or resources to research about other positions. As Tarek left, Cleopatra and Twosret lobbed rotting fruit at him, always under the orders of

Augustuskamoun. Ramses and Pepi weren't much better for encouraging them.

Karim knew that he must make it back to his house and urged Kissa on.

Karim said, "I will explain all as we travel. The pharaohs have already made a conquest of my place, but I escaped because I heard they were coming. They stormed my neighbour's house, looted, and violently evicted them from the place."

Kissa was shocked. "I can't believe this could happen to any of our own relatives or friends, but what about Femi and Keket? They must have had the same treatment," she replied.

They pushed on to the old town, where Karim lived, the next street was his. The property owner next door, once they passed away, had let the place go into neglect. They had been compulsive hoarders, and now there was an accumulation of old carts, roofing tiles, bricks, farming equipment, furniture, and other knickknacks spilling out from the property into the yard and the street.

They used to run a market in the centre, which was well known for its scientific supplies. Bunsen burners, rubber tubing, test tubes with their shakers and holders, and a variety of chemicals in powdered form. Iron, lead, magnesium, manganese, mercury, titanium, and cadmium. Seeing this dizzying array of multi coloured elements, with various properties before him, Karim's head began to spin. So many different uses, but he only needed one to fabricate his homegrown recipe for a buffer solution.

"It will surpass the poorest substitutes we've had over the years, and in previous pandemics."

Karim fell on the booty and collected as many armfuls as possible of what he required, then urged Kissa to do the same.

"With this, we will have enough to make formula to treat the whole country," Karim declared.

"If we go back to my place and it hasn't been taken hostage yet, we will be able to set up a new laboratory for you to work in," Kissa suggested.

Nour was still in the square with Femi and Keket. They had managed to get her to calm down, but she was on the verge of hysteria, losing her husband and being on the brink of poverty was simply enough. She began to have more clarity, at which point she remembered one of the last things Tarek told her before leaving the night before.

"He told me he was sick of this tough existence, having to have three jobs just to pay the bills, and to do what he loves. He was reconsidering how he might be able to have a career that allows him to focus purely in that area. He was doing research and had learnt about people who run mummification workshops. They are well paid, and you just need the basic skills of an artisan, or somebody who could pick up this type of thing quickly. It requires a lot of technical ability, most of the time he will be mixing up compounds that are needed for this age-old process. He will have to go to multiple seminars up and down the country, attend many training sessions, and there is a small outlay. Because it is heavily sought after by the pharaohs, it has been subsidised well, so the amount he will pay is nominal."

Femi and Keket were fully inspired. One of them ran forward and hugged her.

Femi screamed. "This is going to be the answer to all

your problems."

Nour said, "Really?"

"I've got a good feeling about Tarek, he only has your best interests at heart," Femi gushed to Nour.

"I agree. And this Karim and Kissa, you think what they are planning to do is realistic?" asked Keket.

"I don't see why not, they both seem level-headed, I have no reason to dispute their authority on this," came Femi's reply once she had extricated himself from Nour's hug, that went on a little too long for her liking. Well, you couldn't be too careful, could you? She was all for ladies loving ladies, if she wasn't one of the ladies involved.

"You're right, they do seem confident. I can't believe that Augustuskamoun has begun to take over the test centres."

"We saw the virus with our own eyes as it escaped from his body, there's no knowing where it could get to."

"True," said Keket, being careful not to step too near to Nour, who had a very hungry look about her after hugging Femi. "All we can do is try and keep on the sides of Karim and Kissa, as best we can."

"Ammon and Husain seem like a reliable pair," Femi declared, changing the subject somewhat.

"They come from a solid family; I think we can trust in them in the future. They've been through as much as we have, anyway," Keket reminded her.

"True."

The three of them continued to rejoice, as a travelling man with a bugle came through the square. He raised his musical instrument and blew into it hard, announcing that the official spread of cholera had begun, and that the whole population was expected to go into a national lockdown.

Chapter Three

Huda Shawari was a leading light for the fledging feminist scene that was beginning to get underway. Huda usually dressed unconventionally; dungarees made of old sailcloth material, paint spattered vest, and clogs. She never wore a head scarf, to show she stood by her own values, more than anything else. Huda was middle-aged and had splintered off at school from more traditional social groups, preferring to put her own enlightenment before more dominating voices and the overarching narrative of the pharaohs.

During these dark and primitive times of colonial rule, and of the Egyptian dynasties, only males could ascend to the throne. Women weren't allowed to do anything of responsibility, apart from being Queen, if you were lucky enough. Standing around drinking coffee, gossiping, and making babies to build the burgeoning empire, was a woman's reality and Huda was brought up on those stories. The pharaohs weren't so repressive that they had stopped all sources of news slipping through, but she was sick to the back teeth of it. She had heard of the existence of more liberal, forward-thinking countries, and it made her yearn for change.

On a day-to-day basis Huda stood on the corner of some of the busier squares, during the evening once it began to cool a little, wearing a sandwich board and handing out flyers to unsuspecting passers-by, trying to fire up support for an impending revolution. She believed that the current government were asking for it, as far right and backward as they were. Huda stood in her usual spot, when suddenly she heard a woman ranting, and to judge from her tone she was indignant.

The woman was part of a group of three, and they conversed as they walked past. Huda could overhear them.

"And this is the best way to get my life back on track?" one of the women was asking.

"Nour, it's the best way," said one of the other women. "Are you sure your current situation is the only way? It's not just a man's happiness that does such great things, think about your own, too. Try to decide how you can improve it, and don't put the man first."

Nour ignored Keket's impassioned plea and instead connected with Huda's words on her sandwich board. She took them onboard, then went over to sign the petition that Huda was brandishing.

"What's it all about?" asked Nour, as Keket and Femi rushed to catch up with her.

Huda replied, "Women need equal rights, and do you pledge to become more politically involved if need be?"

"I don't see why not," Nour declared, and thought, *if I could get myself onto the political gravy train, I would be a willing passenger. You never saw a poor politician, after all, did you?*

Huda gazed long into Nour's eyes as if to confirm her belief in this issue, then said, "I'm trying to build an army of followers who can be easily mobilised, and at the last minute, so by adding your name to the list, you promise to play a part in the coming rebellion."

Keket heard and jumped forward to sign, too, she was also on the verge of abandoning ship. By heralding the dawn of a new advent, Keket was happy to put her vote behind this new radical thinking party.

The two women continued along the pavement. Femi was caught too, but she didn't want to make the transition, for her forward-thinking remained just that, thinking. She was old fashioned, regardless of how much she looked up to and was inspired by her friends. As Femi caught up with them, they began berating her.

"What's up with you, don't you realise this is exactly what the pharaohs want, less power to the individuals, it doesn't matter what creed, colour, or sex you are," said Keket, indignantly.

Reluctantly, Femi turned on her heel and went back to add her support. "Even if it means a less male dominated society, one that has more of an open mind, it can only be a good thing for all of us, I suppose," she declared, adding her signature to Nour's and Keket's at the bottom of Huda's petition.

As the man in his cloak from another time finished blowing his sad and melancholic news, he climbed down from his cardboard box, packed up his case and began to make off. He carried a rolled-up copy of the Egyptian Tribunal printed on yellowing parchment, and pulling up a nearby deckchair, he began reading. His nose was buried in the newspaper as he searched for other half newsworthy scraps, but he couldn't find any, not that matched the seriousness of his earlier declaration. The pharaohs make small donations to the paper, so its political content is always in their favour, anyway. Irked, he decided to leave. Keket and Femi watched him go.

"How much of an impact will a national lockdown have on you?"

Keket shrugged. "It will affect my freedom of movement, but that pales into comparison as to how we are being turfed from our homes. Can things get any worse?"

"True," replied Femi, wondering what would happen to homeless people during a national lockdown.

"My business will suffer, and God knows if I'll ever see my husband again, once he goes off to do his training." Nour was downcast. Some would say realistic.

"Stop being so negative. My family struggle to get about, this will make things even worse for them," Femi told her.

"Those pharaohs have a lot to answer for, they turfed us out of our homes, then they expect us to stand in line and take orders, as well as to be their runabouts. I've had enough, if signing this petition doesn't make a difference, then we need a new approach," Keket declared.

"At least you know by following me you're trying. I'm sick of being treated like a second-class citizen. Growing up, I've observed a lot about this society and we're always the ones who are put to one side. Now there's a pandemic they are going to use it to throttle us for good." Huda had been following the threesome, sensing kindred spirits, or at least someone to talk to.

"I just want my business to improve," Nour told them, deciding honesty at this stage was the best policy. She was still thinking of rich politicians.

"Your bakery will always suffer," Huda was scathing. "The pharaohs have their thumbs in all pies, nothing escapes their attention. If there's a way that they can make themselves an extra pound or two at our expenses, they will do."

"Are they really that bad?"

In one voice Keket and Huda said, "Yes!"

Then Huda stood to one side politely and was ever so grateful for the gestures they had all made. As a mark of respect and because she began to warm up now, she unbuttoned her collar, eased off her cape, then took off her clogs. The clogs had been handed down by a family member, Antonia, who had travelled far and wide. Huda was very proud of her feats in bringing down such male figures of authority as the President of France, the Prime Minister of England, and the King of Holland.

Antonia had endangered her life to bring the plight of women leaps and bounds ahead. Thanks to her they were out of the dark and primitive times, though Huda still felt man had struck a deal with Satan where women were concerned. Antonia nearly lost her head for her high beliefs, several times; once at the guillotine, then back at the Tower of London, crows, and ravens to witness her feat. Huda had never actually met her, but the infamous footwear with which Antonia had travelled, now accompanied Huda on her way, encouraging and inspiring her adventures, too.

As Huda made to leave, Femi caught her arm. "It might be a good idea to chase up our good friend Kissa. It's easy enough to find her, she should be with a fellow whose name is Karim. They will probably be at her place, just watch out for the pharaohs along the way, though. They want to make it their mission to visit all properties of the lower orders, and give people the option of turning them over, that or having them and their loved one's belongings trashed."

Huda took heed and went on her way. She was a woman of good spirits, generous, and eager to make amends for the downtrodden way in which her sex had been so poorly treated.

"I suppose it's not just down to us, is it?" Huda said out loud.

She left the centre and headed towards the old town

to where she would find Kissa's place. Along the way Huda stumbled into a dry and dusty sideroad, so she decided to stop for a minute. She hired a dromedary for the journey and now let the beast have time to cool down. Huda threw some water from her canteen; it hissed, steaming, as it hit the poor animal's back. The camel spat which meant it was either trying to remove the dust from the back of it throat, or it was angry.

Either way, Huda knew it was best not to encourage the creature any further and waited patiently while it nearly asphyxiated itself. After it recovered, she tried to ease it further along the road, but it was far too stubborn for that. During the short battle of wills, which seemed to be guaranteeing victory for the camel, Huda took off her hood that kept the sand away from her face, and quickly every orifice filled, nostrils, eye sockets, ears. She couldn't hear or see as the the sand and dust levels grew higher and found herself slipping out of consciousness.

Next thing she knew, Huda came to after being dragged backwards down a burrow. She wasn't sure what might have done it, but it couldn't have been the camel because the burrow entrance was too small. There goes her security deposit on the bloody thing! Inside it was cave-like and Huda rushed along at a pace of knots, borne along on the periphery of a crowd of servants, slaves, foot soldiers, cooks, and butlers. When they reached the furthest point of the underground cavern, they threw her bodily down. In the middle of the vast space was a huge bubbling cauldron into which they tried to push Huda.

"Hold on, you stupid fools," Huda cried. "I'm on your side! We downtrodden ones need to stick together. I'm not getting in that.' She eyed the bubbling pot.

One servant said, "This is the pot of King Tutankhamun, and if you want to learn more about his love spells, you must hang around."

Huda said, "Well, you won't get very far if you put me in a pot, you daft bat. I'm one of the rare things that can assist us all in our plight to bring the pharaohs down. If that's a witch's cauldron, then you obviously need a witch, don't you?" She preened herself and watched the other's looking dubiously at her. But they didn't put her into the pot, so her proclamation of not being a witch must have paid off. She determined not to change her skin cream.

Another servant said, "Do you want to know how spells can be cast, on what types of people, as well as for how long?"

Huda was gobsmacked and said, "Yes," eagerly, forgetting that she'd had allegations of being a witch thrown at her.

They didn't seem to have taken much notice, but however, she was curious to gain as much knowledge as she could about the incantations, so she found a place that was out of the way, but where she could still see what was going on.

A cook turned up shortly and told everyone, "It all revolves around the use of the cauldron, if you don't steal it, you won't have a prayer. But of course, you need to know the exact recipe, and just the right chant. The pace must be slow but steady, and some parts performed backwards. Other ingredients that you need are purely of witches' alchemy, such as a crow's wing, foot of lizard, eye of snake, and the muzzle of a monkey must also be sought. To this, a dusting of various powdered chemicals is required."

Huda shuddered, but nodded, taking it all in.

The cook continued. "Once you've got the right balance in the bubbling pot, you can rest on your laurels for a little while, as it takes several hours to reach its optimum use. Thereafter, if it's not made use of within a short while, it's rendered completely useless. Once ready you can take it, strain it, then decant it into smaller vials, that can, at will, be slipped into food stuffs, either liquid or solid. It's also possible for it to be taken orally, via the nostrils, or directly up the rectum, though slightly more painful that way, and, of course, gruesome to perform."

Huda asked, "What type of people could it be cast on?"

"Only on women," The cook told her. "The love spells were discovered in 1896, and they make women's hearts burn until they fall in love with the man who cast it."

"If the pharaohs get hold of these spells themselves, then realise how easy it to make their love lives more prosperous, there will be a public uproar, and no female will be safe! From my perspective, as one who champions forward thinking, this is an outrage! Their design is to encourage women by appealing to their superstitious and heathen beliefs." Huda was, indeed, outraged. Her chest heaved.

Once Huda finished exchanging methods and techniques with the cook, she made off, with such a vast amount of information to keep in her head. She had, of course, remembered well the bit about stealing a cauldron, so she kicked the wooden pole above the open fire that had the cauldron upon it, freeing it, and allowing it to fall to the floor, then she snatched it up, sprinting for the exit and started to dig away at the spongy earth above her. Roots, sand, cactus needles, as well as the dried-out carcasses of bats and birds, began to drop down onto her. She scrambled back into the full glare of the red-hot sun, most things were dead all around her, tinderbox detritus, seed pods, and flower heads.

Huda recalled Femi's words that she ought to chase up Kissa, so she headed towards the old town. She passed through the centre, the wealthy and elegant quarter where most of the pharaohs resided, before reaching an ancient mosque on top of a cliff, where the last rites of many were said before being sent out on their journeys to the afterlife. Osiris was nesting in the branches of a nearby tree.

The ambience was sombre, and quiet. Huda could just see the jutting structure of the pyramid itself as it reached for the sky, surrounded by the archaic looking structures in the cemetery vaults with their doors slammed shut. She scrambled to the top and awaited the awakening of the slumbering personages within, as this was the Valley of the Kings, and until their next meeting, they were peacefully at rest.

Pepi, Ramses, Nitocris, Cleopatra, and Twosret, returned by midnight to the cover of the great pyramid. They settled down for the night and planned to wake up refreshed for another day of making the lives of the minorities a misery again. The meeting hadn't yet been called by Augustuskamoun, who had sent one of his envoys out. After all, he wasn't going to do his own dirty work. Let someone else do it was his mantra!

"Pepi, tell them that a new schedule of pharaonic conferences will be carried out, certain wage increases for us, as we discussed. There will be tax increases for the masses, and slashes in public services," Augustuskamoun declared.

Pepi dropped to his knees in reverence, and gave a cry of servitude, "Yes, sir."

Augustuskamoun continued, "We will also talk about general matters, such as recent employments taken onboard, Tarek in the kitchens, and the non-existent plan to deal with the up-and-coming pandemic."

"Right now, I believe it hasn't even been officially announced," Pepi told him.

Augustuskamoun said, "What difference does it make to the public?"

As Pepi translated the words to the snoozing audience, they began to arise, each had been asleep for aeons since the last public plea for help. This wasn't their standard form of work, usually they passed new bills, and updated laws to make the lives of the poor even poorer.

Inside the pyramid, a central avenue acted as a road, where new treasures could be brought in and out by horse and cart, enabling people to celebrate their own importance and how grand they were. As they realised the import of this recent delegation of work, they began to get on with their everyday business. Each tomb had a plaque with their name affixed, in order of rank and significance.

Pepi strolled past reading them out. "Khufu Robertson - Political Strategist, Nefertiti Frankland – Home Office, Seti Maxwell – Housing, Khafre Davies – Defence, Djoser Collins – Health and Chancellor, Snefru Edwards – Transport, Narmer Richards – Education."

He finished his roll call of the nation's most intelligent and influential men, and then told them, "We will meet in an hour, please be on your way."

Augustuskamoun arranged to come and hold a session with them, whereby they could learn more about his proposed legislation, and exchange views with his cabinet. For this he ensconced himself into the furthermost empty tomb, which lay at the end. His fellow noblemen, Pepi and Ramses, took their own. Once each was comfortably sat in their thrones, hewn from the sandstone, Augustuskamoun made a start. Official minutes were circulated first.

Augustuskamoun said, "Narmer, you are being given responsibility for taking down the fresh minutes, and there will be the opportunity to bring any urgent subjects that need discussing within your own areas."

He skirted around this quickly as he was aware of one more topic that wanted addressing, that of plans for the cholera outbreak.

"Either way, if we want to shirk accountability for it, and pass the blame onto somebody else, or if we just want to carry on as we are in taking over the test centres, kicking residents out, then having them as our own, we can do this. We are also planning to make our own medicine, and if that fails then we will steal it from another group within the country." Augustuskamoun sat back with a satisfied smirk on his face. "This can't go wrong. Can it?"

To this announcement, there was a cheer of unity, all seemed to agree, so, they decided to carry on as they were, no changes to be made.

Augustuskamoun delegated specific roles, "Djoser, you can be responsible for anything that regards health, Snefru and Khufu can help, Seti can assist in kicking people out of their houses, along with Pepi and Ramses. The rest can all be assigned to the cholera team, or as reserves in case anybody drops down with the disease themselves."

At this Nefertiti, Khafre, and Narmer looked about in despair. They were used to a rather more sedate and pampered life, not with the prospect of being at deaths doorstep, on a regular basis.

Khafre said, "Most of us are usually left to watch over the lives of the small people, making judgments over their existence. For the tables to be turned is very strange indeed."

"I can't stand this idea of death; I would feel a lot safer if we could go about our normal duties." Narmer shuddered.

"Nefertiti sits at the border keeping an eye on people as they come streaming in and out of the country, then decides when it is to be closed, how many immigrants are let in or allowed to leave. Do you think she will be able to cope in her new role?" asked Khafre.

"I'll have no choice, will I? I can't even bring myself to feel an ounce of sympathy for them normally." Nefertiti replied.

"What about you, Narmer, you oversee peoples' schooling, currently. Whether the indigenous Egyptians should have to learn English or not?"

"They shouldn't have to, then they can't have a say in their own matters." Narmer smiled rather nastily and then continued. "Khafre, you have a lot of say over the safety of the country. At the drop of a hat, he can have himself and the other pharaohs picked up by horse and cart, then dropped off by train at various strongholds."

Narmer looked around at the others, gesticulating to Khafre, who smiled and said, "They've all been designed and built to endure any attacks, by land, sea, or under other types of fire," he said, of the trains.

"Normally I make decisions surrounding the country's foreign policy with regards to the safety of its citizens, so, if they want to bring further troops in, I am happy to oblige."

"The Egyptians and the English have greased each other's palms for many years now," Narmer commented, thoughtfully.

Meanwhile, Huda was glued to one of the pyramid windows, which were all in the rear plane. There were many, so it was difficult for her to choose one she felt adequate for her eavesdropping. She settled for one which seemed to be less dirty and easier to peer through. Hearing everything that the pharaohs said, she wasn't surprised; she knew exactly what they were planning, *another disgrace*, she thought, when she learnt the latest gossip from within.

As they broke up their meeting below, Huda had to run for her life, as she knew that they'd come searching high and low once they got outside. If anybody noticed Huda tucked away at the top of the building, they would have her down as a miscreant and an informer, the price was too much to pay, she had work to be getting on with and didn't have time to be waylaid. Huda was on her way to Kissa's and was behind with her schedule; she had the cauldron in her bag, when Narmer looked up and caught her sitting on the far edge of the pyramid.

Narmer was aghast. "What's she doing up there? She's an enemy and shouldn't be prowling around behind lines like this. Nefertiti and Djoser, come along, we will fetch her down!"

The three of them were in hot pursuit, they took a ladder made of bamboo pole scaffolding and threw it up before them. Then they began to ascend. They crept ever closer to Huda's hidden away spot, in a crevice. A gutter full of pine needles and fragments of sandstone laid before her, and she began to throw it wildly down, aiming for the eyes and faces of those below. It makes no difference, and they came lurching up after her still. One grabbed for her arms, another for her leg, another pinned her shoulders down. Huda could feel the hot breath of Narmer as he screamed into her face.

"What are you doing eavesdropping on us?"

Huda was too scared to answer, and simply claimed, "I was doing repair works that have been arranged with the proprietor, if you want, I can get a letter, which confirms my story?"

Nefertiti wasn't having any of it. "I'm sick of imbecilic people like you, trying to either con their way into the country, or out of it! Why should I believe a word you say?"

Huda was silent. Djoser insisted that they took her back inside the pyramid where she could explain herself in front of the rest of the kings.

Djoser said, "We will see if she has such confidence then."

They made sure Huda was safely secured to Djoser's back, and slowly scaled down, reaching the ground shortly after. There was an army of men guarding the main entrance below, each carried a warrior's sword, and were mounted on a camel that stood surveying the landscape.

It will be tricky to move these men along, but if I can then that's my ticket to escape, Huda thought. And she did her best to entice the animals with scraps of food lying around. Somebody threw a water bottle, and it bounced in front of her. The camels were so thirsty they leaped on it and knocked the men from their backs. *Now I am home free, and ready to run for it,* and she prepared herself to do so, when at that precise moment, she found all three men bearing back down upon her.

They caught her now and took her into the pyramid, Augustuskamoun and the rest of the pharaohs were approaching. There was nothing she could do, she decided, as one of the pharaohs went through her bag, finding the cauldron.

"What's this?" Pepi demanded.

She wouldn't give a direct answer, but they were well accustomed to getting information and secrets out of people! Khafre lashed her to a torture rack. Within minutes of the handle being turned, her backbone began to twist and split.

Huda gave a scream and told them she was ready to confess all, and said, "The owner of the pot can cast love spells!"

Her captors were wide eyed and curious and wanted to hear more.

Huda was encouraged to speak. "With the right invocation and exact combination of elements, the spell can be cast upon a woman by a man, and her heart begins to burn!"

Their thoughts were boundless, trying to gauge the opportunities this could lend to themselves.

Pepi said, "This is amazing! In terms of being able to conquer and capture members of the fairer sex, we will never need Bastet, the god of fertility anymore."

Djoser had other ideas. "Now we can sleep with countless women and never get caught for it."

"You're right, we can be rogues and dogs and the opposite sex would be like inferior creatures for us, but it doesn't matter as we can bed as many as we want."

This was what was going through the minds of the

majority, each planning how they were going to get away with a life of eroticism, and fanciful afternoons, not to mention the army of babies that would be popped and provide future young men to defend the kingdom.

They let Huda go and she slipped from the rack, wriggling free; she was small enough to be able to squeeze through the bars in one of the windows. Whilst her captors were still debating their life of debauchery, she fled for her life, running back to the safety of the centre, where she knew people, and places to hide. In the eventuality that they came running after, she found a spot where somebody had thrown some old rugs, canisters of incense, spices, and a box of candles. Huda ducked into it and made herself as small as can be, then held her breath and waited. After about an hour, nobody came along, so she thought, *I must be safe* and jumped back onto the pavement to continue along her way. *It is a comfy spot, a good place to let my heartbeat settle, it was in my mouth before.* Huda's thoughts continued along this vein and as she walked, the more familiar the landscape became. She began to recognise building, houses, and other landmarks and was able to breathe a sigh of relief.

Looking up, she saw a huge mural on her left, on the back of the old law courts. It was a precursor to Escher and depicted multiple pyramids, each merging into the next, demonstrating how chaos and insanity are intertwined. Below it was an outcrop of rock where one of the pharaohs had a sculpture of Meskhenet carved. She was the goddess of childbirth. Underneath her sculpture, in Egyptian hieroglyphs, chipped in by a stonemason of great repute, was an inscription.

Huda read it out loud, "With these love spells men will take over the world, and women will be confined to lives of darning, childrearing, being playthings, homemaking, and other menial duties. That's some cross to bear", Huda muttered to herself. "Lots to do, but not much choice."

She was fuming and couldn't wait to recall this to her fellows. Continuing along her chosen route, the words of the inscription were still seeping in, but she knew exactly what they had in store for her kind. She urged herself to carry on, not to fall to the wayside. She was tired already and could easily sleep.

To stop exhaustion overtaking, she kept muttering to herself. "I must speak with Kissa to try to rally more support, we are going to need every ounce of energy we can muster, to fight this evil, pathetic, and over domineering patriarchal society from taking over."

Nour, Femi and Keket were still discussing Nour's dilemma regarding her husband, Tarek, and the intervention of a psychic. Nour hadn't understood why a psychic would do any good, except perhaps to tell her what Tarek was thinking, if he ever did any. But Keket sighed at other woman's naivety.

"Psychics are like witches,' she explained, patiently. "Maybe they even are witches! Maybe they would be able to cast love spells on your husband."

Femi snorted. "If you ask me, the whole of mankind, especially pharaohs, need love spells casting on them. Imagine the difference it would make to them. Right now, if you ask me, they have an overinflated view of themselves, which is not matched by their penis size, however much the exaggerate!"

Keket was scathing. "Exactly! They are all little men

with an inflated image of themselves."

At that moment Huda ran up, huffing and puffing, clearly in a state of great vexation, she was steaming and wanted to vent her anger about what she saw on the way back. So fresh in her mind it was, and how like an open wound, raw, and stinging still. First, though, she had to tell them of the pharaohs plans for women.

"The pharaohs want a situation where we are in their grip, eternally grateful to them for our own pitiful existence," Huda blurted out.

"We are raging ourselves about this. We were just discussing how men have inflated opinions of themselves and how they would use this pandemic and lockdown to assert themselves over women! Why don't all three of us agree to put our best foot forward, to collaborate, throw our weight against this inhuman force, this impenetrable wall of masculinity."

At that, they all cheered.

Tarek was still under the voluntary employment of Augustuskamoun and the men of his estate. They had decided to keep him on to do other mundane and boring tasks, as well as being the general dogsbody who was sent out for spontaneously required goods, usually midnight snacks. Other times they were homesick for English products, like ale, gravy, bread, or Yorkshire pudding. There was a market nearby where all these things could be sourced at an elevated price. The pharaohs had refined tastes and were always after rich banqueting foods, such as suckling pig, gamebird, venison, rabbit, and foie gras.

They made Tarek go out with a rifle to see what he could pick up in the backstreets of Cairo. Often, he came back empty handed, or with other treats, such as snake, crocodile, cat, monkey, or dog. Cholera was proliferating fast, and with the new rules that had been introduced by themselves, he was banned from hunting any wildlife at all, and they must suffer with what they had in storage, usually dry provisions, salt biscuits, bread crusts, preserves, and pickles.

Whenever Tarek wasn't working, he kept remembering the conversation that he had with Nour, the night before he left. When he seemed so sure of his next career step, how he could provide but in a more plausible way. If he hadn't got picked off on the way to the labour market, then things could have been so different.

Tarek muttered to himself mutinously. "I must escape, there is nothing else for it, my life is going to continue in this awful vicious circle, otherwise, money coming in, then before I've even spent it, straight back out again. The first opportunity I get once I can leave the palace; I must find a library or a news kiosk. Anywhere I can get hold of a classified section."

From that moment on, he was looking for the first chance to give them the slip. *It wouldn't be too problematic,* he thought, *between shifts. Usually, the cooks do a handover with the next shift, then the kitchen is at its quietest. I can leave a trail of grains behind me, so I know exactly which way to run, to get to the outside world.*

One afternoon after Tarek had taken out the bins, he came back in with a few pocketsful of scraps, potato peelings, eggshells, bacon rind, anything that would feed him for a few days. Then he dropped some crumbs on the floor, leaving a trail, so that next time, he would know which way to go.

Bang on 7pm., Tarek heard the first set of cooks arguing and cursing. It was the end of the shift, and they were arguing as to who got to do overtime, if anybody is required to stay late. There is a victorious cheer, half dismal, but half overjoyed at the prospect of the extra money. Then Tarek heard footsteps echoing down the hall.

"Now is the time," Tarek muttered to himself, his own voice giving him the courage he needed. "I need to do this before the huge fellow gets across the kitchen, and beyond the fire pit."

Hesitating no more, he legged it. He tripped under the feet of one of them as they made it towards the door, and used the commotion as cover, then darted out into the daylight where he could see better the track.

Tarek had never moved so quickly; he was like a slippery eel, greased lightning, ducking and diving between and behind bags of flour, salt, and sugar, then back out again into the open. Here, he was a moving target, and one cook saw a tiny shadow move. He shrugged, thinking he was delusional and continued along his way. A snake was in the garden as Tarek ran out in a blind panic. Seeing it, he stepped to one side for fear he was going to trip on the beast. Then he stumbled and went headlong into the bushes and brush outside, cacti and smaller prickly shrubs.

"Home free," Tarek screamed as he dodged onto a well-worn path that took him back towards the dig.

About halfway along he bumped into Nour, Femi, and Keket, rejoicing to see his wife and some friendly and familiar faces.

"Direct me to a place where I can buy a paper?" Tarek shouted, after he had stopped hugging Nour and embarrassing the other two women.

They obliged, and Tarek availed himself of a pound. Picking up a copy of the latest rag and flicking to the vacant positions section. There was a whole page special, and he read aloud.

"Skilled workers required to improve their prospects. Starts available immediately up and down the country: Cairo, Alexandria, Aswan, Luxor, Sharm El Sheikh, and Hurghada."

"You've got it made, now it remains to be seen if there is any avenue for myself to make a new living," Nour said, bitterly.

"In these cities. I know that I could build my trade, and my ability to perform mummification to a level that means I could find employment, either within the crown or working for rich English colonialists. You can sell bread to the people on the courses. If they desire loaves for the deceased, they will buy off you and take your bread to the grave with them."

"You're right there, that could be a good option for me, and maybe if they want, I can add a special ingredient to alleviate their pain; arsenic, pack them off quicker."

"I hear of people being buried with their pets, jewellery, heirlooms, clothes, antiques, art, books, why not food instead?"

"Most people think preservation is a way to combat this idea of going to the grave and instead aim for the afterlife. It is just a case of getting the right presents, dedications, and prayers read aloud," Nour agreed.

"If they are to employ a holy man, or somebody to carry out this ghoulish task along the way, then I will be more than happy to oblige. I've not considered what people go through on their death beds, I just want to make a living for you and me, Nour."

Chapter Four

Once Tarek finished reading the paper, he circled back towards where his wife was still conversing with her two new friends.

Keket was saying, "Come on, we've only ever got a raw deal from men, by signing you are at least giving us a cat in hell's chance."

"You're right, but I'm not convinced my husband is included in this. When we got married, we signed a covenant, in blood and in loyalty, that means we carry a torch for one another, regardless of what we go through," Nour told them.

"That sounds romantic!" Femi was impressed.

Nour saw the argument that the pharaohs had overarching power and influence over their lives, but it didn't mean that all members of the male species were the same. Tarek came ambling back up with his paper, and an expression of gaiety on his face. Nour knew that he must have had a life changing experience since she last saw him. He started to speak, and events came tumbling out, not in any order, but stuttered, beginning with his capture.

"Working for the pharaoh's made me realise that we are all under the yoke of the overlords, slaves to the master's voice. If they are around and desire us to run, fetch, and carry, we are always going to be at their beck and call," Tarek declared.

"I really should retrain," he said after a silence.

Nour broke in at that point. "But if you retrain you will still work for them, it really makes no difference what you do, if you make portraits of them or assist in their funeral affairs."

Tarek said, "I agree, but is there no other way that I can get my own back on them, then?"

With the conversation she had had with her newfound friends, and with the thoughts of Huda's petition bubbling away in the back of her brain, Nour said, "Maybe you can come and join the revolution, too? Help us wage the war, so at least they know we're not happy about it."

And with a rousing cry of comradeship, Tarek joined the cause.

As soon as Pepi and Ramses stormed the house of Ammon and Husain, deciding it was going to be turned into a test centre, they arranged for all manner of equipment that was relevant to the conducting of cholera checks to be delivered to their front door. The family took the advice to claim what benefits they could, and headed to the nearest office of reparations, that had been hastily set up and was being manned by Seti Maxwell.

They were forced to sit for hours before Seti invited them in, each taking their ticket from an ancient machine out in the main square, then waiting for their turn to be called. As Husain's wife pulled the lever on its side, she cringed as it spat out dry and dead insects, bees, crickets, mosquitos, locusts, straight into her hand. She was repulsed and pulled her hand away.

"The evil eye must be about, for such an ominous sign to befall us," she cried, in horror.

The family fell to discussing what such a sign could

be connected to, or who they may have displeased along the way. Ammon's grandmother heard from Keket about the experience that Nour had at the dig, what she encountered on the train on the way back.

"She is lucky," the grandmother said. "The curse can affect you in a benign or a malignant way. Nour's business has been in the doldrums and suffering for many years now, perhaps that is what she is hoping to improve?"

There was a murmur of agreement from the rest who were gathered.

A distant uncle said, "The curse has the power to travel around, it tends to alight and ravage its disastrous consequences upon those who are least expecting it, nobody really knows who is responsible for its launch. Some say it's escaped from below the ground and is due to the incessant drilling and excavations that occur."

Once they collected their tickets they filed into an adjoining building to the pyramid. Here was where much of the administrative work was done for the government, and things like filing were also done here by some low paid staff. All new complaints by locals who had lost the use of their homes due to the surge in confiscation of properties, were made at this place. They were allowed to argue their cause, then it was dealt with on a case-by-case basis. If you had family with land anywhere in Egypt, your case was immediately annulled.

In the next room sat Nefertiti Frankland who was tasked with gathering evidence of assaults. Any kind, it really didn't matter. Verbal, physical, or any evasion or breaking of laws; basically, anything that could be used to build up your criminal persona, to eject you out of the country.

New measures towards social distancing had already been put into place. A consignment of facemasks with oxygen breathing devices that looked like elephant trunks, had been left outside the front door. There were also inch thick rubber outfits with grappling arms laid nearby. A telescopic crane rose out of its back, controlled by a pair of handlebars, allowing a hook to be operated at the end of a long pulley, so that they could safely pick up and bring items closer for inspection, without touching them. It had been left for the workers who were converting the premises, and they were to be distributed throughout the house.

The front room was assigned as a waiting room, the kitchen a place for taking breaks, the garden for smokers, the cellar to be used for the hiding of tests. Word came through from Augustuskamoun that a certain number of tests, regardless of their result, must be rigged. He did not consider the moral implications. He just didn't want people in the future investigating his affairs, trying to bring legal proceedings against him.

Another room was designated as a place to hold spontaneous Christmas parties but was located deep within the confines of the house, where no eye of the public or newspapers can pry. A sauna on the roof had been designated top secret, admission by invite only, for all night hummus and baklava orgies.

Ammon's family took seats in the first room they saw in the main hall. They were sat for a few minutes, before a screeching voice called them through. The family all got up and filed into the next room. As they entered, they were ordered aggressively to take seats.

"My name is Nefertiti Frankland and I'll be responsible for chasing up your case and ensuring you're able to claim any benefits that you're entitled to."

Husain said, "That's a relief, just what we came here for."

Nefertiti gave them chance to sit down, then she let them have it.

"I'm not even in charge of giving out benefits, but we are so short-staffed that I'm having to multitask, which I always struggle with."

Husain replied, "Pardon, I thought we were in the right place."

Nefertiti said, "As you have a long since dead relative who was the owner of a smallholding in the north, you won't be entitled to a penny."

Husain replied, "That property and lands been taken over already by the English."

Nefertiti said, "What does that matter to me. Do you want some sympathy?"

Husain replied, "It might be nice, but I can see it's probably not going to happen."

Nefertiti said, "You are only entitled to money if you are Egyptian, and not an immigrant. Otherwise, you'll be out on your ear, without even time to think about it."

Husain kept quiet.

Ammon stood up next to plead their part. "We've been kicked out of our home and so we are homeless. What can we do about this?"

Nefertiti ignored Ammon completely, "My only concern is whether you are legally in the country, or not," she said.

Ammon replied, "Two pharaohs came to our house, and told us that it must be converted into a test centre. Shouldn't we get some sort of compensation?"

Nefertiti thought about it for a minute, then said, "In one word, no."

"Did you hear that, Father? Now we truly are out on our ear. Left to survive on the street."

Husain's wife stepped over, then gave the two of them a hug. "Things can't get much worse than this," she said.

Nefertiti's grating voice went on like a monotonous din.

"Right then, the lot of you, up and out of here at the double. Quick march, quick march," she cried out.

Ammon gave one last pleading look at Nefertiti as if it might make her melt a little, and change her mind, though he could see she was set like stone.

Ammon said, "Let's get out of here whilst we've still got the full use of our legs and arms."

Quietly he motioned for his family to leave.

As they walked down the street, Husain turned to his son, Ammon, and said, "We lost the land already once to them, who are they to revisit this pain? Adding insult to injury."

"Father, the English have always been at our throats. We must do what we can to suppress their desires, their need to rule the world with an iron rod," Ammon replied.

"Too right," Husain answered, dejectedly.

Escorting his family towards the nearest lodging house where they could get a room, their circumstances having changed from 'houseowners' to 'homeless' in the blink of an eye, Husain was aware they needed a place to rest, to lay their weary heads. The first lodging house they came to was operated by a distant relative of Pepi. When she saw them coming, she found it difficult to contain her glee.

"Looks like we've got a lively bunch here. Straight out on their ear and looking for digs." She just about prevented herself from doing a little celebratory jig. "After all, one man's misfortune means a lot of money for another!"

She'd been tipped off by an informer who worked between the social security offices and her own establishment, helping to put business her way.

"They're homeless," she cackled, clapping her hands in a queer and uncontrollable way. In them, she saw a vulnerable target, ripe for the picking.

Husain and his family didn't have much choice. The sun was already down, and with older members in tow feeling heavily fatigued, they unloaded their bags and knapsacks. Some of the group chatted congenially and compared notes about the incredible succession of proceedings that had befallen them, making bets if anything worse could happen still.

One said, "I remember the face of Seti surrounded by gold and stripes of azure, eyes like black saucers, a prominent growth coming from his chin. He had the careless expression of a rich man."

As they left, they were sure that he had been spitting

lumps of screwed and chewed up papyrus scrolls at them, because they hadn't paid enough respect, they thought. Husain and Ammon came over to see what all the fuss was about, some of the others were quite irate about the whole thing.

"It's always been the same, ever since they took our lands over. Now we never get to see any of our treasures, or anything of value," Ammon moaned.

Husain agreed. "I'm not surprised, I've been around long enough to know how things are," he said, bitterly. "They want to replace our laws and history, take our culture for themselves. Now with the advent of this cholera outbreak, they will use it as a smokescreen, so that they can get away with blue murder, and it will all be perfectly legal. They want us to be a pair of hands for the rich, so they never have to touch another reeking and unclean bin, kitchen door, signpost, road lantern, or place for sending telegrams. They don't want to have to go out to any public place, markets, temples, or mosques, so they won't be exposed to the lousy stinking virus. Our future will be being their butlers, their doormen, their servants, for eternity. The disease will trample upon our clean hands! If you ask me, we are heading back to the ancient times!"

Ammon thought that was a bit of an exaggeration but went along with it because he sensed his father was in no mood for dissent. He listened with what he hoped was an interested expression on his face.

Husain continued his tirade against the establishment. "I feel frustrated by the nature of the situation we keep finding ourselves waking up in. Another day like a bad dream, feeling like we haven't witnessed this before, but then realising it is a repeat of every awful nightmare we've ever experienced."

"Being at the mercy of the Pharaohs, the mocking and talking down to, the summonsing to do their every command, as they so wish. A man or a woman might think they have freedom, but really, we have none," Ammon had to agree. It was the truth.

As they sat outside the boarding house, word was getting around about Huda and the revolution she wanted to begin. As they discussed it in further detail, the family agreed that this could be a way to make a difference.

"We need to seek them out to find out what the next step is. It's true for sure we aren't in such a bad situation as the women of the world, but if we bring our forces together it can only help,"

Ammon declared. "Come, the boarding house woman is signalling that we may enter. Let us put the elders to bed, we can return outside to have a deeper conversation about this."

They continued in this vein putting the world to rights once they were out in the street again. It was one o'clock in the morning, and the only shapes in the landscape that they could distinguish were of ragged palm trees, ripped flags fluttering and, towering overhead, a temple dedicated to Thoth.

As they passed under it, Husain said, "That's the god of wisdom, writing, hieroglyphs, and the moon."

It looked quite wondrous, they thought.

"It's been carved out of sandstone as one gargantuan figure, with the head of a baboon, and the delicate and elegant body of the ibis," marvelled Ammon, eyes on stalks taking in the features of the temple.

A battered sign stood above them pointing to an empty tomb where people went if they were feeling frisky. Curtains had been hastily erected over the door, so it gave some form of privacy. They passed beneath it, finding two avenues that split in opposite directions. Considering which way to go, they found themselves meandering towards the nearest square.

"I have a vague recollection that we are supposed to be searching for Huda," Ammon commented.

"We are," Husain told him, and made a big show of looking to his left and right, when in fact, he had forgotten all about the blasted woman.

They waded into the immense gutter. It was full of the pods of dried fruit trees, mostly date, lotus, mulberry, and tamarisk. A heavy coat of dust covered the lot; they disturbed it walking through. Eruptions of seed-like clouds were thrown into the air, blocking their vision.

It was whilst they were stumbling through, unguided, that they came across the well-defined outline of a trapdoor in the floor, covered with daubing of symbols, images and letters. As they brushed away the debris, they tried to figure out its meaning.

"If I recall my schoolboy days, my errant searches for truth and knowledge," Husain mused.

Ammon said, "Go on!"

"Give me a chance," retorted Husain, tetchily.

Suddenly, it hit him what the true message was. He could dimly make out outlines of the letters R, O, S, E, T, another T, and an A. As he brought together the syllables, vowels, and consonants in his mouth, Husain spelt it out.

"Rosetta!"

Ammon was silent for a moment; the word had no immediate effect on him. Husain with his maturity of approach knew more than he cared to and said, "Just uttering the word can be the beginning of a long and dark curse falling upon you."

Ammon replied, "Oh marvellous! That's all we need in our precarious situation!" He wasn't impressed.

"I've heard accounts over the years of whole families splitting up, mostly because of a breakdown in communication, caused by misunderstandings, via different parties," Husain told him, darkly.

Ammon looked at him with a shudder, but then said, "It is imperative that people can comprehend one another, this is one of the basic foundations of all human civilization, I suppose."

"To talk, read, write, or discuss, to gauge whether one person agrees with another, or if a reasoned argument is needed," agreed Husain, completely forgetting about curses.

He leant on a tree and heard the grinding of stones, as the whole slab with its inscriptions continued to roll away. There was a gaping hole which led to a tunnel, gradually burrowing its way down, and wound up several hundred feet underground. They were brought out into a central chamber which had been reinforced with scaffolding, and hastily plastered on concrete to stop its walls from caving back in.

As they took in their surroundings of letters and numbers engraved into the walls, Ammon said, "I'm completely blown away by my lack of ability to be able to bring things together, in any cohesive way."

As he elucidated this to his father, Husain, never one lost for words, he immediately shared his own deliberations on the matter, that of the highly sought after and revered Rosetta Stone.

"To be in its company is highly sobering and humbling. It's known for its capability to improve one's own intellectual prowess. This room is used as place to carry out mathematical and numerical formulas, to arrive at new words to understand and reason with the world," Husain declared, and he began to decipher the words and symbols around him, to offer a translation to his son.

"As far back as I can remember the pharaohs, regardless of dynasty, always aim to keep us out of their affairs. They've done this to ensure people remain stupid and in the dark, to put it bluntly. If they can make the stone more readable then we all can benefit from its collection of curses and superstitions. Just recently two men cracked the code, it's brought a whole new light to the matter, given people new tools to access its hidden depths. The stone is used to decode ancient languages, such as Greek, Latin, and Egyptian, which nobody but the pharaohs speak," Husain told his son.

"As soon as Augustuskamoun and his legions hear about this, they will oppose it, so that they can keep it for themselves. Rumour has it they want to use it during the ongoing cholera pandemic, too. God knows how?" Ammon asked.

"They will have the power to keep the general public's grasp of the situation to an absolute minimum, because nobody understands what exactly they are proposing or want to get away with," Husain replied, thoughtfully.

Once Pepi and Ramses finished commandeering people's homes, Augustuskamoun delegated them with the task of making sure each test centre had the necessary apparatus, and the correct staffing levels.

"The best way for us to hire the staff, is for a man to stand with a sign on his back, directing would-be employees to enquire within the pyramid," Ramses said.

"That will be an astounding success!" Pepi was enthusiastic.

Within days, they had hundreds of centres up and down the country manned, and all were ready in or around the potential start date that Augustuskamoun had set.

The following Monday morning, which was the day the centres opened, when the doors were flung open, they were faced with a growing number of people who had symptoms of cholera. Ranging from food poisoning, diarrhoea, nausea, and vomiting, as well as severe dehydration, low blood pressure, rapid heart rate, and muscle cramps. This was to be what would happen more and more in the coming days.

"As each candidate tests, if they are found to be positive, they will be put into a section of the house, which is sealed off for the use of quarantining," Pepi said.

"All other people following their test are allowed to leave and resume their normal lives, usually with a written note to prove that they are safe to return to their daily duties," declared Ramses.

"This will be more efficient than the suppression of the Indians by famine," laughed Pepi.

Ramses guffawed.

A memo came through from Augustuskamoun that a great party was to be organized.

Pepi read it directly from a long scroll of papyrus that he found in a small chest dangling between the feet of a dove. "It will honour the dead and the dying, the efforts made by our own members towards securing the health of the masses."

Pepi barked out instructions to the nearest officials, Seti and Ramses. As the order came through, they ran off making mental notes to contact various other pharaohs, other minions who can be used to cart most of the equipment and supplies that were required. Pepi and Ramses headed off to find a shop where they could pick up a plentiful supply of bandages.

As he left, Ramses said, "They will be used to wrap people's bodies in. We will roll them up until their air supply is cut off, then unravel them before the blood comes rushing back to their heads."

"I like it; dark, twisted, and dirty. Even though it is billed as an official work meeting, we want to be ready for any kinky ideas that are thrown at us. Invitations will be sent to old flames, ex-wives, and divorced partners, and we want to track down Huda with her magic cauldron, as we hear from the rest of the pharaohs that this is something that can serve us well." Pepi sounded excited.

Off they went in opposite directions, Seti to chase down Huda, Pepi and Ramses on a mission to bring all they needed to ensure the party went with a bang. As Seti left the pharaohs headquarters, he encountered a group of homeless people on the street. One of them was begging alms and was sat on the ground with his two hands cupped in front of him. His fingers were gnarled and bony, and it was obvious that the lockdown and closures were influencing food supplies. He was badly undernourished. Seti pretended that he hadn't seen him, then continued his journey without even thinking to offer them a tip for their trouble. The group looked at one another then spat in the sand at his retreating shadow.

Seti walked on and soon came upon a group of people who were taking their daily exercise, a nicety which Augustuskamoun had decreed to those incarcerated indoors due to the lockdown. He stopped to ask them if they had any idea where he might find Huda.

Seti told them, "She is wielding a petition and wants to stir up anger and discontent within the people, and against the rulers. Huda's a nasty piece of work and we would do well to be rid of her."

The description didn't register with any of them, but when he went into more detail about her appearance and that she carried a cauldron, some of them laughed.

"She sounds like a witch," one of them cried out.

"Not far wrong, she's capable of delivering more than just bad curses and spells upon us," Seti replied.

Seti walked off without a word of thanks to the group.

"He's gone the wrong way," one said.

Minutes later, in a grimy cloud of dust and dirt, Seti skidded back up to where he left them.

"This time give me the right direction; I'll make it worth your while," he cried.

They had seen him flip a silver pound coin out of his robe. This worked as an incentive as they scratched their heads in unison, searching for information that might prove right.

"I saw her earlier on," one said, "she sauntered past with the rest of a group. Now she's hanging around in one of the tree-lined squares that surround the central pyramid, and fronts with the market."

Seti didn't have to be told twice; he was down there in a jiffy. As he approached the looming triangular structure that soared for miles upwards, he thought he could hear somebody cry plaintively, in a bleating tone about the government, and what they had in store for the masses.

Huda wailed, "They are going to make use of the pandemic by hook or crook to do their own will, and they will use the Rosetta stone."

Next to Huda's sandwich board and belongings, was a battered and worn copper cauldron. Seeing this, Seti threw himself upon it, stashing it safely away in his robe. Now Seti had what he was looking for he could report back to the others, and he made off on his merry way. It didn't take long for him to arrive back; he coincided with Ramses and Pepi who were bringing a bounty of seedy goods from the store. They had been waylaid down near the old statue of Thoth.

A madame ran a brothel out of the back of the unit. Brothel ladies had been designated as essential workers, and when times were hard the girls reduced their prices, so they'd all had an invite to the party, and now Pepi and Ramses just had to secure a room far from the testing areas, without access to any lowly paupers who might wander by. That or where other workers might stumble in.

A room deep underground was chosen for its obvious connotations with a dungeon. Pepi and Ramses rigged the room accordingly, lights dimmed and switched for red bulbs; Mattresses had been tied to the floor and the walls, to protect people as they pass out and tumble down. Stocks, chains, and shackles lay scattered about for the lewd imagination of the partygoers to put to their own use. It was going to be a lockdown party in every sense of the word!

Seti brought in a cauldron along with a handwritten note that Huda left in there. It gave plain instructions about how its powers can be summonsed, the exact ingredients that were needed. Ramses was sent on an urgent errand to collect the various requirements. Once he returned and popped them into the cauldron, they fizzed away nicely.

With this Ramses uttered, "We can make all women fall in love with us, make their hearts burn until they do so." At that, he began to chant rhythmically and stared deep into its depths. "The young girl whose name is to be dragged through the mud is Dendera, it will happen tonight."

Augustuskamoun agreed to turn up at 7pm. He was punctual and brought along two floozies he had met on the way. The other pharaohs began to arrive shortly after. There were queues of them snaking down the stairway, each dressed in resplendent headwear and cloak, with a feathered staff whose purpose was to give tantalizing pain and pleasure, in equal amounts.

Ramses said, "Now the party is flowing, and the sauna open."

"A barrelful of hummus has been left out with pitta for guests to help themselves, and to smother it upon their partners, kinky devils!" Pepi grinned.

"Too right. Plates of baklava have been left in strategic places too, they are hoping some may use the stickiness to glue bandages and other edibles, such as the bread to one another."

"Whatever turns them on," Pepi shuddered, and disappeared in search of some fun.

He found it in the form of Dendera, a woman of lowly rank, an underclass, and particularly poor. These things made it much easier to persuade people to do things they would not otherwise have thought of doing, Pepi knew, and he went swaying over to her with a sticky treat in one hand and a triangle of hummus in the other. Veering towards her, he smeared the concoction across her naked shoulder, taking advantage of the moment to force himself bodily onto her.

Ramses, who was watching from the shadows, called out, "Watch out! A newspaper hack is concealed behind an old and worn copy of the Egyptian Satellite, a hard right tabloid."

The journalist started snapping away merrily to steal the front cover of the early edition. To spread the news far and wide that Pepi had been caught in flagrante, seen canoodling with a new love. What a scoop!

The next morning a cloud of shame hit the ears of Pepi's beloved wife, Twosret, causing her great agony and giving her the opportunity to forgo any future relationships with the man.

Chapter Five

As the party wound down at the house, the pharaohs skulked off in various directions. Some headed for home, others back towards the pyramid; to its interior where they could find their governing throne. Pepi, Ramses, and Seti agreed to stay behind so they could manage the test centre for the day, whilst Khufu, Nefertiti, Khafre, Djoser, Snefru, and Narmer trooped their way back.

Nitocris, Twosret, and Cleopatra were on their way from some far-flung place, within the grounds of the palace. Cleopatra had had a copy of the newspaper waved under her nose on the way, and upon seeing the pictures and the accompanying headline, she decided the best course of action was to confront the issue as soon as she could. She had little or no consideration to the sensitivity of the matter.

Cleopatra walked up to Twosret, declaring, "This is outrageous behaviour! What man ever treats his wife in this way?"

"This is the first time I've heard it, but the partner is completely in the wrong. It's all the newspapers' fault. It may not even be true; but you know how these things can be organised to put people in a bad light," Nitocris declared, grabbing the newspaper and feasting hungry eyes upon the contents of the front page.

"It reminds me of the time when Ramses was out philandering with one of the cook's assistants, who'd been recently employed. The minute folks turned their backs he decided to take advantage of her," Cleopatra said, rather unkindly.

Twosret gave a horrified snarl, determining his punishment herself. "Well, I don't care what Ramses did, but if Pepi comes grovelling back, I will never accept him. If that's what he wants, he's welcome to it!"

They continued along their way, making haste as they were to meet Augustuskamoun in exactly half an hour. Twosret's anger made her quicken her step.

Nitocris said, "Hurry, hurry, if any of us are late he can be petty and intolerable, so I've heard."

They pressed on and as they reached the outer confines of the pyramid, they ran into the other returning pharaohs.

Narmer cried, "Augustuskamoun awaits us."

"His Majesty has arrived," Snefru announced.

They hurried down a dusty corridor. It was early, but the temperature was already creeping up. They were all perspiring, fetid air pervaded the space, combined with the scent of rosewater and other perfumes that they wore. As they reached Augustuskamoun's throne carved from the sand, expecting to find him there as arranged, they peered in and saw nothing. There wasn't even an air of warmth to the lair, nobody had been sitting in his casket, not recently anyway.

They scratched their heads, and Cleopatra said, "He must have left for some other business, it's that or he's playing away from home."

Cleopatra took a deep breath of the interior, to help her decide, based purely on the blend of smell, and sweat leftover, whether anybody else was present. Not spotting any belongings either, she was happy to step back, let the others crowd around. Most of the pharaohs are used to being disowned by their ruler.

Narmer said, "The best thing for us to do is step for our thrones, we can take refuge there by having a nap, then continue with our duties."

Snefru agreed. "Hear, hear! I think most feel safer this way, than having to be out on the streets with the public, that dirty heaving mass. Out there, the chance of them catching cholera is much higher, all they must do is stumble across a disused test, or another infected possession, the disease can easily pass on that way. Then, all they need to do is touch or inhale the virus and come breathing or touching us!"

As they pushed on, they ran into a small group of visitors who were leaving from the party. They assured the group that they had missed all the excitement, that the allegations about Pepi which were flying about were one hundred percent true. Twosret seemed to shiver with rage, then steam started to pour from her ears. Her eyes rolled back, her fury growing, a crime of passion discovered, making her bubble up in anger.

Augustuskamoun suddenly appeared and boomed, "I left the party much earlier, took an underground passage that led back toward the house. I was hoping to catch Pepi, Ramses, and Seti before they left but it wasn't the case. I heard something of the events of the night before, but in amongst all the fun and frolics with which we were entertained, it was all very unclear. I arrived at the property, in the underground layer to be precise, where most of the incriminating proceedings had transpired. I felt no guilt as my mind tried to dimly string together what had ensued."

Snefru encouragingly coaxed a few more words from their master, who clearly was trying to claim he had had no part in any of the proceedings but had haplessly stumbled upon events.

"What happened next, then?" Snefru carried on with his interpretation.

Augustuskamoun replied, "I remember arriving, then being assailed with large quantities of wine, before being coaxed up the stairs to the sauna room. Apparently, I didn't make any protests according to Pepi and Ramses, who escorted me along. Beneath the multiple layers of hummus, bread, and baklava, it is far more difficult to tell what happened. I have a dim memory of pushing Pepi into the arms of a young girl, but then nothing. There was an oath of vengeance from Pepi, then I succumbed."

Pepi screamed out, "You liar, you're going to destroy me!"

"Tell them about the love spells, Pepi, how we had to pursue Huda for the cauldron. Our battle to track down the recipe and with what ease all women can be rendered powerless."

Pepi, eying Twosret nervously, said, "Just imagine, every time you call forth the spirits, their heart burns until you set them free. Woman's ability to succumb to our baser desires, but under our control, our jurisdiction. No more of this silly and frivolous activity of falling in love, such a waste of time, its hopes, its disappointments. Then the setbacks in men's careers! No more, though."

Augustuskamoun joined in with a hearty cheer.

"With this, we can free ourselves of these unruly

women, that and the rest of the population."

Tarek sat at the end of a bench, with his wife Nour, Femi, and Keket huddled together in the middle. He read the newspaper he had bought to search through the classifieds. As he finished, he folded it back and gave himself up to catching up on current affairs. One of the pages was dedicated to a story about a new liberal government in Egypt, its potential effect on the country, the other an update on the cholera outbreak. He finished reading and they left the bench, heading back towards the dig.

Tarek called, "Nour, you must get back for the next bake day, me to gather my possessions, make last minute preparations before setting out to attend my first seminar. It is to happen in the northern city of Luxor and means a ten-day trip by canoe along the Nile."

"I'm so worried about you, your trip is fraught with its own dangers; crocodiles, alligators, and plagues of locusts that you may encounter, and to make things worse, you are going on your own."

"My plan is to pack all the vital camping equipment that I require, then I am going to pitch up at various places with my hammock, swinging it over any convenient dates palms that happen to be hanging low," Tarek told them.

"I bet you're dreading clouds of flies and mosquitoes descending upon you in the night, on your journey," Nour shuddered. What she really meant was that she would dread clouds of flies and mosquitoes descending upon her!

"I am, but I must set my worries to one side. I have reading to get on with and making notes for my coming class," Tarek replied, nonchalantly.

"Is there anything in particular you must learn?"

Tarek nodded. "There are recipes and a variety of ways they can be conducted, and techniques that range from ancient to present day. One that is recommended for us to try, features sesame oil, a balsam type plant - can be root extract of bullrushes, plant-based gum - a natural sugar that may come from Acacia, and conifer tree resin."

"Good luck finding those, then!"

Tarek replied, "I will make a notation of its process, a mental note to look out for those ingredients on my travels the next day."

The sun rose and he rolled his sleeping equipment up, packed away his stove, put away his meagre supply of food. Nour had only given him four loaves, so it was guaranteed that he must keep his eyes peeled for places where his provisions could be replenished. Tarek had not seen a soul since he began the journey, his only travelling companions were a swallow, and a crocodile.

I suspect the latter is tracking me for no other reason than being hungry, too. I've heard that crocodile once grilled on an open fire, removed of its leathery armour, can be tender, juicy, and flavoursome, most think it tastes like chicken, Tarek thought to himself as his newfound friend was never far away, and once he has gotten over his fear, he decided that crocodile meat should be his next priority.

Food, of course, was essential, and even more so when you were on a journey alone and provisions were low. Tarek slipped down the muddy banks of the river. He had taken with him a length of old rope that he had tied into a huge slip knot, and he ventured down towards where he thought he would find the crocodile's lair. As he got closer, he lost his footing on the mud, and before he knew it, he was out of control. He slid past where the crocodile was snoozing peacefully, short puffs of air coming like locomotive notes out of its scaly snout.

Getting as close as he dared, he threw the rope with practised aim, over the crocodile's closed trap. Tarek thought, *it can't do a thing; its eyelids are rolling back and its black eye blazing like coal. There is an immense strength in those muscley forearms and legs, though!* Suddenly, realising it was caught, it sprang itself like a peg that had popped, launching itself violently into the air, flying claws, teeth, and gaping gullet, towards Tarek.

In the heat of the moment Tarek somehow managed to remain calm enough to divert the flying beast as it toppled him to one side. Its leg was still caught in the rope, so, he gave it another yank. This time, the crocodile lost its footing and went crashing down onto the bank, a combination of reeds, grass, and a quicksand bog.

As soon as it landed, it began to sink.

This is it, thought Tarek. *This is my last chance to ensnare the animal. It's going under and will probably suffocate. Then I'll pull it back up when it's finally squeezed of oxygen.* But this time when he pulled, expecting the croc to be out cold, Tarek's fears were confirmed! The crocodile was full of life and gave a huge swing of its tail, before going into a death roll, whereby it submerged itself under several feet of muddy water, before it gradually began to pull him back in, inch by inch, until he was left grasping and clutching at any available vegetation, shrubs, or bushes onto which he could grab. *Nothing makes any difference, though,'* Tarek thought, as he sped past another bush. *This could be curtains for me!* The rope around the crocodile's trap slipped and the animal was able to snap and gnash. *Well, he's not gnashing on me,* Tarek thought with determination.

As Tarek was about to be pulled into the swampy murky deep for the last time, he had the luck of seeing a fellow human. Somebody was out on the opposite bank of the river washing a bundle of clothes, with their basket.

Tarek yelled, "Throw your basket!"

It was made from toughened reeds, and Tarek was convinced that it could be used to wedge into the crocodile's mouth, to stop it snapping shut.

The basket came sailing towards Tarek and he grabbed it, then stuffed it as best he could into the creature's feeding cavity, which gaped open, as it flailed from side to side. *It seemed to be working,* Tarek thought. *What a miracle! The gods must be smiling upon me today.* He used the opportunity to land himself upon a solid piece of concrete, where he could get his footing better, then did his best to pull the awful, struggling beast back onto the bank.

Once out of the water, Tarek left the basket in its mouth, then used some lengths of sharpened bamboo to hoist the animal up at both ends, by its tail and snout, so its belly hung down. Then he slit it lengthways from throat to belly with a knife he had in his pack. The blood, which was almost black in colour surged out, then pulsed for many hours, throbbing out slowly.

The battle is over, Tarek thought, as he saw that the pumping of the crocodile's blood had stopped. *That was some conquest.* He hauled his prey further up into a place where it couldn't be seen, smelt, or carried up into the air by vulture or other carrion eaters. He proceeded to skin it for its most usable assets; everything would go to good use; he had learnt well from Nour. The carcass of the animal itself was an ideal candidate for practising his mummification technique.

All entrails and innards were removed with medical precision, as if conducting a dissection and each part was named. The brain was put to one side, as well as the internal organs. It was lucky that Tarek had ample supplies of salt, and he caked the whole body. According to the recipe, it must be left for several days, to be entirely preserved. Then he buried it in the sand knowing that this is the best way to ensure no other predators might find it themselves.

As soon as Tarek finished, he left its body, then made off to find the integral parts of the recipe he wanted to carry out. To keep himself company, he talked to himself along the way.

"They should all be relatively easy to source on the banks of the Nile," he muttered and continued his recce. "Most of the ingredients grow in abundance in this part of the world, especially so out in the wild."

He had not been walking long when he came to a huge Balsam bush, which he dug up to expose its roots, then used it to take his cuttings from.

An Acacia was the next tree that he saw with its

branches drooping low.

Tarek spoke under his breath. "That's where the sugar comes from. If I remove the gum from the bark, it can be derived from there."

A conifer was next on the list. He had been wandering for a mile or so, when suddenly he saw a huge clump of evergreens. Heading towards them he went to collect resin that dripped directly from their trunks. *The last one could be trickier,* Tarek thought. *Sesame oil and linen. It might be easier for me to go and trade them with the villagers.* It was at this point that he stumbled across a man herding his cattle back home.

"I'm desperately in need of some sesame oil and fine linen. I can give you crocodile steaks in return," Tarek told him, without preamble.

The man was no fool and said, "For food, I'm happy to answer your request, with no questions asked."

As Tarek stood waiting for the man to come back as promised, he gazed out over the river. There were many folks trying to fish. A huge heron stood amongst them with its wings spread. Tarek watched the heron until the man returned with the spoils which Tarek had requested. Then, he set off back towards the place where he last made camp, on his approach he saw an immense cloud of flies, which helped him to ascertain the exact position he had buried his corpse, his soon to be embalmed volunteer.

Tarek used his hands to dig around it. Uncovering first its tiny claws, then its snout and its underside. The whole thing was squirming with maggots, which he took to be a good sign, because it meant that any last residue of meat would have been cleared out. Then he began to unearth it properly, tugging it gently from the sand.

It was well ensconced and took some pulling and pushing, until he could slowly prise it from the ground. As the last of the sand fell from its body, Tarek noticed its eyes had turned into wrinkled and tiny knotholes, its mouth too, as if it had been sewn up, with all signs of healthy tissue long since removed.

The next step was for him to combine all its components, so Tarek went in search of a pestle and mortar to grind up what he needed. *Everything will just melt with the warmth of working it, gradually combine,* he thought. When the oil and the resin were mixed, it gave an antibacterial property that protected the body from decay. He poured a smaller quantity into the mortar and took it around to where he had set up his temporary workshop.

Tarek started to dab it in with a brush, working it into the various cavities and grooves of its head, its neck, and the wrinkles of its gullet. *It goes further than I thought. I can do most of its body with a thick and even pasting. I will top up my mixture and tackle the underside. It will create an all over seal once it's done, that also functions to kill bacteria.* It was just left for Tarek to finish the final wrapping process, by rolling fine linen around its body, then it would take on its true mummified state.

The mummy and its shrouded body could now be left for a duration, to be dug up many aeons in the future. Tarek wanted to take it with him and show it to the other members of the group. If any of the other students learnt from it, he would be grateful.

The next day he packed away all his belongings, and

realised he still had an epic journey in front of him and wanted to set off early so he could beat the midday sun. As soon as he rose, he went to check on his canoe, for any leaks or other repairs that might need to be made to the delicate membrane of palm tree leaves that make up its exterior. There was none that he could see, so he went to collect his possessions, then packed them away securely, pushing the small, mummified object up into the front part of the craft.

Once off, Tarek could only paddle for a short duration before the heat became too intense. so, he let himself glide down the river, with the oars laid across his legs. He thought, *it's a good thing that the waters are so calm and still.* When the temperature abated much later, he felt his energy returning and decided to push on. He was in a shady part of the river, where the trees stretched their limbs out to their furthermost points, interlacing and creating a canopy that gave him optimum protection from the relentless sun.

All Tarek's supplies were running low. Matches, wood, kindling, water, food, salted snacks, fruit, and vegetables. He worked hard to ration these out; his intention was that they should sally off hunger and attacks from wild animals. On day eleven, one day over his deadline to arrive, he romped up at a beach just outside Luxor. As he dragged his canoe from the desert, a herd of camels greeted him, it seemed as if they were being led along. When Tarek hastened to slow down and make himself known he met an elderly Bedouin who was driving the beast's home.

Tarek called, "Where are you going, my good friend?"

"We are heading for an oasis just on the outskirts of the city, where it is promised there will be plentiful supplies of all we can imagine," the Bedouin replied.

Gasping and red-faced Tarek uttered his gratitude and joined the caravan. They were an uncouth and stinky lot, constantly kneeing and kicking, as well as braying their displeasure at the hostile surroundings in which they found themselves.

The leader promised they would make it in a day, but he hadn't bargained for a storm that blew in from the west. Tarek pulled up his scarf to protect his face from the biting conditions that prevailed, but all was in vain as his view was blocked, and within minutes he had lost the entire group. There were dunes to his left and to his right, but in front of him it was less easy to define. Tarek sensed that they must be in front of him because he seemed to be protected from the oncoming winds. *If I follow this line,* he thought, *I can be provided with cover for the rest of the trip.*

Barely able to hold himself straight and battered to and fro by gales that blew backwards and forwards, Tarek was crippled with pain. He had to gradually limp back to safety, to the respite of the small lake and the shelter of the trees. In front of him was the Bedouin with his loyal herd of camel.

"Now they will be rewarded for their efforts fighting through the inhospitable desert," Tarek said.

He drove them towards the water's edge, where they gulped and gurgled until their thirst was quenched. After that, the Bedouin tied a nosebag to each camel, and let them have their fill, until the next trip that must be made, anyway.

"They have two humps so they can maximise their storage capacity. It optimizes their ability to make long journeys again," the Bedouin remarked.

Tarek emptied his canoe out and gave everything a good wash. It felt good to refresh his own body, as well as his equipment. He took great draughts of water to restore his shrivelled and parched body. So many days out in the open, under the oppressive sun, his body was a mere shadow of its former self. He had lost several stone, gained a few more grey hairs, but he had made it.

Now, as he revived himself, his vision and goal came hurtling back towards him. Tarek knew he must make it to the grandest pyramid in Luxor, where a meeting had been arranged at a dilapidated building in the centre of town.

It was a place where artisans came to practise their art of carving sandstone, before attempting huge religious and other culturally significant commissions, such as the one of Thoth at Cairo, Anubis at Luxor, Isis at Sharm El Sheikh, Osiris at Alexandria, Horus at Aswan, and Amun at Hurghada.

Out towards the back was another artistic looking establishment, in a small shabby shack, a shelter where regular meetings took place for the Society of Mummification. They ran workshops and other related events, and it was here that the seminars were due to happen, the first was arranged for that evening. Tarek was the first to arrive, so eager to display his keen attitude.

The institution was one with lengthy and bureaucratic links to government, which was good as it meant all Tarek met would put him in good stead for his lengthier object of acquiring a full-time position, either through them or with a different organization. He went and sat at the back and made copious notes whenever the lecturer spoke, and making drawings to the best of his ability.

Tarek wanted to know the best ingredients to use, as well as other substitutions, if the best could not be sought. At the end he had a barrage of questions to ask the lecturer, who had travelled a similar distance to himself, though did not look half as battered. Tarek wanted to show him his recently mummified crocodile, to see if he could gain an expert opinion on it, if he was doing everything as he should.

"I'll be back in a second," Tarek shouted.

Then he ran off to where he had left his goods. He returned, diligently dragging the trussed up and parched looking body. It was covered in fine material; its outer shape could still be made out. The lecturer was pleased to see that Tarek had made such great efforts of his own accord.

"We don't usually get such willing attitude," he remarked, and made some notes of his own, so he could visualize this memorable character in the future, what an impression he created.

"Let me make further inspections," he told Tarek, and he began to unravel the material, peeling away the various layers of skin, congealed blood, and salt, which had come together to form a hardened casing.

"With the addition of the resin, sugar, and oil, it made hasty work of cleaning and forming a new coating, one that can keep its poor inhabitant in stasis for many generations," commented the teacher. He kept picking away at the dead skin of the wound, as if this action would help it to heal.

Suddenly, he cried out, "Whoever has done this work has made an amazing job of it! I would expect this specimen to outlast any dynasties that might surpass it."

Tarek ran back over; he had been deep in conversation with some other students, trying to ascertain their own approaches, and whether he needed to consider them competition or not, as most were keen for a job. Did he now have an advantage, he wondered.

Chapter Six

Once the seminar finished, Tarek made his way back towards where he had left the Bedouin. He wanted to ask for some advice on anywhere half decent to spend the night. Although it was sultry and warm, with a breeze picking up, there was word a tempest may be coming. He knew he couldn't face another night out in the open, not if there was a serious storm.

Back at the Tavern with the Bedouin, he was given directions to a widower that took in the odd traveller. The next session happened the following day at the same location, and he didn't want to stray far.

Tarek didn't have much with him. Only a bulging folder and a bundle in which he carried his sample. As he rapped on the door, he heard a quivering voice.

"I don't let strangers in so late at night, have you got any credentials?"

He showed some drawings from his folder through a crack in the door, explaining more about why he was in town.

"I'm hoping to begin running mummification workshops soon. Back down in Cairo."

She was keen to learn more and unbolted the door immediately, swarming him with questions.

"My name is Eshe, nice to meet you. Will you spread out your papers and elaborate further, please? This is something I am curious about as I am making my own funeral arrangements now. I am investigating all the options that are open to me, and I've heard a lot about this specific type of afterlife care, whereby you leave your body to the hands of the gods: any gifts and presents that are left to them, the more favourable they are on you."

Tarek was happy to admit, "I'm no expert in this field. But my knowledge is built up from time spent at work in the houses of pharaohs and wealthy merchants across the city. I hear countless conversations about these matters, that leave you assured if you want to live for eternity, the best way to do it is down this route."

Eshe listened intently. She made careful mental notes and asked questions. Then she blurted out, "How much does it cost for my body to be embalmed? You said you are learning how to do this yourself?"

Tarek was in shock. His initial idea was he would target wealthy families and royalty, rather than having to work for peanuts in these impoverished surroundings, but as Eshe seemed so friendly and congenial, he softened a little towards her.

"Do you know of any other people who are on their deathbeds? That could possibly donate their bodies towards my humble acquisition of knowledge within this ancient art?" he asked, thinking on his feet.

"I've lived in Luxor for many years now and know a great number of folk. I'm not sure it's the avenue that most of them want to go down. But if you will cut me a deal on the cost of my own treatment, then I can go around and see if anybody is willing to give it a go." Eshe said.

Eshe worked at the central pyramid doing administrative tasks where she helped to look after internal affairs. This gave her a lot of contact with the ruling classes every day. She was happy to put the word about with them too, and it was agreed that she and Tarek would meet up again in a few days' time, giving her time to make enquiries on his behalf. She told him she would have to do a little research and broach the subject carefully to get a measure of peoples' interest.

Business concluded, Eshe bade him goodnight and rattled off upstairs into the darkened room of the attic. She slept there because then it meant she was out of the way of the lodgers. Sitting in his room, Tarek took out his pack and overnight supplies, climbed into bed and pulled the grimy sheet up over his nose. *I'm sick of working for these people,'* he thought. Suddenly he was transported back to the hellish din. The unceasing noise of the dig.

Shaking his head, he said to himself, "I've got to get out of this way of life. Maybe if I can earn enough with this mummifying skill, I can take Nour away with me, too."

With that, he drifted off into a fitful sleep. Tarek's dreams were broken by flashbacks of ending up working back at the mine for pennies or having to graft again at the palace. He heard the barking of orders from a chef; he ignored it and escaped the voice.

Dawn was just around the corner. It had been a restless night, with Tarek drifting in and out of consciousness. Before he knew it, there was a brief knock at the door, and he was being bid downstairs for breakfast. As he headed down to meet Eshe, she stopped him in the corridor and blurted out her dreams.

"I slept a lot better," she said, "but the afterlife can provide me with a fitting end. My own peaceful passage can be ensured by leaving treasures out in a specially built tomb. When I awoke, I was overcome by the indignity of life. It made me feel I am succumbing to an existence of intolerable toil, waiting on the hands and feet of others."

Eshe started running about for what Tarek required, then wearied. Eventually the lodger seemed happy, and Eshe left him, heading to her workplace at the pyramid.

Tarek stared straight out of the top window, but Eshe was lost within seconds of leaving. She turned down a short sharp alleyway that ran alongside the house and soon transformed into a labyrinth of mazes. They were constructed from mud bricks made from the receding flood waters of the Nile, with a mortar of dried sticks, sand, and a cheap form of plaster containing hay, loosely daubed over the top. The sun was still low, and she found it difficult to see, its rays shining directly into her face.

Eshe decided to pick up a flatbread along the way, pulling up to a vendor that she knew well. He had an umbrella to give himself some shade and wore a scarf to keep out the dust.

"Typical inhospitable conditions," she muttered under her breath. "How's the poor fellow to make a living working the streets all day. He must be on peanuts. It's only because people like me take a liking to the guy, that he has any income at all. Most people would walk straight past him. If with two jobs I'm struggling to make ends meet, he can't be doing much better."

Eshe pushed on towards the pyramid, she could just about see its tip peeping between a row of buildings. A newly erected statue of Anubis, the god of death and the art of embalming towered above her, the figure of a man with the head of a jackal, who carried a staff. Eshe stared up in wonderment, awe, and memories flooded back from her childhood days at school. *What is the role of this individual?'* she thought.

As far as Eshe could recall, he guided the souls of the dead to the Hall of Truth and was part of the ritual of the weighing of the heart of the soul. *A heavy responsibility,* she thought. *But then with most of these gods it is. The fact he is half wild dog makes him appear aggressive, but really, he is to be trusted.* She made a mental note to speak to Tarek about this later.

Arriving at her workplace a few minutes later, the guards greeted her at the gate. She had to show a card with her thumbprint smudged onto it with red ink, before they let her through.

It's always the same high security around here, she thought. As she headed to her workspace, she gazed up at the point of the pyramid, which was completely concealed in a yellowy grime. The breeze had picked up now and the appearance of everything was changed, making even the most recognizable things difficult to discern.

Eshe left her belongings at the door, as you weren't allowed to take anything into the building. Security was always tight, for fear of attack, only the previous year there had been a poisoning incident involving the pharaohs. Most unsavoury, although some would say necessary. They were strict about all of this, most of the workers involved that year were sacked immediately. Any with immigrant heritage were deported back to their own countries. Eshe was lucky, she had been born and brought up in Egypt.

She hung up her own clothes and got changed into the generic outfit worn by all. Jewellery had to be removed; apron and sandals were to be worn. After that, she headed towards one of the central chambers that was lined with ancient typewriters. They operated with huge rolls of parchment which needed changing once it ran out, it was her job to replace it. Papyrus scrolls on vertical arms rotated about the room, the whole sheet winding constantly around.

The administrators tore off small sheets to record what the pharaohs said they should be doing that day on their rounds. All that were based there had to come and pickup their instructions for the day. Another part of Eshe's job was to make sure that they were all collected on time. There was a huge ornate table of carved marble where they collected their sheets, and she sat to one side giving advice and updates, as well as any other additions that had been made.

Eshe's day was busy with a new wire from Augustuskamoun, and multiple other tasks were to be carried out, too, including writing up new laws and sending them down to the pharaohs for stamping and signing. There was an archaic system in operation, involving a huge, heavy stone which she struggled to lift, let alone bring down with enough force to ink the paper. Audits must be carried out of all supplies in the pyramid, from the back offices to the tombs and sleeping quarters.

A new decree had been received from Augustuskamoun that stated as with the poisoning case, all workers of immigrant heritage were to be turned out on their ear. No reason was needed to be given either, just an explanation that they were dirtier, and with them it was easier for the virus to spread. This had been a contributing factor in the mass spreading of pandemics for many generations before. Because Eshe was of Egyptian nationality, this did not involve her, but her heart went out to the vendors in the street, servants, butlers, guards, slaves, all minorities, plus people whose livelihood it was to look after the nobles.

Suddenly Eshe remembered that she told Tarek she would keep an ear out for potential candidates for mummification, and she began to think about death.

How and where would that leave me? She decided the best thing was to speak to the pharaohs as soon as she could. *Hopefully they will want to discuss the afterlife. You never knew with these pharaohs, though,* Eshe ruminated. *Sometimes when you have money you are quite happy to think about your demise, but the average worker is too busy living in the moment, they don't have time for such considerations.*

She threw herself to a wall as a troop of pharaohs sailed through, in a cloud of dust, all high opinions and berating the immigrant workers for spreading disease. *Maybe once they calm down,* she thought, *and after a drink or some food, after their bellies and extensive appetites have been satiated.* They sauntered past and she listened to their receding footsteps as they disappeared around the corner. She sprung up after they left and followed them down to the great banqueting hall.

This was a medieval affair where great quantities of mead, roast game, and any other delectable organ that can be pulled from the insides of some rare and exotic creature, was served, and consumed. The chefs from the kitchen had been out the whole day with their nets trying to trap these poor innocent creatures, so that they could be served up on a platter with a silver spoon to the overlords. As the pharaohs burst in with huge royal bellies, and an air of self-importance they literally took over the room.

Eshe chose to wait until after they had eaten, knowing they would be more likely to talk about life, and more appropriately, their death, once they were fed and watered. After, she hoped they would drop to their knees with the sheer weight of what they had consumed, and then struggle to hold themselves upright, wobbling, and standing wearily. Eshe saw this as being a point of entry, so she stepped forward to offer the afterlife services of Tarek. Approaching Narmer, Khafre, and Snefru, Eshe began her pitch.

"Have you ever thought about what comes in the next life?"

"Most of us already have long standing arrangements, ones in place for many years which we cannot get out of. I could potentially offer the lives of some of my more menial staff, doormen, slaves, kitchen hands, gardeners, people who are more expendable. If there's something in it for me, then I will be quite happy to make an agreement for some of them to be transported down for his use, and to brush up on his skills, for what he is doing, no doubt, is of indubitable importance," Narmer told her.

He hollered for one of his foot staff, who had been quivering in a corner and demanded that they take a piece of parchment bearing Tarek's particulars to his palatial home, in order that he could talk to his staff and suggest they took up this offer. Narmer and Snefru fell back to talking. Eshe found herself fending off the attentions of Khafre, who was in predatory mode, which seemed to be the only mode he used when women were concerned. Regardless of whether she wanted to speak, Khafre wouldn't let her anyway. Eshe spoke it was with sense, but he treated her to his usual belittling demeanour.

Where did the pharaohs get their lack of manners and respect for women? Eshe thought. She'd been around long enough to know how things operated in this type of relationship and knew that only if she offered something of herself, or another potentially appetising treat to him, then he might become more malleable in her hands.

Putty was what Eshe wanted, and she began to sing a lullaby that had the effect of an aphrodisiac on him, causing him to throw his arms around her and whisper sweet nothings in her ear. The word of the love spells had spread from Augustuskamoun, Seti, and Ramses throughout the land of the pharaohs. Even though they knew that the cauldron was needed for the spell to be cast properly, this was enough for some of them.

Khafre's head was in a passionate haze, and Eshe was the poor unsuspecting female that was unlucky enough to suffer his advances. Eshe didn't have a clue about the lustful thoughts of Khafre.

I'm going to throw myself upon her, Khafre thought, as she sat there talking about the afterlife. With that he lunged for her, but she ducked and managed to butt into the conversation of Narmer and Snefru instead. They were innocently discussing how to contact Tarek, and how awful Nefertiti was to work with.

As Eshe broke in, they hadn't even noticed Khafre was practically salivating in her ear but having not gotten a response from the po-faced Eshe, he decided he would be better off having something to eat.

After they had their fill, Khafre and Snefru decided to leave. They discussed the odd character who had approached them earlier on, claiming to be able to make their journeys to the afterlife so much easier. Khafre was curious to know more, but whether that was because he was interested or because he was still wanted to try his luck with Eshe, he wasn't sure.

Narmer joined them and an animated discussion on their lives and working conditions ensued, and although Khafre nodded, he wasn't listening properly, answering carelessly, "I've heard that Nefertiti can be a bully, she can make our lives hell with that."

"Apparently, Nefertiti was responsible for personnel a while back, and each was given their marching orders well before she was done with them. They weren't even given the opportunity to explain themselves. They had been out on a work trip in a distant part of the country, and nobody was around to record what happened, let alone argue their case. It was said that she'd had the bodies disposed of in the nearest channel of water, a tributary that leads up to the Nile." Snefru glowered. Khafre gulped.

The three of them went their separate ways. It was late, so they headed back to their individual tombs for the night, ready to rise early again the next day. They all slipped out into the darkness, there wasn't even the screech of a nightjar to break the silence of the streets where they saw the homeless sleeping. They didn't feel a tinge of compassion for them, there was always a whole ghetto of people living in impoverished circumstances, what difference did it make to them.

"I'm more concerned about the spread of cholera and how quickly it will spread in the city," Snefru declared.

Khafre elbowed his companions and uttered, "This will be like wildfire."

The other two juddered and fled to their own quarters where they needn't encounter the masses.

Another new law repealing their right to travel freely around the country had just been issued, and all pharaohs were told not to leave the pyramid. It was being done for their own benefit, but they all knew the reality of it. They were supposed to be giving a good example to the people but instead wanted to continue with their own important and highly superior lives.

That day, Narmer, after he finished his meal, went to find Djoser and Khufu. He couldn't resist retelling the tale of the administrative worker who had so much to say about their future. Khufu wanted to know more, but Djoser had been put in charge, and he didn't want them frittering their time away, chatting about irrelevant matters.

"There is work to be done, run here, run there. Get yourselves moving!" Djoser commanded.

But Narmer and Khufu had no intentions of doing any of the running around for themselves, for this they approached their own minions, after all, what was the point in being able to delegate, if you didn't delegate?

Djoser was chancellor, as well as responsible for health, and he was even more cutthroat than any of the other pharaohs. If he must slash figures and budgets to get the country out of a crippling economic slump, he was quite ready to do so. He was planning for more cuts and improvement measures. He didn't have an ounce of sympathy for the public, or cholera patients.

He had learnt from Augustuskamoun that shaking their hands was just a way to make yourself look good, implying that your own health doesn't matter. *What about the imbecility of it all, though, that is a thing that goes by the by,* he thought. *What does it matter if I expose myself to the virus? It will probably just boost my immune system anyway, maybe everyone, even the elderly should do the same?*

Narmer was another who saw the pandemic as an opportunity. For him, he wanted to keep schools running, risking the spread of cholera amongst teachers and the children. He thought, *they can all keep going in and spread herd immunity amongst themselves. This is the best way I am convinced, and I will make this known to Augustuskamoun.*

Augustuskamoun didn't need much persuading. If there was a solution that meant that the problem was solved, but at the expense of other groups of people in society, such as the lower orders, he was happy to push it forwards. In fact, it sort of killed two birds with one stone, he decided, happily. 'Herd immunity' was just another buzzword for spreading the disease, and in doing so, it would reduce the population, which was the whole point of pandemics, after all.

Khufu Robertson, who had the lordly title of Political

Strategist, had no real tasks or duties assigned, apart from giving advice in areas which he knew nothing about. He had been given the job of researching various places that they could go to as the pandemic got underway, somewhere that they could elope to with the smallest of fuss, and without people noticing. In other words, he was plotting with the rest of the pharaohs to completely ignore the lockdown and go on a jolly.

For this, he decided to embark on a countrywide trip to a variety of different and pleasurable destinations. With this rather satisfying task ahead of him, Khufu retired to his tomb for the night, and the next morning he arose with the larks and set out to a private boat on the Nile. The boat would take him up to the northern city of Desouk, within a few days. Having planned well, Khufu had made sure his craft was laden with every delectable goody, treat, and luxury imaginable, and there were women, wine, and lashings of fun and depravity to be had, too, he thought to himself.

Khufu was on his own but had arranged to meet a rich merchant he knew. The next day, the merchant arrived on the boat, bringing with him a whole bevvy of young Arabian princesses, various intoxicating substances, liquors, and other presents to tempt the palate and the guilt free consciousness of Khufu. Pandemic? What pandemic? Lockdown? Not on my boat, he grinned.

Now, Khufu was a man respectfully married, and he had been for many years, but like most pharaohs he was partial to a lap or belly dancing session, knowing that in this part of the world it was a thing that men loved.

They dined together exchanging political views, and how they could assist each other in their own mutual ways, and then the ladies were brought forward. It was the way of the world; he placated what little consciousness he had about his wife and their marriage. She probably had a young slave to keep her amused, anyway, and with that, he didn't give her another thought.

One of the women came springing into Khufu's lap, a bunch of grapes in each hand, jewels dangling from her navel. She was heavily made up and looked like a dancing girl. She gave him a smack on the lips. Khufu was delighted and returned the compliment, however, despite being from an outlying region, and not having a great command of the English language, she managed to make it known that she was expecting a tip. *Curses!* Thought Khufu, *they are always after money.*

Pulling a gold pound from his pocket, he dispensed it to her, and she went on carousing and dancing. It seemed the merchant was also having a whale of a time himself, and it wasn't until many hours later that they got the chance to compare notes once again.

"She's a lovely girl," Khufu said, and the merchant agreed. "We are lucky here; there's no danger of anybody getting wind of our private party."

They both shared a secretive grin and went back to their carousing, neither concerned that they were breaking the recently made laws because, of course, neither of them thought they would ever be found out. Who was to tell, after all?

The next morning the merchant left the boat at the city of Kafr El Zayat. He had urgent business to attend to, there was a marriage being conducted by a local Imam, and he, as a distant relative, must put forward his best sentiments. It was his wish that a flock of sheep, ten goats, three sacks full of corn, plus a hectare of farmland be issued to the couple the next day. As the merchant left, the dancing floozies departed with him, they were to bring more ill repute to the next social function he visited. Generally, they followed him everywhere.

As Khufu waved them off, he started making plans for the next leg of the journey, as far as he could, for what he might encounter and need upon his arrival in Desouk. He still planned to call in at as many different places as possible, so that upon his return, he would be able to tell the pharaohs about all his travels and what he had gotten up to in each place. He could then make recommendations for which places they could go and recharge their batteries.

That had been his instruction from Augustuskamoun, and he wasn't likely to stray from those orders. Judging from this recent experience, and since he had set sail at Cairo, he thought that this might be a great way to carry on, and so he arranged to call at every port on his way, for action, love, sun, sea, sand, and sex; as well as any other business that could be carried out for his own selfish needs. The fact that a pandemic was ravaging the lands itself didn't seem to worry him a bit. *This is just good practise for what we can all be getting on with in the future, God knows how long this pandemic and lockdown might last,* Khufu thought, and then carried on his business as though nothing was amiss.

Chapter Seven

Meanwhile, back in Cairo, Karim and Kissa stole away from the place where they had found the equipment and chemical supplies. He required them for setting up his own laboratory.

Turning to Kissa, Karim said, "Lets head to your place, where I can begin construction of my laboratory."

Kissa agreed, and they set off. It wasn't so far to her settlement on the outskirts of the city, and as they walked, they discussed how quickly the cholera pandemic was spreading.

"I believe that within days it will surpass any suppositions that have been made about its duration," Kissa said, thoughtfully.

Karim replied, "Yes, I believe you're right, it will spread like wildfire. I've been doing my research and know what's out there. One of the things most likely to spread the disease is that test centres rely on primitive technology. Kits are produced at a low cost, and a lot are not accurate at all. I can develop one that is one hundred percent successful. This will mean far fewer deaths, because people who are ill will instantly be told to isolate, thus keeping the chance of spreading the disease to a minimum. With what we secured from that dump of scientific supplies that we were lucky enough to find, I believe I can build a testing kit within a few days. Prototypes will have to be made first, then we can begin getting them out to the public."

"I promise that I will do my best to help," said Kissa,

but at the same time she was wondering what would be in it for her. A girl had to plan, she decided, and they continued along their way.

"If we can get to one of the test centres, we could see one for ourselves. I reckon I would be able to use their test kits to base my own, much more efficient design, on. Then we can play the pharaohs at their own game, and it won't mean we need to be so reliant on their methods and ways."

Kissa saw he talked sense and said, "Sounds like a plan that requires a lot of luck, and things going like clockwork. If things are even a little off kilter, then we might have to call it off. Let's go and drop everything at my place first, then we can head out to see what we can find."

They quickened their pace, both keen on what benefits such a plan would have on their own fortunes and before long they were at Kissa's house. They stopped for a moment outside, both a little paranoid that the pharaohs might have got there first and be ransacking the place, or worse, turning it into their own centre. It seemed to be quiet, so Kissa slipped through the courtyard, then unbuckled the chain that hung around the gate, to stop it from being pulled open. Using her key to unlock the latch, she let herself in stealthily and tiptoed around the house checking each room before alerting Karim that the coast was clear before rejoining him outside.

There were only two floors and a basement which Kissa thought would be most suitable for building a laboratory in. Here Karim could have space to bring in all his specialist tools, those that he needed to manipulate plastics and cut them. Karim hadn't resolved his design yet, but from how he explained it to her, a larger vessel must have a hollow cut into it. This is what the used swabs were dipped into, before finding out if the result was positive or negative.

She called to Karim, indicating that the coast was clear and together they transported all the gear downstairs, before either of them could retire for the night. It seemed to Kissa that Karim would be working late most evenings, so it made sense for her to get to bed early, so she could awaken refreshed and ready for an early start the next day.

Kissa headed down to the basement the next morning, and could hear loud banging, sawing, drilling, and snapping plastic as it was continuously being twisted to its limit.

"I am testing the strength of various materials to be used," Karim told her by way of explanation.

"I can see many models that are all slightly different in design, hanging from a washing line, using pegs," Kissa observed, staring out into the small courtyard at the back of her digs.

"They are at various stages of drying, having been glued and pieced together earlier on. Now I am waiting to continue my experimentations for the sturdiest plastic that can be used."

"What is your next task?" Kissa was curious.

"I must work on the formula itself that is needed to determine the result. This will be a combination of various chemicals," Karim told her.

"Looks like you're going to have a full day in the basement then," Kissa sighed. She had rather liked their sojourns out into the avenues and squares.

Karim nodded and said, "Yes, but I will need more equipment for this part of the process."

And he went off to collect oversized test tubes and Bunsen burners. Soon he had them bound together with rubber straps at various points and bends, and chemicals in liquid and powder form could be seen bubbling away in conical flasks, before being put into petri dishes to cool down and potentially be reused. Either that or act as research for what he had and hadn't tried. At times, they would explode and be fused together, reacting in exactly the way he wanted.

Quite often Kissa returned to the basement and saw him scratching his head, his hair stood up on end as if he had just received a jolt from a Van de Graaff generator. In those moments of enlightenment, where he was seen staring into space, he was making calculations that were combinations of algebra and long equation. Then, he began spitting chemical numbers of various metals, compounds, and alloys out at night, during his sleep. Kissa was superstitious, and in these moments, she hid under the bed!

A few days later, Karim said, "Eureka! I've got it, after puzzling away the whole night, debating whether to use one powder or another."

"Got what?" asked Kissa, her heart going nine to the dozen after his sudden loud cry.

With a glimmer of excitement, Karim announced, "The experiments I set running a few hours ago, seem to be doing something interesting."

Kissa looked blank. All the experiments seemed to look the same to her. "You'll need to explain more?"

"One has bright blue bubbles foaming out of the test tube, and I take that as a sign that I'm on the right path."

Kissa who had an elementary scientific knowledge said, "That's genius, if the liquid begins to dry, you can see faint watermarks on the paper, which proves it is exactly the balance you're looking for."

"Now it seems the days will blur less quickly into one another!" Karim grinned.

"The pace of your work has become more gradual and less frenetic. Now might be the right time to have a day off, to go and see what we can find out about the beds. I know you want to make one of those too, so we can have the holy trio."

"Good thinking, sometimes I get too caught up with the practicalities, forget the bigger picture. Come and collect me tomorrow morning and we can be on our way."

The next day, Kissa did as she was bid and called downstairs to him, "Karim!"

There was a grunt from below.

"Do you think we should go and pay a trip to the test centre? The nearest one is only a few blocks away, but on a broiling hot day like today, the effort used to make our way up there will be fatiguing indeed," she told him.

Karim gave a nod of acknowledgment and said, "Yes, of course, why not!"

They pulled on their cloaks, scarves, and hefty boots to protect them. There was always a westerly breeze where they lived, and a constant stream of sand blew into the eyes and faces of anybody who left the building. As they mounted their camel, Karim attached their kit containing water and other dried provisions for the day, as they were both targeted by an endless blasting of sand.

Through a crack in his cloak Karim said, "That was incredibly painful, and now we can't even see to manoeuvre up the street."

Kissa was more optimistic. "There's the vague outline of a neighbouring building that we can follow. That of a mosque dedicated to the God Bes. It has bow-legged dwarves with large ears, prominent genitals, and who are shaking rattles. They can just about be seen standing on top of two huge columns."

Karim craned his neck to get his bearings the best he could, knowing that in normal conditions, this would only be a five-minute ride. The animal itself was struggling. They threw a rug over its face to guard it, but it could see less than they. They thought better of trying to complete their journey and decided to wait, pulling into the next shelter, which was under the shade of a temple. A huge lump of marble hung precariously above them and looked like it might fall at any moment. Realizing this, Karim pulled hard on the reins and choker of the camel, in the hope that they could divert the tragedy, but to no avail, and it came crashing down! What a palaver!

Karim scowled.

They managed to pull free in the nick of time and were back on their way again. The breeze had abated a little, and was not so constant, or intense, and now this was an opportunity for them to make a run for it. He urged the camel on, it lunged with its huge brown muscular body and its lanky long legs towards the corner, where it pulled in. They had arrived at their destination.

Even from there they saw a queue that snaked around the building twice, back up the street and around again. It was composed of all citizens of the city, and most had their scarves wrapped tightly around their heads, partly to protect themselves from the weather, but also from the danger of passing on any strain of the disease that they might had. That or risk picking it up from somebody else.

"There are workers from the pyramid, slaves with their shackles, holy men with their books, foot soldiers, and gardeners, all with their weapons and tools laid down at their sides," Kissa observed.

"It looks like they've been waiting a long time, as they've began to set up their own little bases and dens, using any implement that they can find, to build shelters and block the sun," Karim replied.

"Ingenious." Kissa gave the waiting hordes a compliment that probably they wouldn't have appreciated. They just wanted the queue to move! "Right, what's the best tactic then?" she asked Karim.

"Let's pretend we have the disease already and join the queue," he suggested.

Kissa didn't look impressed. "I think this is too dangerous and I don't want to risk our health."

"Good point, well made!" Karim replied. "Alright, let's circumnavigate the building and try to access the centre a different way."

They led the camel behind them, and as they turned the corner, there was a kiosk where a man sold grocery goods, newspapers, tobacco, and other confectionery.

"It's a small wonder he is still doing business in the middle of the pandemic, but as he is, let's hasten and purchase water and sugary treats from him," said Kissa, thinking he must be classified as an essential supplier to still be trading.

Karim appeared to have read her mind, because he told her that even essential street traders, such as he, would have to now comply with new, tougher lockdown regulations. Only the bigger stores with permanent locations in buildings would be able to remain open.

Kissa looked at the street vendor and sighed, "This guy's commerce is doomed."

Karim knew she was right. "The effect that the tougher lockdown is having on the whole country is cruel and the introduction seemed malicious. The control of the pandemic was getting unpredictable, and any more regulations are putting the fear of God into people, who are worried that they might lose their lives, homes, livelihoods, everything, in fact. Although it seemed the pharaohs didn't think about this sort of impact. So long as they were alright!" he said to Kissa.

"They are happy to get on with their self-important existences, travelling up and down the country, visiting relatives, even going to group meet ups with their own kind. The social distancing rule hasn't seemed to affect them, only the lives of these people," and she gestured around at the queue and the people gathered by the street vendor.

Having purchased some water and some sugary treats to give them energy, Karim and Kissa kept on searching for an entrance, when suddenly above them shimmering in the dust and heat, was an opening in the fence. They both peered in, then Karim leashed the camel onto the nearest post, and said, "Let's see if we can squeeze ourselves through?"

He scampered up to the gate and offered Kissa a hand, who followed, then he escorted her through the narrow tunnel of bricks. It was tight and clouds of dust fell upon them as the mortar crumbled, but they made it through, and then the light was brilliant, clear, pure, and they could see for miles.

Karim shaded his eyes, scanned the horizon. "I can see two structures, one must be the test centre, the second is smaller, that must be where they are doing quarantine," he mused.

He strolled on, with Kissa at his heels, keeping his eyes peeled for a bed. There was no danger for them of being in there, the worst that could happen was getting thrown out by one of the pharaohs. Suddenly, he spotted a bed right in front of him, beckoned to Kissa and said, "With this we will be able to develop our own fool proof version."

He slung the bed over his shoulder, and they made off, leaving the street vendor to serve more hopeless people in a never-ending queue of other peoples' hypocrisy.

Eshe's day at the pyramid finally finished and she was eager to leave. She had much to tell Tarek about the research she had been carrying out, because it seemed there were a few firm candidates who he could make use of. She hung her uniform up and collected her everyday outfit, which was a linen tunic. As she left work, she threw on some bracelets, picked up a wicker basket, put it on her head, and then she was ready to go.

Leaving via a small doorway cut out of a stone partition that formed part of an extension in the building, an oppressive wall of heat hit her. She was knocked back by this and slunk into the shade of sheltering corridors, here the temperature was lower as it was in the darkness. Eshe ran her hand over the stone to keep herself cool as she passed and thought about the errands that she must run on the way home.

I want to pick up melon and other thirst-quenching fruit, she thought and then she remembered an old blind and dumb hawker who sat up near the Avenue of Sphinx. He was normally in the shadow of the small orchards of rowan and mulberry trees that rose majestically into the sky overhead. The outline of each was delineated by the bright sunshine, and she had difficulty in the supposition of his awning, but after searching swiftly about, found it and pulled up, greeting him inconspicuously.

"Hello, I'm looking for several items, and please tell me about your family?" Eshe asked.

The hawker replied, "I'm down to the last of my stock, so you can't be too fussy. Most of my family have already been taken away."

"I'm so sorry. Is there anything I can do? I would be more than happy to oblige."

The hawker was grateful and told her, "Not really, but thanks for asking, anyway."

Eshe smiled sympathetically and then bought the last of his provisions, not because he had anything she particularly wanted but because she wanted to show him solidarity and help him provide for the few family members he still had left. Then, she headed directly back to her place, throwing herself down a winding alleyway that turned out near the towering statue of Anubis. She thought, *I must remember to speak to Tarek, seeing this god of embalming has reminded me.*

She skirted alongside the base of another immense pyramid that rose nearby; its brickwork steps seemed to stretch off into the relentless, azure sky. On the steps she saw many citizens and became even more incensed at what was happening within society – she spotted a road sweeper, sweeping around a girl who was sitting on the cobbles brushing her hair. She watched as a woman counted beads, and a man hawked his wares to an invisible clientele. *It is pitiful,* thought Eshe, *and it makes me angry.* These people were all victims of the pandemic. There was more than one way to lose your life, she mused. Instead of the area near the pyramid being heaving with life, with people meeting, conversing and socialising, it had become a socially distanced existence. Nobody dared break the new regulations, but equally no-one wanted to catch the virus.

Eshe felt a tinge of sadness welling up in her, but instead of letting it spring out she went back to her duties. "A few more blocks and I will be there," she told herself, hoping and praying that Tarek hadn't gone out for the day.

In fact, Tarek had been in the house the whole day. He didn't want to risk going out, so was happy to place himself under voluntary quarantine. It was the dead part of the day, the afternoon, when nothing happened because everybody was paralyzed by the sun. Now, as the evening approached, the district began ringing with voices, singing in the streets and from balconies. If no-one could meet in the streets, they would meet from their balconies or courtyards. The din caused Tarek to make his way into the front room, also knowing it would be cooler in there as it had been sitting out of the sun's rays for the duration of the day.

The whole place had been carved out of the rocks and was classified as a cave dwelling, each room was on the cliff face side, and an exterior stairway ran up and around it. The stone construction meant that once Tarek had seated himself in the front room, there was an amazing amount of sound insulation from the neighbours. Even if they were singing, copulating, or marching up and down in their houses, not a note travelled through the solid walls.

Vast Arabian rugs were laid down on each floor, each with its mesmerizing print and geometric pattern. Tarek makes himself comfortable with a drink sitting cross legged on the rug, then the thought struck him, *Eshe will be back shortly, and she can see to my dining requirements.* He grinned. It would make a change someone else ministering to his needs. As good a wife as Nour was to him, she did not always cook for him, and of course, his stint working for the cooks had put paid to any culinary ambitions that he might have had.

Right at that minute, he heard somebody running up the steps outside, and suddenly, Eshe appeared and unloaded her basket full of fruits, offering some to

Tarek in a gesture of hospitality. Tarek was parched and took what he could, enjoying their succour before he felt less dry mouthed. His vocal chords were eased by the moisture of the juicy fruit. Even though he hadn't left the house, he was eager to talk.

"The clients for embalming, did somebody drop in a card earlier from Narmer, offering the bodies of his staff for this process?" he asked.

Narmer was based in Cairo but once he went back, Tarek could easily make use of this kind and wonderful offer. But then a question struck his mind.

"How can Narmer have such little disregard for his staff, offering up their bodies in that way? Don't they have any say over their final rites, and what can be done with their own bodies?"

At that Eshe who had been listening intently, replied, "They're slaves! They have no say over what happens to them afterwards, it's as simple as that."

In deep shock, Tarek said, "I agree, it would be stupid for me to forego this opportunity just because I feel strongly against it, my future career depends on it, after all." But all the same, he did feel uneasy.

Chapter Eight

Pepi, Seti, and Ramses had been at the centre for the whole day. It had been crazily busy, and a new record of people testing had been logged, so in addition to getting used to this, they had to also deal with all the positive test results they were seeing. The Testers were streamlined to one side and put into isolation rooms at various places around the house, then their figures documented on a yellowing sheet of parchment, to be passed on to Eshe later, who had the job of keeping records of all these tests back at the pyramid. No-one else had access to this data, only Eshe and the pharaohs, who of course, had to have access to it in case they wanted to doctor the figures to suit their own agenda.

As they got out of their protective equipment, goggles were dropped to the ground, gloves, aprons, breathing apparatus, and tubes of medication.

There were people going around collecting all that was disposed of, and throwing it directly into great chutes, where it collected outdoors, in piles. Further workers then picked it over and put all contaminated items to one side, anything else was thrown into the normal sewerage system, gradually ending up out at sea. The workers were entirely disposable themselves.

The risks in doing these sorts of jobs were countless, from accidently being stabbed by soiled needles, to encountering contaminated tests. That or ingesting waterborne particles that came into their faces, as they weren't wearing masks. It was all so dreadful. They were so desperate for money; they had no option about whether they took the work or not.

Pepi, Ramses, and Seti laid in the various sun loungers dotted about on the terrace, that were available for their own exclusive use. There was the shelter of immense walls that rose on all sides and blocked out the sun, but the heat was still intense. A few wilting palms were haphazardly positioned around the edge, suffering as they never got any sunlight, and there was a pool that had long since been emptied of water. Whilst they reposed, they discussed the days results, how each of them felt, and what gossip was going around that had been triggered off by the party.

"This is more fun to discuss. I'm happy to shirk responsibility by talking about the virus, and the disease that is in full swing right now," Ramses smirked.

"The party was epic, and having those love spells really threw a new spin on the night's proceedings," Seti grinned.

"I agree, do you think Pepi will lose his job over the whole business?" asked Ramses.

"Well, it's enough for him to lose his wife out of this, let alone his job," Seti observed, recalling the events that had taken place.

Ramses leapt to his defence and said, "Wouldn't you have done the same in his situation?" *Wouldn't anyone,* he thought, lustfully.

Pepi had been lost in reading a newspaper, where he found a series of pictures of a barely discernible couple, dripping with hummus, the remains of a baklava, and pitta bread strewn through their hair. The text printed beneath, read. *Not much mystery about Pepi and Dendera, who appeared as a couple at a recent government party.* Pepi was fuming, and his rage shot out at the other two, who were grinning like a pair of Cheshire cats.

"I don't deserve to lose my job over this, this is ridiculous!"

In sympathy they agreed, then Ramses said, "You were just unlucky."

Changing the subject, Pepi asked, "Do either of you know where Augustuskamoun has got to? He hasn't been seen since he left the party in the morning. Only a few people have heard anything from him, he's been a perfect mystery, where could he have got to?"

"Probably at the pyramid," Seti guessed.

Ramses said, "Keeping out of trouble, planning the next step in the fight against cholera, I should think!"

The other two looked at him as if he were mad. "No, but that's what he should be doing, though," said Seti, raising his eyebrows.

As they sat there, a summons came through from Augustuskamoun for Ramses to attend in person, an invite extended purely to himself, that he couldn't refuse.

The other two laughed, and Seti said, "On pain of death if you don't."

"How nice for me," he muttered, facetiously.

Ramses was curious but not foolish, so he packed his things once he finished talking with the other two, then went on his way. It was evening by the time he slipped through the streets, and the sun was setting; buildings and a nearby statue were infused with a pinkish glow. With him, he had a small number of tests and buffer solution left over from the days' testing. His slave carried them, sweating profusely in the still humid evening air.

The heat made Ramses decide to stop for a drink on the way home; he knew a small place that was open purely for the pharaohs. As they pulled over, he rapped hard on a stone door which had an iron ring hanging down. He heard the patter of feet and then a small letterbox was opened in the door, and a voice came ringing out.

"How can I help you, my royal?"

Ramses barked through the door, "I demand to come in!"

He didn't have to show any identification. His attire and his attendance by a slave were enough, and he was let in at once. The door was slammed shut behind them, as Ramses entered the front room and bid his slave to put his belongings on the floor. The owner went to grab him a drink as specified; he had heard of similar visits that had resulted in licences being revoked, if you didn't co-operate, or even worse punishments being meted upon you, such as prison, or having your body left out for the vultures. Not fancying any of this, as he had a small family, he was aiming to please. He had heard that his own path could be paved with gold potentially in the next life, but only if you did good things for a pharaoh. Sometimes it came back to you in a good way, meaning your passage to the afterlife was ensured. He didn't want to ask outright but was wishing for this in the back of his mind. He brought water for the slave too, though as he was about to hand it over, Ramses grabbed his arm and pulled it back.

"No water for him, he'll survive!"

The owner was in deep shock, *I can't believe that anybody can be considered generous that keeps their own staff in that way,* he thought.

However, that didn't deter him from seeking to appease Ramses more, who requested food, then wanted to see dancing girls, too.

"I know a small establishment around the corner," he told Ramses, who nodded and tapped the side of his nose in a secretive fashion. Then, the bar owner sent Ramses and his slave on their way, thanking his lucky stars to whichever gods were responsible for him having gotten off so lightly from this brief experience. *I've been extremely lucky this time,* he thought with relief and several whiskies to calm his nerves.

Once Ramses left, he made his way to the next street corner, where there was a towering statue, and beneath that, an entrance that had been dug out of the sand and was supported by concrete and corrugated iron boards. It had been hastily put up by the owner, and his place catered purely for pharaohs; he was well used to dealing with royalty. As soon as Ramses began to go down the stairs, a stone door was pulled to one side to allow him access. It was now the job of the owner of this establishment to ensure that Ramses' every need was serviced and all wishes granted. *Let's hope he doesn't ask too much,* thought the owner, giving Ramses a shifty look. *I can probably manage the impossible, but as they say, miracles may take a bit longer!*

He strode over to Ramses, and proceeded to show him the belly dancers, and other types of entertainers too, who had come from far and wide to work in this establishment because of its link with the pharaohs.

After all, what little girl doesn't dream of one day being a princess? Belly dancing was his favourite to watch, and he pulled Ramses down a corridor of velvet and sequins, with all manner of glittering beads and embellishments, then pulled him into a room where there was a low curtained ceiling that hung down, and walls made of lavish drapery, fine silks, and satins. He had these shipped over from the far east when the place was first established, and they were the most expensive, rare, and resplendent he could find.

As Ramses made himself comfortable, cushions were thrown down, and a drink was brought over by a new girl who had just started working there. She ambled back over and asked him if he wanted a private dance, at which he answered in the affirmative. Then, springing up, she seized his hand gaily and threw it in the air, spinning him about wildly.

She began rising and falling, wobbling her hips and her belly in perfect rhythm. She'd learnt this dance from her family, generations before, and knew every nuance of it, like the back of her hand. She didn't even need to visualize it; she just kept her eyes closed and let the melody and the tune take her there.

She whispered sweet nothings into the ear of Ramses, and he was putty in her hands, ripe for the taking. Despite her dancing for him, it was as if he was the prisoner. *Now I know I can get my own way, I can have anything I wish from Ramses, that is how it always works,* she thought. *Men of power, money, rank, and distinction often come here to lose themselves, and end up losing their wealth to me. In this state of partial hypnosis, it will be easy for me to command anything I want from him.*

She said, "Bring me vast amounts of rubies, bracelets, diamonds, silver, and gold jewellery."

He did as he was bid and ordered for huge showering's of riches to be made her way. It was as if she had a treasure chest into which every coin that was thrown, multiplied a hundred times when it bounced back out again. She was eternally prosperous and never had to worry about having to dance again, now she could set herself up with a nice little business, for when she is older and had less energy to plough into more energetic pursuits.

Ramses said, "I feel good about being able to support you in this way."

"I promise anytime you want to come back, just give me a knock. My door will always be open for you," gushed the dancer, clearly not wishing to lose her newly acquired meal ticket.

Ramses waltzed off into the night with a light step and said to himself, "My appointment with Augustuskamoun is tomorrow, it is late, and I must rise early to be on my way."

The next morning around five o'clock, Ramses crawled from his tomb. Narmer, Nefertiti, and Djoser were still slumbering, and hadn't stirred yet. He wanted to be off before any of them woke, as he knew they will want to know his movements for the day. Then he heard an enormous grunt, it was Djoser, and as suspected, he began bugging and plaguing him for what he had planned. He had the makings of a fine gossip, did Djoser, but not today, thought Ramses!

"I'm on my way to see Augustuskamoun, he has a

special request for me," Ramses told him, by way of explanation as to why he would not stay and reveal any information. That, and the fact he didn't want Djoser blabbing his business everywhere and adding any embellishments he pleased.

Djoser said, "Fair enough, you best be on your way."

Ramses excused himself, saying, "I will be at peril if I don't get along shortly."

He bade his slave to attend him, the poor man looked done in, and they both made off before Djoser began another round of interrogation.

It was a two hour walk at the crack of dawn only because the streets were usually quiet. Even in lockdown, you would still find plenty of people about later, enjoying their daily exercise, queuing up at the dole office, or looking for a shop that was allowed to open, for whatever provisions the pharaohs decreed could be sold today. Quite why you couldn't purchase a parchment newspaper or clothes during a pandemic was some strange regulation no-one had yet managed to fathom. However, Ramses didn't particularly care if the whole of the populus had to go about their business naked so long as they kept out of his way.

The sun was just about visible at the tip of the pyramid, a small glimmer of pink and gold that cast a glorious glow down its extremities, slid from step to step, before cascading across the city floor like spilled jewels. Usually this was an area where street vendors hawked their wares, and there was life and vivacity, but today with the advent of new lockdown restrictions, the sole visitor to the pyramid was a nightjar. Its tiny beak tweeting piteously, as its minuscule skeletal body pecked desperately for crumbs that weren't there, as nobody had been around to deposit them. It wasn't just humans that were suffering with this pandemic, nature was, too. Other areas had been known to rewild naturally, huge groups of crocodiles and alligators crawling up from the Nile and making themselves known in the streets and squares.

Nobody dared to leave their houses as a rule, because it was rumoured that they were even hungrier than usual, as they had been deprived of their food staple of small mammals, snakes, lizards, and birds. All of these having left themselves in search of other food sources. Even the birds down at the Nile were usually fed by villagers who threw large handfuls of grain to them, but now nobody was coming out anymore, and they were all beginning to starve. Some had decided to migrate to other territories, and therefore they came into the city. Ramses hurried past without even a thought about this, he was caught up in his own self-important matters as usual, and only worried for whether he will be strung up on a line himself. The nightjar watched him carefully, then tweeted his disappointment and continued its desperate pecking.

As he neared the central chamber where Augustuskamoun was said to be at his throne, Ramses slowed his pace and threw a few prayers out. He wasn't strictly a religious man, but with this meeting, he had the fear of God in him. He approached from the back of the pyramid where it had been flattened, and a huge trench carved out of the sandstone. Two immense seats being installed into the void left behind. In one he saw Augustuskamoun, and in the other his good and resourceful wife, Nitocris. Ramses caught his breath and dropped to his knees, in reverence and as if giving praise for his greater glory. Augustuskamoun's eyes flashed with a vicious look in his direction. There was nowhere to hide, and he and his slave stood out like sore thumbs. Nitocris took pity on them and said, "I recognise you; you are one of the lesser pharaohs. You are welcome to sit down and proclaim your news."

Ramses took the invitation literally and flopped himself down promptly in the shade, then the stories came pouring out, in a high pitched, nasally whine.

"Since the party, Pepi's good reputation has been tarnished. He's outraged by the whole business; he's going to lose a lot over this whole shenanigan. What was meant to be a little fun soon blew out of proportion."

Augustuskamoun, who had heard about the whole thing, burst into laughter, making it known that if Ramses wanted to garner any pity from other pharaohs, he was barking up the wrong tree, doing it around there.

"You were in the thick of it yourself and loving every minute of it!" Augustuskamoun protested.

Ramses went quiet and looked like an animal caught in headlights. He wasn't sure which way to run, or what to do, and decided the best thing was to just gloss over the whole thing and pretend it hadn't happened.

"How am I supposed to be assisting with encouraging punters and shoppers back out from their homes, and back onto the streets again?" he asked, cleverly changing the subject.

At least he has seen the error of his ways, Augustuskamoun thought, and glared at him as he gave a roar that tore right through him, consumed with rage and despair at this idiocy.

Then he told Ramses, "You will have to do mummy unwrapping's in public places where normally markets and shops are. Because of cholera, they have all been closed for a while. Hopefully people will see you and be fooled by your words, and because they see you without a mask on, they will assume it's safe to go back out again."

"That's genius," said Ramses in a tremulous voice.

"I know," grinned Augustuskamoun and went on, "Then, we can be sure of two things – they will either die of cholera, in which case an immediate result, or we can arrest them for breaking the lockdown, throw them in jail and they will die in there either of the disease or starvation. It's brilliant! All you need to do is kit yourself out with the relevant equipment, a body for embalming can be stumbled upon easily enough, I believe. Just call in at Narmer's place, and he can supply you with one, that should keep you going for a while."

Humbled by his presence with the great master, Ramses nodded his agreement, gathered his belongings and made off, pulling at his slaves' shackles and tugging him along whether he wanted to come along or not, whilst explaining to him exactly what he must do and the sheer ingeniousness of the plan.

"The first stop is to collect a body from Narmer, I think we should be able to find him back at the pyramid," Ramses said.

It was another baking hot day and now the sun was fully up, walking felt like wading through melting toffee.

Ramses urged his slave on with a whip made from a leather thong, and they pushed on until they began to see the furthest reaches of a huge building. It had the name Society of Embalming and the Afterlife chipped into a tablet in huge letters and placed high above the main entrance.

"This is a whole new government department dedicated to this process and all the related administration that must happen," Ramses told his exhausted slave.

In a voice dripping with sarcasm, his slave said, "Sounds fascinating, tell me more?"

Ramses didn't really do sarcasm, unless it came from him, and fell for his slave's bait. "Inside there are great lists of rules and regulations relating to every aspect. They have a vast database of artisans from across the country who can be brought in at the least notice."

Leaving his slave out in the street in the burgeoning heat, Ramses set off for the pyramid, not caring that he looked as though he might flake out if left under the scorching sun any longer. As Ramses entered the threshold, pyramid administration staff rushed at him from all directions, they could see he was a pharaoh and well respected.

"I was looking for Narmer's place so I could pick up a body but stumbled in here assuming that they might be able to help me with my plight."

One of the older men with the frame of a skeleton crept up to him, he had pursed lips sewn together, crinkled eyes, and tiny screwed up ears.

He shrilled, "How can I help you, my good sir?"

"You can help me look for a body that I can take

away with me right now," Ramses told him, looking with disinterest at the older man's rather shocking features.

A body was brought up that was to his liking, then a deal was struck. Ramses said, "Instead of paying, we will invoke the name of Augustuskamoun."

"I swear never to mention this trade again," said his co-conspirator.

Ramses stole out of the door to where his slave was panting heavily outside. If he was lucky, Ramses thought, the slave might have enough energy to carry the body back to the marketplace, where he had arranged to be the next morning. They set off, the slave with a body bound to his back, and Ramses in his tunic carrying a royal feather across his chest. He had on an extra collar that day which signified war. A few mortals passed by and fell to their feet grovelling and picking themselves up at the same time, trying to get out of his way.

"Sometimes if you are in the imminence of a pharaoh, it's better to move, than be struck down by one of them," one said.

The others agreed as they stumbled down the street in a cloud of dust.

Ramses shouted at them, "From tomorrow at seven, I will be at the market. Go and tell your friends and family."

They all sped off in different directions, and the word of Ramses the pharaoh was spread like wildfire across the city.

One said to another, "Ramses isn't wearing a mask."

"Not wearing a mask," came his friend's reply. "Is

that even allowed!"

Another replied, "Well, only for pharaohs, not the seething masses, only they have the sway of whether they must wear one or not. The likes of us just have to do it."

"This pharaoh must be a clever and intellectual man if he can go around giving us orders in that way," someone else proclaimed. "Let's keep spreading the word, and we'll see how many we can pull down tomorrow."

Ramses carried on tramping the streets with the sun baking on his back, and his slave by his side. They headed towards his tomb so they could rest for the night.

The next morning, regardless of lockdown restrictions, it was surprising to see that there were vast throngs of crowds in the street. They'd been trying to push their way down into the main square since dawn. People were still pouring into that part of the city, to try their luck. Because they had heard an announcement was to be made, by a figure who was hugely feared, and they were intimidated by that man. Ramses chuckled as he prepared to go up onto his podium, to address the crowd.

"Minions, lend me your ears, I have news that can affect your sense of freedom," he declared.

A few folks heckled him from a distance, but he carried on. His slave was behind and at that moment came up bearing the body, which he threw to the floor. There were gasps at the disrespect being shown to the body, but they allowed Ramses to carry on speaking.

"This mummy has been donated to me by the

government, and I am going to use it to carry out an unwrapping."

There were some shrieks and screams in the crowd, as some had heard of the terrible and gruesome process, and of it being carried out in other places. One person cried out.

"For this to be done in public and surrounded by hundreds, maybe thousands of people, surely that's not right, and especially in the middle of a pandemic."

"Well, anyway, the body probably has cholera, but that's not an issue. I wouldn't be worried or scared anyway."

Several people jumped and leapt away in fear.

"That guy is a liability," one called up. But it didn't seem to avert Ramses' progress, and he carried on with his mission of scaring the living daylights out of the crowd.

"If there are women, children, men, people of milder temperaments, or with higher anxiety levels, I suggest you leave now or stay the course," Ramses warned the crowd.

A few people tried to leave, but security men in heavy robes were stationed at all entrances, and there was not a chance of anyone escaping.

"Just sit back and enjoy the ride," Ramses cackled, and began unravelling the body on the table beneath him.

Bandages fell to the left and to the right, powder, caked on bits of resin, all began to flake away more easily. A shrivelled body sat there with nothing to cover its shame anymore. Ramses yanked its head which came off, and he held it high aloft in the air, and a steady trickle of sand came out. Some of those watching seemed stunned, and there was a low gasp.

"The body has breasts and vagina, but it is a prince," Ramses declared.

"You're a liar and a necromancer!" shouted a member of the crowd, and they were carried off and deposited far away by security.

"How can you tell if it's had a sex change?" another shouted.

Ramses replied, "You don't need to believe me, just take my words as gospel."

Another in the crowd said, "I'm confused."

"We've had too many years of conservative ruling, we aren't ready for such far sighted ideas," came another cry.

Others in the crowd just lapped it up, they nodded and cheered, talking amongst themselves about the openness Ramses displayed. Others were more sceptical.

Someone said, "I'm happy to see Ramses as a liar, somebody that might pull the wool over my eyes in the future. I'll just live in the belief that anything he might say or do be taken with a pinch of salt."

This was much of the reaction from those gathered, and a stir went around the crowd, low mutterings and mumblings hummed in the morning air.

There was another shout, "Ramses is a character who is supposed to be our leader, but we can only trust him as far as we can throw him."

"Why don't we return to the shops and marketplaces in great numbers, and throw caution to any wind with regards to current rules put in place?"

"Hear, hear!" The cry went up from the crowd as more and more took up the mood of disbelief and dissent, playing exactly into the hands of the government. Ramses smiled to himself.

The next day the streets and squares were bustling once again, nobody was wearing masks, as they had observed Ramses without a mask, and they believed the buffoon.

Someone said, "Ramses' imbecility is incredible, and we've had it on higher authority that he really is talking out of his rear. How can one man be so influential?"

It was only weeks later that mask wearing became almost obligatory again. Was being mask free a mistake or a deliberate government ploy that had paid off?

Chapter Nine

The next morning after sleeping late, Tarek and Eshe rose at approximately the same time. The conversation went on late and long, and he had taken pleasure in speaking more about Nour, and how he was sick of having to graft for the pharaohs any longer. He told her his plans to improve their lot by putting his best foot forward, and that he wanted to become the breadwinner.

"I know it sounds old fashioned," Tarek said, "but I do think this would be a very favourable way forward, and as for Nour, she brings a lot into the relationship and shouldn't need to do anymore to balance it out."

Eshe listened attentively, uhhmming and aahhing as she listened to Tarek's misogynistic ramblings.

"We've had our ups and downs about this over the years, and it always comes down to the fact that I'm not bringing in enough, and then Nour is perceived as the head of the household, but all this can change if I bring in more income."

Tarek seemed convinced about this. Eshe didn't try to argue, she could see he wanted to get it all off his chest. Instead, she said, "I want to talk about the embalming. But it seems as if you are stressed about the whole thing."

Tarek ignored her and said, "Our lives could be so much better. Ever since the pandemic started, our lives have been turned upside down. It wasn't so bad after the first lockdown, I had extra money coming in from a scheme for workers, and we were doing okay. I wouldn't say we were rich, but we had enough to live well. I am helping her out in the bakery most days, things could be tough sometimes, and we had blazing rows, but now several months later, I think it has made us stronger. When I get this new role, it will make things even easier. My usual income from selling trinkets up in the old town under the cover of the pyramids has dried up. There is not even a trickle of intrepid explorers and adventurers around, let alone any that might spare a dime on a souvenir for the loved one back at home. I am high and dry and must think fast what I can do, and the only option is to help with the bakes."

Eshe nodded. "Things must have been tough at home; otherwise, why would you be so far away trying desperately to improve your lot in life?"

He murmured in agreement.

Eshe asked, "Do you want a tea?"

Tarek accepted her offer, so she hurried off to prepare traditional sweet mint tea. Minutes later, she came back with a small silver gilt tray laden with crockery, and miniscule cutlery, of which each one's handle was finely carved with an inlay of ivory.

As Tarek stirred his tea, he stared into the ever-decreasing circles below and began to fall into another trance. It was as if he was being hypnotised, and he uttered words and numbers that didn't make any sense at all. Eshe came closer and mopped his brow. The heat of the hot beverage combined with the rising temperatures outdoors had taken effect, and he was perspiring heavily.

"Are you okay?" Eshe asked.

No sense came from his mouth, but when she

listened more closely, she began to pick up some barely intelligible words.

"Curse of Augustuskamoun… Nour was on a train this morning and she peered into an open casket; it seemed as if that was where the bad spirits were issuing from."

Eshe was alarmed and cried out, "What is that, then?"

When Tarek didn't respond, Eshe continued, "I know he is the ruling pharaoh; he has recently risen from the dead during an unwrapping in a back street of Cairo, and that word is going around it is he who is to blame for this latest outbreak of cholera. People say that Augustuskamoun brought it with him, carried under the surface of his skin, deep in its cells."

Tarek, who had gained some clarity now, said, "I've heard similar. As he awoke, fine powder evaporated from his joints, and from the bandages as they fell to one side in a heap. Apparently, they sat there fizzling away, then as soon as he began spitting and gobbing trying to clear his throat, the first few germs came flying out."

"That doesn't surprise me at all. They say that they gravitated towards a small crowd of visitors that were gathered. There weren't any other pharaohs, only some workers, so the newspapers were hushed up with a few well-meaning words." Eshe shook her head.

"They don't want them getting the wrong idea that any pharaohs are responsible for its spreading, they are always trying to make out it's the dirty immigrant workers who are the ones to blame."

Tarek sighed before continuing, "Constantly, they

gather in large numbers and living ten to a room, how else does the virus spread?"

"I'm not sure, but I know many people whose lives have been ruined by the outbreak, whether they suffered any deaths or not," Eshe was incensed that the ordinary people should be treated so callously by the ruling classes, and she began to give the example of her friend the vendor. "He's a perfect contender. Every day out on the highway in that suffocating heat, now that's a hostile environment. Nobody is going to help him out, regardless of the pandemic."

Tarek nodded gravely as he was thrown back into his own dire circumstances. His mind took a dark swing, and he was picturing how he made his daily toil, within seconds back in that no win situation. He said, "All I can ever hope for is to please the pharaohs, that and be paid back with torrents of abuse. Whilst I was at the palace every day, they used to pour scorn on me, and the cooks weren't much better."

He'd never really experienced being bullied all his life, but now these converging events were coming together to make him realize that this was what happened to him.

"I had to break away in the end, I couldn't take it any longer, and I was spurred on by the thought of my beautiful and diligent wife, Nour." Tarek gushed.

"Once I cottoned on there are alternative ways to make a living, I've been better. I am unlucky that I got picked up by one of the raids out looking for slave labour. Chances are it would have been a racket supported and paid for by the pharaohs to clean up the problem of joblessness and make themselves look good because the unemployment numbers are going down, whilst giving heavy subsidies to their own organizations."

Eshe was lost in her thoughts; her concentration had gone completely from the conversation and was now back to balancing up her own poverty-stricken life. Numbers shot across her brain, the cost of the rent, bills, rising price of food, and medicines. Eshe was agog, and her ideas stuttered as they strung themselves together in her head. Gradually she began to calm down, but she'd always had to work for the pharaohs, she was lucky that they've never came asking for anything else. She thought of some horrendous stories from girls who used to work the circuit at the brothel on the corner, and how well she knew the ruthless, vain, ignorant way of the pharaohs and what stuck up arseholes they could be. How sometimes they looked at you like you were camel dung from the boot of their foot. She recalled at the pyramid, stories were rife, ten a penny of pharaohs taking advantage of younger employees, in particular women and she thought of her own tale about Khafre and his wandering fingers.

Rumour had been going about that the pharaohs wanted to use the love spells to be able to take over the whole of the female race, to make every one of them incumbent upon an egotistic male. Eshe shuddered as she thought about this but was duly overjoyed as she heard word of the efforts of Huda. How she had been going around enlisting help and trying to drum up support to rise and beat the pharaohs at their own game.

Our odds are short, Eshe thought, *but I'd happily put my name down too, if it means that we can push for a revolution!*

With that final thought lodged in her brain, she went off in search of Huda, before she had to go to work.

Tarek had arranged to go out for another session of training for his workshop. So, Eshe found herself leaving the house alone. She turned onto the street that led to the town centre and walked alongside a wall topped with ancient plaster that had sagged in the heat and now reached the floor. She leapt over it and beat a hasty retreat. The sun was at its highest point, and it cast no shadow, not a single living thing escaped its beam. From people bustling at the bazaar, to cats concealing themselves within the steps of the great pyramid itself, and they were usually the last to retreat from the noon day solarium.

The masses were making themselves known in the markets, and within the shady concrete units, life and business was flourishing, the trading of a smashed-up typewriter for a pound of dates, anything that can be bought for a barter. Since the recalling of regulations by Ramses, the crowds had flocked back to the shops, and nobody thought twice about whether he was pulling a fast one or not.

A man was heard to say, "He's to be trusted regardless of what he did to that mummified specimen the other day."

Another agreed, "Even if he lies about its sexuality what difference does that make to him as a moral being?"

But others were not so sure, and a hot debate ensued.

"It's precisely because of that tendency to stretch the truth they should never give him another chance."

But then another cried, "He's a pharaoh, what do you expect!"

Eshe passed the men who were talking and carried along her way to a smaller square, a lot closer to the main pyramid, and the Avenue of Sphinx. There were huge flags here that unfurled themselves in the non-existent breeze, they were mostly dominated with hieroglyphics and rudimentary diagrams. Upon one Eshe saw the symbol of a pair of goggles, a mask, and a pair of gloves. Eshe looked on and suddenly there was the blast of a military fanfare from a small trumpet, it was the man who was the herald of news.

"Another update to cholera regulations!" he cried. "We must aways wear our safety gear whenever in the company of others."

Eshe muttered to herself, "I am aware of this."

Then she suddenly became aware of a commotion down the street, far away in the dust. She found it difficult to distinguish what it was. As the noise came closer, she saw a woman leading several others, it looked like they were all carrying placards and banners. As they finally came close enough to read, Eshe saw that they were protesting the pharaohs, the all-seeing power that they had, and wanted to change this, to make a revolution, to bring an uprising against them.

This is something you rarely see, she thought, *never really.* Eshe was inspired and wanted to know more.

As the commotion passed, she called to someone, "Hello, my name is Eshe, who are you?"

"My name is Keket," said a woman, approaching Eshe. "This is my friend, Femi. We have a petition between us; do you want to sign it? It says that you can be called upon in the future to help once we have enough resources to battle against them."

Eshe said, "Certainly. Why don't we meet at the giant obelisk that sits in the shade of a smaller terrace, we can talk for longer there?"

"Good idea, we will come up on our donkeys," Keket told her.

Keket and Femi approached later checking nobody was following them, so they could talk more freely.

They settled down and Keket began to pour out their story. "We met Huda, and she has been an inspiration to everybody, and we've vowed to get our own back."

Eshe listened intently, she had only ever seen repression during her years, every dynasty that came forward seemed to be even more backward than the last. Women getting less power instead of more.

"I work at the pyramid," Eshe told them. "And I must deal with their gross misconduct all day long. Because they are in their own environment, they think they can get away with it. They only need to click their fingers, and the servants come running, and so do the rest of us. Nobody is free from their tyranny. I am on my way back to the pyramid as we speak, and I can pass along the word to see if we can rally more troops."

"That's a grand idea, next time we see Huda we will tell her what the next step is, see how she wants to go about with rising against this common fiend."

They bade farewell to one another then went on their separate ways, Keket and Femi heading back along the road where they knew Huda to be. They had left her at the one of the grand squares near the plaza, Huda told them she wouldn't move until they got back from campaigning on her behalf. They had been doing this prior to meeting Eshe. Huda had given them a huge bag full of parchment flyers, each with a neatly inscribed image of herself, a small hieroglyph that stood for the enlightenment of women, and another symbol that described power to the people. Keket and Femi had been out the whole day since dawn, making their way up and down the streets until they were lost and confused, and didn't have a clue which way to turn. They had been out for several hours, asking random strangers the best way to get back to more familiar territory. When they met up with Huda, they told her about some of the people they had met during the long, hot day.

They had been in a rich and affluent area where all they could see were villas and palaces, there wasn't even a path for them to walk on, just a dirt track. Keket had tried knocking at one of the doors for access, and to drop a few flyers, and as she approached, all she saw were cats, a man reading his newspaper, and a woman darning clothes.

As they approached, the man looked over and asked them, "What do you want?"

"He doesn't seem friendly and keeps barking at his wife to not look up, and to keep sewing," Femi said.

"She is exactly who we should be targeting, it's women who are seriously repressed, they are the ones that need the greatest help," Keket replied.

Femi agreed, "I don't want to go back and make a big scene, I am afraid of how he had accosted us."

"I think they may be administrative staff from the

pyramid," Keket said. "Most of the people who work there, apart from the more menial staff, are nasty people who don't act much better than the pharaohs. Those staff are a bad example, as likely to spit and talk down upon you as anyone else, such nonsense, and double standards."

Huda nodded and instructed them to continue with their efforts, delivering flyers and generally campaigning on her behalf.

Keket and Femi had continued handing out the flyers, pressing on until the sun beats down on them fiercely at the midday hour. They both flaked out in corners under a small lotus tree, the scent from its fragrant fruit passed beneath their nostrils as they slept. On awakening they had their fill of the delicious and sweet treat and were on their way. Both felt revived and more energized after the short nap, and they set out to a new residential quarter of the city.

"It is miles from the centre, but this area has its tales, many people from immigrant families live here, and it is a good and safe place to be, unlike those haughty neighbourhoods earlier on."

"Really?" said Femi, in some surprise. She had expected the opposite, if she were honest.

"It's so stuck up and snotty there. We are far more likely to find people who will support our cause around here. These are people like us, they have the same struggles we do, they just want to have simple lives, unaffected by such things as a pandemic, and they are the least likely to be able to make their way through it. Some have small businesses in the city, they'd much rather work for themselves than take charity, especially from the pharaohs, not that much is offered, anyway. These people are so proud."

"They sound like our types." Femi had to agree.

"This isn't so far from where Husain and Ammon hail from. Now with the pandemic, the whole area has been changed and dominated by the pharaohs more, they have turned houses into test centres and turfed whole families out."

"That's outrageous," said Femi.

Then Keket began to roar and cried, "Many have lost their lives, not just through cholera, but also with the pharaohs ineptitude at dealing with the problems. Many are sick of this, once again the country's poorest and weakest members of society, and those who have the least rights, are being made scapegoats for the whole thing."

Huda nodded and thought to herself how not a day went past when a front-page story didn't unravel that didn't undermine their efforts to make a half decent living. Regularly there were new stories going around about how it was their fault for spreading the virus quicker, overcrowding in rooms, or the way that they shouldn't be there in the first place. She turned her attention to the others, as they continued their story.

Keket remained quiet from then on, putting one foot in front of the other, making her way slowly through the afternoon haze. The temperatures were in the fifties now, and the mercury had popped from the thermometer many hours before. There was a sundial nearby and it read three o clock. The angle of the sun beat down upon their backs mercilessly as they walked down the road. A few more gates and fences, and they were ready to throw themselves into the respite of the shade of a shadowy underpass, where the overhang of a building made a roof for their heads.

"Let's try this place," said Keket, and Femi followed diligently.

She rapped at the door, and after a short pause a young woman opened it a crack. She looked to be of mixed race, possibly of African or Iranian descent.

Keket showed the woman the flyer and began explaining their plight, and within minutes she wanted to sign up too, and said, "Things are getting worse, before we had no respect from the pharaohs, but now it's even less."

Femi stood at her side like an arrow, straight and tall, she wanted to give the impression that they were to be trusted. The woman promised to pass on the word to her family, friends, and work colleagues.

Keket said, "The pharaohs can't be allowed to get away with this anymore."

"We work at a small flower stall in the centre. We are completely reliant on business from the pharaohs, but we hate it and would much rather be free of their dominant ways. Every day they come in, then walk straight back out again without paying for the flowers, or they promise that some small favour will be paid on the other side, but who's to believe that nonsense! Just because they are lords with all their wealth and riches, it's like they feel they can command us still from the grave."

She hooted with laughter, half with fear. "Imagine that!" she said, with a terrified giggle.

Femi was quaking, but Keket was a lot more solid in

her beliefs. She knew what powers they had but saw the battle they would ensue with one another being in this world, not the next, and with that, they departed from Huda and went on to continue their campaigning for a better life for women in this world, not the next.

Augustuskamoun, after finishing early with Ramses that day, decided he had better make amends with his wife, Nitocris. He was always in the bad books with her, and it didn't take much to realize why. His philandering ways at the recent party had reached her delicate ears, via the gossiping do-gooders, and she had given him a severe dressing down.

Twosret and Cleopatra had been doing their best to fill her head with tales of misdemeanour, and ill repute from their recent night's excursion. Apparently, a young nubile thing was caught in the arms of Pepi, and Twosret hadn't spoken a word to him since. Augustuskamoun's behaviour wasn't much better they both assured her, even Cleopatra seemed convinced, though she hadn't seen her other half yet.

Augustuskamoun left his tomb and headed back to the palace to try and swoon Nitocris that way. He wanted to make up for all the muck that had been flung at his name, sullying it, and wanted a clean slate. He was pretty sure that in amongst the lavish settings of the palace that he could convince her that she was wrong. Nitocris would be fooled by the hum of riches that pervaded the air, because she had become blinded by the shine.

It won't be difficult to bribe her even, Augustuskamoun thought, *another clock, watch, bracelet, gold necklace, women are so easily bought.* With this last thought, he headed for the pawn shop.

As soon as the custodian realized who it was, he was humbled by the royal presence of the greatest ruler the nation had ever seen. He laid down prostate and gave up prayers for his own impoverished self.

"Have mercy on me," he said. "May Allah protect you."

Augustuskamoun roared and bellowed with rage, adapting a voice that he was used to applying in the presence of the minions.

"You are a blithering fool, bring me some of your finest treasures that have been used to pay the way for other people's misfortunes."

He didn't miss a trick and found it mildly amusing that so many people were struggling beyond words, must come and sell their worldly goods to make ends meet. In the confusion the man ran hither and thither, he dashed downstairs, then back up again. He had been rooting through chests beneath the ground but now found exactly what he was looking for.

A week ago, some poor soul had called to see him. The man was in debt and wanted to trade something that would gain him better access into the next life. He had left a monkey with eyes of deep azure, carved from the finest marble, an eagle with glittering feathers that reflected the light, and a small statue of the god Anubis.

The shopkeeper handed them to Augustuskamoun with glee in his voice.

"They were taken by me, then the man never came back."

Augustuskamoun boomed back, "These are ideal for

what I have in mind, they will put a smile on the face of my Nitocris."

With that he left the shop, and all was quiet.

The shopkeeper's wife came out and asked him what had happened, and he replied, "I think we have just signed a deal with the devil."

She said with fear in her voice, "What do you mean?"

"I gave him the monkey, the eagle, and the statuette which I believe has a curse placed on it."

"How did you know about that?" his wife asked.

"Because when the poor fellow came in the other day, you could see it in his eyes, he told me a story that he'd been up at the archaeological dig that day, and whilst underground, he has fallen in with some unsavoury types. They made him swear to hand over his business in return for the very goods he gave me, not realizing that they are cursed. He thought them to be worth a great deal and that he would never have to work again, but it turned out not to be the case. When he got home that evening, he left them in his satchel bag. His family were around, having a meal, and when his brother walked past the bag, he sees the eyes glowing green and pouring with steam. They urged the man to get rid of it quickly before any ill will befell them, and the very next day he brought it back to the shop, so now I have given it to the pharaoh, to be rid of it for good. So, now you see the curse will fall upon the pharaohs, too."

"But what kind of curse is it?" His wife asked.

"The man said the stranger had mentioned it is supposed to rid you of your manhood, your masculinity."

His wife nodded. "I've heard of similar curses, and they don't treat men too well, they are rumoured to have been started by one of feminism's late and great leading lights. She is said to have been the first, way back in prehistoric times, who managed to outwit a man in battle, with the use of a fossilized eagle and a monkey's skull. She set a trap with the use of some honey to act as a lure, on a table, then as the skull clasps closed, the eagle came slamming down too. The man's finger is then stuck forever, and he can't remove it again. It stays with him to remind him of the stupidity of his ways, and that the woman has beaten him at his tricks."

The shopkeeper fell silent, before saying "Does that mean that it can have the same power over the pharaohs?"

His wife murmured in assent, then went on with busying herself in the shop for it was getting late, and they were closing for the night.

Augustuskamoun went upon his regal way, sending out a message for a legion of servants and slaves to be ordered, and for them to wait on his every wish and command. He waited at the corner of a vast avenue that looked out over the desert in one direction, and over a vast sweep of the city in the other. A warm wind was blowing in from the east, and Augustuskamoun twitched his nose in a knowing way, smelt the air, mingling with the scent of women.

Later, I will assail my Nitocris, he thought, *but until then I have much to do.* A whiff of cholera passed beneath his nostrils, and also disinfectant and hand soap, a combination of palm tree and ground up dates. These were sworn on by the locals, but he didn't rate it. The only reason he used it was because of Nitocris who seemed to be more pandering to their ways, believing that they must have some knowledge after all.

The stench that followed was carried from the recently dug open grave on the outskirts of the city, and he could see vultures wheeling around in neat slow arcs. *How can they fly so close to that thing,* Augustuskamoun thought, and wondered if he should reopen another mass grave.

"I could open it near the archaeological dig, where nobody lives apart from the itinerant traders of rugs and other treasures that have been brought up by the explorers," he said out loud, as his mind goggled over how this could be a boon to everybody's lives and made a mental note to tell the other pharaohs next time he saw them.

In a huge cloud of dust, they arrived, and men and women started fanning him, availing him of his heavy robe.

"He must be put into more lightweight attire, then we can put him into the back of a chariot, cart him back to the palace," they said.

Augustuskamoun sat in a tent that had been temporarily erected using ropes and canvas that they had with them, and he was put in there to cool him down. Two women in full Iranian costume were sent to please his every wish, one had a small bunch of grapes in her hands, and on her nipples, she wore tiny golden tassels.

Thoughts of Nitocris evaporated from his mind, and

he was enveloped in an all-consuming cloud of lust, seeing only the colour of eroticism. His slaves left him to his misadventures for a while, then sent in two men who were to take orders for what appetite he had built up.

Augustuskamoun had a raging hunger and shouted, "Bring me two birds of prey immediately, and a platter of smoked meats."

Within minutes the meats and birds of prey were carried in thrown across the shoulders of a young vixen like woman, she was brave and eager to do battle with the great man.

"If he wants food, he will have to pay for it," she told him.

Augustuskamoun said, "Pay for what? And with what?"

She said, "His life, by taking me on." She paused, then said, "Augustuskamoun, you are an imbecile, Huda is planning a great revolution!"

Then she stopped in her tracks.

Augustuskamoun said, "What? Did you say what I thought you said?"

"Huda is a friend of a friend; many people have already signed up. They want to show how forceful they can be," she revealed.

Augustuskamoun was in shock, after the eyeful that he'd just received from his two previous visitors, this was something entirely different.

"She seems plucky, not that that will get her far, though," he said.

He arranged for her to be dropped off at the quarantine room of a test centre, where she would be guaranteed to catch cholera herself shortly. One of his men came running over and squeezed her tight to his chest, then made off with her.

Augustuskamoun, after all the fuss, wanted to get on his way, so he ordered for his belongings to be packed up, and for the whole procession to assist him back to the palace. It was dusk when they arrived, and as he walked up the polished granite drive, he could hear the distinctive churring song of the nightjar. He didn't normally pay so much attention to nature, but in this case, he was duly hypnotized by the beautiful sound, and it put him into the mood of whispering sweet nothings into the ear of his dear Nitocris, with the aim of wining, dining, and ravaging her.

As soon as he was in the house, he called for a bottle of fine vintage wine to be brought, together with some small treats to satiate her hunger, then he proceeded to climb the grand staircase and crept to the master bedroom. Once outside, he rapped on the door lightly, and he heard her cooing voice from within.

"Augustuskamoun, please enter, you are the man of my dreams."

With that he threw the heavily velveted door open, there were cushions of lace all around, and a huge, deep, and luxurious rug.

"Welcome to the boudoir," Nitocris purred.

As Augustuskamoun was about to fall upon her, he was stopped in his tracks. It was as if an ice cube had been dropped down his back, and every thought of want and desire left his body. He had been assailed by an anti-sexual entity, something beyond his own powers of comprehension.

Even Nitocris was looking sorely non plussed.

She said, "What's just happened?"

"I'm not sure," was his reply.

"You had red hearts in your eyes when you walked in that door, now all I see is a void."

The pair of them began to rearrange their robes and try to make the best of it, composing their faces, and hair. A stone eagle and a monkey skull with glowing green eyes dropped onto the floor with a loud bang, alerting them both to the sound.

"What are these?" Nitocris cried.

Augustuskamoun replied, "I was going to give them to you as a present to apologize for my wayward behaviour at the party."

Nitocris, it seemed, was better versed in the word on the streets than the great pharaoh, for she understood the gifts he had brought with him had a malignant curse attached to them, she knew the mythology surrounding the artefacts.

She began to explain. "This thing targets your groin, your scrotum, your testes, those glowing eyes have bored out all trace of any of them, there won't be any left."

Augustuskarmoun reached down to scratch and inspect but couldn't see anything amiss.

"You won't notice anything," she said, watching him with pitiful amusement. "Its work has already been done. If we let this spread, then it can bring down the whole monarchy, all our best men at any rate. There will be no more babies to be sired or lineages to carry on."

Terrified, their eyes met in horror. When they had talked about wiping out the population,

Augustuskarmoun had not meant his own.

Keket and Femi, after finishing their day of delivering flyers, made it back to the safety of their own neighbourhood. They had arranged to meet Huda again, later that night, down in one of the palm lined squares. Huda would be on her own and wanted to update them about her latest plans, they also had much to tell her.

Around 9pm., the sky was pitch black, only a crescent of a moon could be seen. Cats crept about on their nocturnal prowls, and there was the occasional howl of a whirling dervish from a nearby dwelling. *I can hear genies whipping around in the air, chasing one another, tail to tail, like blue bottle flies,* Huda thought.

In amongst all this, her thoughts began to crystallise; Huda had been contemplating her next move in quashing the pharaohs. Two familiar voices came to her ears at that point, and she recognized them as Keket and Femi. As they walked past, she called softly for them to turn, and they stepped over to see her.

"It's our old friend, Huda," Keket said.

"What a relief to see you two," Huda replied. "You don't know what a time I've have had since I last saw you, the worst of it was when Narmer, Nefertiti, and Djoser were chasing me down for the cauldron I found underground. It was so that the love spells could be enacted."

Chapter Ten

The great Augustuskamoun was flummoxed at the thought that he may have lost the ability to recreate, and in a depression wanted to get on and let his minors know. The quicker he could get information out, the more likelihood that somebody would have a solution, or could shed light on the matter. Even though Nitocris had fully convinced him of the gravity of the situation, he didn't believe her fully and decided he will have to enlist some young females to inspect his gonads further.

"Farewell Nitocris, I have rounds to embark on," he told her, eager for this inspection to take place.

With that Augustuskamoun flustered and flurried out of the room. Nitocris had arranged to meet with her friends later, Cleopatra and Twosret, they wanted to catch up about the party and whether Augustuskamoun had tried to butter her up.

Several hours later they arrived and were all sat in the saloon as the evening drew cooler and ordered drinks that might refresh them.

"I'll have Limon with a shot of ouzo in it," Twosret said.

She gave a playful pat on the bum to the young slave lad who walked in, who had been fanning her patiently, until she decided she would have a drink.

"Order me the same!" cried Cleopatra.

The three of them carried on conversing, asking questions based purely on their value for gossip. They all went silent for a bit, and the murmur of the desert could be heard outside.

Not noticing how beautiful it was, because Nitocris wasn't paying any attention to it, she cried, "He was about to give me a present, when it fell to the floor, magical trinkets that turned out to be cursed, and now he has lost his testosterone."

They listened without an expression between the two of them, then they were in hoots of laughter.

"This is brilliant," Cleopatra cried. "Finally, he has got his comeuppance."

Twosret couldn't stop laughing. "If only the same fate could befall my Pepi, life would be sweet."

Cleopatra was wiping the tears from her face, but managed to get out, "You're right about that, that man is a liar, and a cheat."

Nitocris was confused, she had never really thought of Augustuskamoun in that way.

Twosret started shouting, "You must be mad to trust him, I wouldn't trust him as far as I could throw him. As soon as they leave the palace, pretending to go on errands, or that they must go away for night or two, they are at it with some other woman. Didn't you hear about the one who took a trip up the Nile? They are saying he was sent up to do a reccy for places that they could escape to in the event of a full lockdown, it is reported that he'd made it to some small town halfway between Cairo and the Mediterranean. Word has it that he's been on a vessel on the river living it up to his heart's content, and has no plan to return to the drastic situation the rest of the city finds itself in. It seems like he wants to forget it is going on at all."

Nitocris's reaction was of horror, she couldn't believe any pharaoh would do such a thing. She began blocking out the arguments and opinions they were dropping on her. She put her fingers in her ears and called to a nearby slave to gather her things because she wanted to get off. A few moments later one arrived, and she was carted away on the back of a golden chariot, with her presents.

Even though it was late she swept through the city streets at great speed, she was angry and wanted to get her rage out in some way. She called at the slave to throw a rope over the stallions and tether them close by. She wanted to get off and stop at a favourite location of hers, an overlooked beauty spot.

He pulled up towards the end of the road. It was dark, and the morbid smell of death pervaded the air. Her nostrils twitched: she was enjoying its fetid aroma. The slave was almost choking, he knew it was because the daily fatality rate had just hit one hundred thousand. When Nitocris looked back, he was retching, and she looked with disdain upon him.

"How are you so easily affected by this?" she asked.

He was too busy spewing and couldn't answer back, but she knew that this type of thing was always a weak spot, for the common man. *They always seem so pathetic,* she thought. She used to have this discussion a lot with Augustuskamoun, and they had both agreed. He used to say, they don't make them like they used to.

After Nitocris finished gazing into the night air and with distant thoughts of Augustuskamoun on her mind, as well as the fate of the pharaohs, she got another odd feeling, because she could see some similarities between herself and the people. She thought, *it's not just us who get a hard time, it's the slaves, the kitchen hands, and the administration staff at the pyramid. The pharaohs are up on their pedestal, preaching down to us, being deceitful, and passing on their wicked ways to the children that they sire. Biding time until they go to the next life. If I could only connect with other women and smaller fry, at least in that way, we could build our forces stronger. I could even tell Twosret and Cleopatra, we are all in the same boat. I don't know if they will believe me, though. Mind you, they think they are out to get us, so maybe it is a good idea to tell them.* The thought grew in her mind until she was determined to go ahead and get her own back.

Augustuskamoun thought he would enlist Narmer, Nefertiti, and Djoser. *They will be at the pyramid,* he thought. *I can go and speak with them in the morning, but now I must go and get some rest.* And with that he hollered for his slave who came running, throwing his possessions onto his back.

Augustuskamoun drew out a whip and flourished it in the air before lashing him heavily, the welts stung and ached for several days after. It was almost midnight and as they stole through the quiet streets and squares, the tiniest glimmer of a moon gave them light. It glanced off the back of familiar statues and landmarks, and at once he had a great feeling of home and pride. *The people don't understand this,* Augustuskamoun thought. *Most of the retches are half castes or immigrants, what would they know about pure blood?*

He grinned, as he took another look at the pain he had inflicted on the poor man's body beneath him. *He deserves it and so does the rest of his family, and with a bit of luck they will all get cholera. It will tear them apart limb by limb with its great strength, and their bowels will be rent by great convulsions too. One of the worst and most noticeable side effects of this disease is that it causes you a looseness of stools, most people can't even make it to the door of their own dwellings, let alone go about their daily business,* Augustuskamoun thought. *Then, he'd soon be dead, like the rest of them and the depopulation would be continuing.* He never once thought that if the pandemic killed off all the lesser mortals beneath the rank of pharaoh, there would be no-one to do his bidding. He had yet to realise that the pharaohs and the ordinary people had to co-exist together, that one was only great because the other let them be. Leaders were only leaders if there was a population to lead. However, Augustuskamoun was not equipped to realise this and when he was finally back at the pyramid, he drifted off to sleep with pleasant thoughts of a peasant cull on his mind.

He was rudely awoken several hours later by a rap at the door. Somebody pulled a coiled piece of velvet that acted as a chime and was now trying to access the palace. The butler let them in and escorted them down to his bedroom. Leaving the visitors to their own devices, he made off. Then, Augustuskamoun remembered, and roused himself. It was the two young women who they had been called upon to further investigate whether Augustuskamoun had anything to worry about in relation to his gonads.

As soon as he dropped his pants, one who was familiar with curses and their effect on people, screamed. "Oh, my God, this is something very serious, sir!"

"Don't you realize who I am?" Augustuskamoun

shouted back.

The girls continued talking between themselves, comparing notes and experiences, and trying to work out whether there was anything good they could pass on. But neither could think of anything positive to say.

One whispered, "Great ruler, you are in a very sticky pickle here."

"Why?" Augustuskamoun screamed.

"Well, we've seen this happen many generations before, and it leads to a horrible onslaught of masculinity loss, sire. This is serious indeed. Cohorts and dynasties of rulers lose their ability to breed, not a single child is reared for the duration of that time."

Augustuskamoun cried, "What! Something like that can never happen, you two must be witches."

With that, he cast the pair out of the door.

"Never set foot near this house again," he roared.

The women, who had had a lucky escape, ran for their lives.

"I don't think he realizes the import of this," one said. "The power of his testes has been removed. It's strange because they are still there, so he still feels a certain pride in their existence, but at the end of the day, they are just empty shells now."

The next morning, feeling bleary headed and with eyelashes ragged with grit, Augustuskamoun woke, called for a glass of water, or something to quench his thirst whilst his mind raced back to work, and he began planning out his day.

He arranged for several slaves to meet him in the main courtyard; it was another fiery morning, and they wanted to get off before it got any hotter. The sun was raging like a furnace, and as he waited for them to pack his belongings, Augustuskamoun understood their wilting.

Even I'm struggling here, in this heat, he thought, *but the men will be okay, they are used to it. They've been carting royalty about for generations, they know nothing else.*

One of the slave's signalled to him that they were ready, and he waved for them to come closer.

Augustuskamoun ordered, "I want picking up from this very spot."

They pushed their golden chariot towards him; it had great runners that allowed it to sledge on the sand. It came slipping and sliding across, the men bowing and curtseying to Augustuskamoun and his great presence. As they saw his shadow looming in the distance, he urged them on despite the heat. They sidled over, gradually parking in a gutter by his side.

"What took you so long!" Augustuskamoun cried, without a shred of irony.

Chapter Eleven

The meeting with Huda went on longer than Keket and Femi planned, they had so many misadventures to compare. Huda had a run in with the pharaohs, was imprisoned, escaped, and had her own personal encounter with the love spells cauldron. Keket and Femi were amazed and began giving her their own thoughts about this.

"So, you think the pharaohs want to use them to control the entire female population? That is so dark." said Femi. "Is there anything we can do to stop them?"

Huda replied, "The best way is to keep drumming up support in as many different areas of the country as possible, and not just amongst women. We are all in the same situation, whether you are a slave, a footman, a soldier, a prostitute, or a cook. We need to keep spreading the word, try to build our numbers, then maybe we will have a way to fight fire with fire. Right now, we are in too much of a disadvantaged position. They have every power over us, and most people live in fear that they may lose their jobs, be thrown to the lions or the vultures, or be left to die a lowly death of cholera."

"You're right," said Keket, "and we will keep passing on the good word."

The hour was late, but it was still hot, the palms above them were interlaced and had managed to hold a lot of warmth in from the day. They looked about them and all they saw was a man holding a post decked out with local newspapers, each hung like an unfurled flag in the non-existent breeze. Keket felt sorry for the man, so went over to purchase one. She was talking with him for a while, and he explained that all his family currently had cholera.

"I don't think things can get any worse," he said.

Keket didn't know what to say, she had been relatively lucky herself, nobody she knew had been struck down by the dreaded virus.

Keket, Femi, and Huda decided they would go and get some food as they were famished, and they set off to a small place that they knew in one of the souks. Usually, it was a hive of activity, heaving with all manner of transports, bicycles, people pushing carts, and vendors sitting at every corner hawking their wares. They chose a place where they could get Egyptian and middle Eastern fayre, ducked in and ordered a falafel each, taking it to a quiet spot out of the way, so they could continue their conversation.

The eatery was in the loft space of a huge granite building, that used to serve as a marketplace, somewhere for butchers and fishmongers to bring in their daily produce. It still had that same clammy and stinky air, and you could see scales, blood, guts, and entrails sprawled out on the concrete floor. Femi gawped to one side, staring into space, then she caught sight of two familiar faces on the lower level near the entrance that consisted of two doors fashioned out of stone, with huge wrought iron rings across them.

The people she recognized had just walked through and were standing below, Femi knew they looked familiar but couldn't bring their names to mind. *It must be somebody from our neighbourhood,* she thought. *I don't know too many other people in the city. Maybe if they come closer, I would recognise them.* She looked over and took one of them for her old neighbour and family friend. She called his name out.

"Ammon!"

He looked up unaware of who it was. He seemed to be with another figure much older. *Perhaps it's his dad,* she thought. As he caught sight of her, he realized who it was. Ammon searched for the nearest stairwell that took them up to where they sat. He popped out at the top and strolled over to where they were. It was around midnight now, so the place was quieter, most visitors and workers had gone home for the day. This time she screamed his name out.

"AMMON!!"

It had been so long since they set eyes on each other. Keket looked in their direction and her eyes lit up, Keket knew him from times of old. The three women invited Ammon and the other man to sit down and ordered drinks from the owner of the bar below.

"It's been such a long time since we last met," Keket said, "but we've been through a lot."

"I have plans to take vengeance upon the pharaohs. Sexist pigs, but it's not just us they've got it in for, societies been dying for a long time, lets ring in a change," Huda said.

There was a short silence.

Ammon chimed in with, "They took over our house, we were lucky to escape, but the rest of the family were beaten by the guards who came to convert the house. We were lucky that none of us had cholera or another life shattering event! Do you know, everything the pharaohs do seems to bring some form of bad luck, and despair. Now, we need to do something about it!"

Huda plucked out her petition, thrusting it high into the sky.

"Sign this and at least you know you're trying," she said.

They both agreed and signed, Femi and Keket gave a rousing cheer as they grew their numbers.

"My father and I undertook a lengthy journey underground and found out the secrets of the Rosetta stone," Ammon told them. "I didn't even know what it was until then, it is only because my father has some murky recollection of knowledge, from times long gone."

"Your father will always be handy," Husain cried, indignantly.

"The stone renders all that interact with it deaf and dumb, so they cannot understand a word of what they are reading, their powers of comprehension and intelligibility go. The pharaohs are planning to use it to blot people's knowledge of current affairs, and of any sources of news that are truthful by replacing them with falsehood and lies," Ammon said in disgust.

"Nothing new there then," Huda commented, "and exactly why something must be done about this tyrannical reign."

"How can we join forces over this, then? The stone has a particular power, but if we can harness it, then we will be able to unleash it in our own way, we just need to take it by force first. If I go back to the place where I first saw it with Ammon, we can recover it quickly and bring it back to make best use of it," Husain said, eagerly. "We know not to try to interact with it. We will not talk to it or honour it, we'll grab it, cover it with a cloth and return with it so we can use its power for our benefit, not our downfall!"

Ammon was favourable, so, they agreed to set out at once, and not return until they come back with the stone.

"Can you remember the way back?" his father asked.

Ammon was sure his sense of direction and powers of recollection were good enough, so he answered in the affirmative.

"We should sleep, though, before setting out again," Ammon said. "It's been a long day, and I know Keket and Femi were both delivering flyers long into the night. Working in these temperatures takes it out of you, although I guess we should be used to it. Huda, where are you planning to stay tonight?"

"I haven't even thought about it. We can go and stay at a lodging house near the centre, I know plenty," Huda replied.

They agreed to follow her and make their way to a lodging house located near the Avenue of the Sphinx. It was an area where the dwellings were covered in inches of dust, and there was noise that kept them awake from a nearby encampment of pagans. The pagans were sleeping in traditional yurts with prongs of branches poking out of the top. They were visiting because a religious holiday was about to take place, and there were people from up and down the country, who had come for miles.

Some of the pagans had made a special trip to see

displays, rituals, presentations, and incantations that were being made to honour various gods, and to bring forth their spirits. There was a plan for various sacrifices to be given, they would be made at the site of an old temple, and at other spots that were spiritually connected. The pagans wanted to leave gifts for each of the gods, a cat for Bastet, a serpent for Apophis, a scarab for Khepri, and a crocodile for Sobek.

Some of the group wandered out with curiosity at the noise, wanting to find out where it was coming from. Huda was still sleeping, but Keket and Femi had risen, slipped out of a back door, and were roaming through open plains that neighboured the site. They left the other two, Ammon and his father, slumbering as they knew they had big plans for the next day. Getting closer to the pagan camp, they began to move lower to the ground, trying to disguise themselves against the bare thorny shrubs.

They could almost overhear voices talking. Femi said, "Can you hear what they are saying?"

Keket replied, "I can't make it out."

But the more they both strained their ears it was possible to discern the odd word. The pagans were talking about animals, discussing how they might collect the various ones they required.

"Once they have all been brought to one place, they are saying that they will read a blessing over them all, then take them out to the places that have been designated for their untimely end," Femi said.

"Wouldn't it be great to tag along if they would ask us," Keket mused.

At that, there was a crackling and snapping of

branches and they heard and saw a great kerfuffle. Somebody was trying to stamp down the bushes, to warn them off.

"It must be the pagans!" Femi cried, and they both turned tail and ran!

They leapt through the undergrowth as fast as they could, until Femi got her foot stuck in the loophole of a root in the ground, and fell, tumbling forward. Keket tried to reach and grab to catch her, but it was to no avail, and she stumbled anyway. Femi fell through the thorny bushes and found herself emerging in the central area of the pagan's camp. There were sticks of fire burning brightly, tied to various posts which were rammed into the ground. Femi looked about and saw a group of people walk past; they were dressed in animal furs and carried clubs.

They look barbaric, she thought, and ducked under a nearby bush. Keket had done similarly, and was doing her best to conceal herself, but one of her legs was sticking out, and as they walked past, the pagans caught sight of it.

"What do we have here?" One of them said.

They pulled roughly at Keket, and she fell on top of them.

"She's very light," another was heard to say, and he cradled her in his arms. "What's wrong, my sweet?"

Keket answered, "I'm not spying on you!" Although she was, if she was honest but she was paranoid they might do her some harm. "I'm totally innocent, there's another of us, my friend, Femi."

At that she called her name, "Femi!"

She turned back to the pagans and said, "I've lost my

friend and I've no idea where she is."

Femi's voice issued from a bush in the darkness, and the pagans hastened over. As they stood about with Keket directing them, they found its source and owner. One grabbed carelessly at Femi's hair and pulled her bodily out, under the flickering light of the fire. The pagans could see fear in Femi's eyes and wanted to do no harm, so told her.

"We don't want to hurt either of you."

Keket breathed a sigh of relief.

One of the pagans said, "We are here for our annual festival that takes place in the desert this time each year. It's always held under the shadow of the pyramid and sphinx, as we feel it helps to focus on our aims of gathering the relevant creatures that we need. It's like the gods are smiling down upon us, from on high. We want them to show us their charms, and to encourage that we present each with a small gift: A cat for Bastet who is known for protecting the deceased and the living. A serpent for Apophis who has powers of dissolution, darkness, and non-being. A scarab for Khepri who has powers of rebirth and creation out of nothing. A crocodile for Sobek who is responsible for all life in Egypt, as he is the creator of the Nile. Would you like to come and join us on our task of finding each?"

Keket smiled broadly, Femi could see that they were in safe hands. The pagans wanted to leave immediately so they set off towards the river to see if they could find the reptile they were seeking. As they reached the water's edge, they heard screaming, and upon getting closer, they saw two villagers wailing. Keket stepped forward to console one of them, but the villager shook her off. Then one of the pagans stepped forward, asking what was wrong. The villager gave no answer, but then a young boy came skipping past, whispering.

"The largest crocodile ever leaped from the water and pulled a woman's son under. He was helpless, he didn't even come back up for air. The whole village is racked with cholera, and they have been taking water from the river because they thought it is safer than drinking it from the well."

"They were just unlucky, then," Femi said.

One of the pagans, regardless of what just happened, went crashing towards the water's edge. He seemed to have a devil may care attitude. As he got closer to the water, he started shouting and screaming, beating his chest. It appeared he wanted to avenge the poor woman's son, too. The woman looked with pride, urging him on.

"Is he really going to do it?" asked the woman.

"Yes, I think he will," another replied.

Then there was the sound of waves crashing into the pagan's calves as he waded deeper.

"He is walking to his death," Keket said, in horror.

He went deeper and deeper until he was up to his chest, then began calling for the crocodile to show itself.

The pagan shouted, "You family wrecker! You're worthless and of ill repute. Nobody fears you, least of all me."

Suddenly, there was a crash of water and the thrashing of scaly skin, muscle, sinew, and the animal came surging from beneath. Like an arrow, it aimed for his throat, because it knew that that was the quickest and swiftest way to wipe out its enemies. It worked with the young boy earlier, too. The pagan gave a garbled scream and went under, then there was silence for a bit, just ever-decreasing circles on the surface of the swamp. Suddenly the pagan came shooting from the middle, blowing out mud, sand, and scum from the bed of the river. There was a cheer from the shore as the others realized he was still alive, and then they watched in amazement as he took the creature into a headlock.

The pagan tucked its snout deep under his elbow because there it won't be able to snap. It seemed to work. The others could see the crocodile's black, emotionless void of an eye flickering as its lid tried to shut, and as it struggled to break free. The pagan came limping towards Keket, Femi, and the small crowd, and they were clapping as he came closer.

"It looks like he's going to come out the victor," someone said.

The animal was thrown to the ground as the pagan cried, "This is for our celebration, with this we will put on our best side for the gods, and they will pay us handsomely."

"You mean in attributes?" someone shouted.

"Yes," he answered. "With this we will gain the life-giving powers of the Nile. Animals, families, gods, the poor, the pharaohs, cholera sufferers, and those who are fine. People will come for miles to visit us, because they think we can assist or heal them."

"But can you really do that?" Keket asked.

The pagan gave a mischievous grin and said, winking,

"Of course."

That was all she needed to hear, and she was convinced it was a good idea.

Keket arranged for the pagan to go back into the dangerous waters, recover another limp and long reptilian for them to use as their own gift to the gods. Soon he came swaggering back over and threw it roughly down on the sand.

"This one is for you," he said, grinning.

Keket thanked him, then the pagans slung a crocodile up between their shoulders and make off. Keket picked up the other crocodile and, following the pagans, she dragged it along behind her.

"It can only work in our favour."

Then Femi interjected, "How can we use it to fight against the pharaohs, though?"

Keket scratched her head and thought for a while. "Maybe, when people realize what great things we have done to help, they will want to reward us in their own way. The sky's the limit, anything is possible."

"True," Femi said, hoping fervently that it was.

They were both thinking that this was something that could be used in the battle against cholera, and each was too excited to talk much more about it. Leaving the pagans, Femi and Keket walked back to the lodging house, and continued their talk.

"It's true, this could be the cure for the common cold, the miracle that the people have been waiting for. But who do we go and speak to about this?" asked Femi.

On the grapevine they had heard news of Karim and Kissa, their plight to find a solution that could be so efficient for the tests, that it may save many lives.

Femi continued, "If we can present them with this possibility, they may realize that we are onto something. That or tell us that it is spiritual stuff and nonsense!"

"Let's go and speak with Huda," Keket said. "Our knowledge is too sketchy."

With that they pressed on. They had been out the whole night and now the sun was climbing from a shimmering horizon, as the heat rose like a wall in front of them.

"It's only early," Keket said.

They tried to keep to the shadows, hopping from one foot to another in pain, because of the temperature of the sand.

"Maybe, another hour and we should be back," Femi said.

Keket and Femi looked up and saw palms as far as the eye can see, stretching off into the distance. The rows bent and twisted in the strong light, making it look like a mirage. The top of each tree was crowned with vegetation and had the nest of a vulture within it.

"Am I seeing things, now not only a vulture is before my eyes, but a serpent also," Keket said, shaking her head.

The snake wriggled itself under the sand before either of them could get close. It burrowed under the surface where it was completely hidden.

Femi knew a little about them and said, "I think it's a black mamba. It's the most poisonous snake."

She gave a little shudder.

Keket wasn't listening, she was thinking more about their quest for Apophis. "If we can catch one and sacrifice it to him, we will improve our powers of dissolution, darkness, and non-being!"

Laughing, Femi asked, "What does that mean?"

"It means that we can break up any form of law, politics, relationships, or religion. The pharaohs will be powerless against us," and with that, Keket also burst out laughing.

Keket threw the crocodiles limp body onto the ground. Before Femi could stop her, Keket ran off and scrambled in the sand, her hand thrust deep into a burrow. She pulled up her arm and the black mamba was caught between her fingers and thumb. She was holding it in such a way that its body pulsated, trying to escape from its captor, hissing, and squirting venom from its fangs.

"The poor creature," said Femi. "Its fate has been sealed."

Keket kept squeezing her fingers more tightly around its neck until it gave its last two gasps, then ceased to wriggle anymore. She opened her knapsack and tossed its body into the bottom of the bag. The two of them picked up the crocodile and continued along their way.

A short while later they spotted a scarab beetle pushing a giant ball of dung.

"This is the greatest of miracles," Femi said. "To see this is the equivalent of a human pushing a pyramid. They used to do it, but they would need many men, and complex contraptions to keep its flow going."

"Never mind that," said Keket. "We are witnessing a great feat."

Keket threw herself prostrate on the ground so she can study its movements more clearly.

"Look at this," she said, and Femi drew closer to see what she was pointing to.

The beetle's tiny little legs pulsed with insect-like muscle, its iridescent body glimmering. The upper part of its body was merely a shell. "It would be so easy to crush it," Keket said, but she was so impressed she didn't. "That little creature has powers of rebirth and creation out of nothing. Unbeknownst to its size, we can see it has great strength, this is how it pushes such a large ball of dung. If we could have those same proportions, toppling the pharaohs would be easy, just imagine one person upturning a pyramid!"

Carefully Keket cornered the vulnerable beetle, and it stopped in its tracks, unable to move. Femi approached from the left, and between them they tricked it into walking into Keket's bag, that she laid down before it. The insect was trapped, and they could get on their way again. The sun beat down relentlessly now, the hour was nearing noon, and this was when most activity stopped. Animals and people went and sheltered in makeshift tents for a few hours, until the day cooled a little. The two women did likewise, finding a rockface with small holes and tunnels to conceal themselves in. The sun moved around them like a vicious sundial, trying to penetrate every place they were hidden.

They retreated as far as they could into the cracks. Two or three hours later, and they ventured back out again. They had lost a lot of water, evaporating in perspiration. Both were feeling dehydrated after not a drop to drink, and they struggled to speak to one another. Their throats were rasping and dry.

Keket managed to say, "We need to push on, we must still find a cat."

There wasn't a sound from Femi, she merely followed. They had been walking for a short while when Keket saw what she thought was a cat, even though they were out in the desert, and this wasn't normally the place to find them. "Maybe it's a wildcat," she said, "either way, this is what we are looking for."

She slunk low to the ground, scuffed the sand, and sent it up in arcs around her. The cat heard the commotion and coyly looked over. It wasn't acting like a feral cat; this must be the traditional variety. She had a beautiful arch that flowed down the line of her neck, traced her back, and ended in a graceful twist of her tail. The cat was sitting perfectly upright now, and this was Keket's chance to move in swiftly and scoop it up into her arms. The cat then sat lovingly nuzzling her ear and purring heavily into its chest.

"This furry and cute companion of man is well known for protecting the deceased and the living. Even though she may not look it, in our day-to-day world she has the ability. All you need do is put her in a hospital, a crematorium, a burial ground, anywhere where death lurks nearby. Even with cholera raging," Keket told Femi, who had finally caught up and was rewarded with a glimpse of the feline, and its newfound owner.

She remarked, "How can she help us in our plight against the pharaohs?"

"Wherever we leave her, or come across her, she will protect us against death. Pretty puss! Everywhere, on the tops of posts, fences, walls, and around the back of chairs and tables, she's almost better than a black cat for good luck. Not that I'm superstitious," laughed Keket.

They made their way off, heading back towards the lodging house where they had left Huda, Husain, and Ammon.

Chapter Twelve

Once Snefru and Khafre left Eshe's place in Luxor, they set off to Cairo. They had a long journey ahead of them, at least a week of travelling. They had been summoned by Augustuskamoun, who wanted them back at the pyramid before long, apparently, as he had a new mission that concerned them. Fearing for their lives, they prepared to leave at once, they weren't too precious about packing their belongings carefully.

They arrived at the pyramid and went underground. A gradually sloping concrete path took them under, then the temperature dropped as they plunged into the coolness below. The men leapt up and began alleviating the pharaohs of their robes, giving them fresh ones and perfume to scent their bodies with.

Snefru was escorted down a temporary ramp by one of the slaves who had set it up, and he gave his arm to Khafre so that he was safely supported as they descended. Now that they had been refreshed, they knew that they must harken to Augustuskamoun, and they set off quicky down one of the endless passageways that drew out labyrinthine from there.

It was only a matter of minutes after passing through cold, dark, and narrow corridors, that they suddenly came across a huge, bolted, sandstone door, with wrought iron handle and marbled plates to strengthen it. They stepped towards it and Snefru tapped lightly at the door, partially afraid of the response that he might get.

Khafre was quaking in his boots, too. *If the men could*

see what fear was wrought in them by the great leader, they would be laughing at the bottom of their souls about this, he thought miserably. A spider that must have been in collusion with the men ran across in mortal dread, too scared to throw down a web.

There was a rasping, throaty sounding cough, a clearing of phlegm from the lungs, until the breath came easier and more settled.

"Enter," came an authoritarian voice that boomed through the door.

The entrance was flung open as if by magic and slammed heavily into the walls of the underground lair. Dust, mud, and sand filled the small chamber and caused the owner of the voice to choke once again, then he motioned for them to pass through. There was a musty stench, the decaying aroma of centuries of putrefying flesh that had been slowly rotting around the edges of his tomb. It was only as he climbed out, knocking this, and sending off fresh permutations of the smell that Snefru and Khafre were momentarily shocked, sickened, and stopped in their tracks.

"All hail the great Augustuskamoun," they both said in unison and dropped to their knees.

Prayers passed over their lips begging for forgiveness, that he might not be able to read their own private thoughts and actions. There was a long pause and then Snefru said, "We are here, we have come as you requested."

Augustuskamoun answered, "I have a new ruling which I desire you to spread, from this moment forth, pass onto all other pharaohs and members of the public, as you so wish. From this day forward special hunting laws during the cholera outbreak will apply, that only the pharaohs will benefit from."

"How do you mean, hunting?" Khafre asked.

"Any activity that involves the cruel and pointless activity of hunting for game, rather than for the primary source of food. For foxes, falcon, eagles, vultures, birds of prey, big cats, large land mammals, and other desert fauna, all are only tolerated to be shot on the spot, with catapult, poison, traps, or fairly chased down with the aid of larger animals of different species."

Snefru grunted a reply, as Augustuskamoun went on. "I want to arrange a hunting trip into the interior of the country within the week, that will include your good selves and me. Tomorrow at dawn we will meet at the outdoor mausoleum, to head out on our way."

With that, Augustuskamoun disappeared off in a cloud of dust, slamming his tomb shut as he crept back in, and pulled the huge stone slab over.

"I'm not to be disturbed until the morning, not even by Nitocris," he commanded.

Snefru and Khafre both decided an early night would be sensible. But when were they ever sensible? They could not resist staying up for the rest of the night, drinking and taking pot shots at animals that they saw fit to practise on, for the up-and-coming trip.

"Why don't we go out into the desert?" Khafre suggested.

"I'll order our gang of reprobate slaves, foot soldiers, and servants to bring with them our fine array of hunting tackle," said Snefru.

"Wise idea."

They stood gazing up into the darkness of the night; there was a beautiful crescent moon, and an abundance of stars lit up the sky like a constellation. They were discussing the most probable creatures they would stumble upon.

Khafre said, "We might be lucky to see a Saharan Striped Polecat or an Aardvark. They're both nocturnal."

Their equipment was brought out and set up, traps and ropes with loops littered the ground. Apparatus was wedged and nailed to trunks; hoops of elastic suspended between the two that allowed them to fire large rocks out from the trees with. The men were sent back to the pyramid so that they could be sure of absolute silence, and then Snefru and Khafre took their respective places behind convenient rocks and boulders nearby.

They had only been tucked away for a short while when they heard a familiar sound, long claws being dragged along the ground. It was bizarre and gave them the creeps, worse than fingernails being dragged down a blackboard. There was breathing as if interspersed with a vacuum.

"It must be coming from its snout. Probably making its way through the undergrowth, searching for anthills and termites," Snefru deduced.

Khafre, with practised aim, ran for a temporary lever that had been set up, sent a giant missile flying. Over it went at high velocity, homing in on the poor creature's temple, then crashing to its target. It hit the ground quicker than the speed of light and sent the beast careering off into a bush.

"Now it's up to us to go and claim our prize," Snefru cried gleefully.

The pair of them crept over to where they believed it had fallen, and it was still gasping its last. Khafre seized it by the neck and throttled it. "This will make a fine trophy or a shield."

Once they finished with the evening's fun, they gathered their equipment and hollered for the men to pack it all away carefully, and to bring with them the poor animal's body. One of the slaves threw it over his shoulder, and its hooter hung low, swinging to and fro as they walked back towards the pyramid.

Finally, Snefru and Khafre retired for the night, it was late, but they thought they will get a couple of hours sleep before dawn. Before long they were both snoring long and hard, dreaming of entrapping all manner of rare and extinct creatures. A voice that grew louder the longer it carried on, eventually brought them back to their senses.

The sleep had been fitful, but Snefru wasn't happy at having been awoken from his slumbers, where he was so purposefully raising hell with the animal population. He decided to take his animosity out on the two women who had been sent with food and water to revive him.

The two women came closer, trying to pass a morsel of meat and wet his lips with a lightly dampened sponge, but he gave a bloodcurdling scream, and the pair jumped out of their skin. It sounded grisly, and as if he might have dismembered some weak and defenceless creature.

Snefru gave a groan as he came fully around, shouting

for his left-hand man, "Khafre!"

"I'm here," came his reply. "I suspect one is suffering from the morning after the night before," and he grinned as Snefru continued to moan, until they were heading out to the allotted place for the meeting with Augustuskamoun. They arrived first and were left waiting for several hours, much to Snefru's discomfort, before Augustuskamoun reached them, sporting a pig headed and arrogant grin.

Khafre said, "He's here, but what kept him?"

As he approached, you could see he was being followed by a group of men, one of whom was carrying a sack. Inside was stuffed with the inanimate forms of taxidermized animals.

Augustuskamoun said, "These will act as my lures for when I'm trying to tempt a creature closer, then it can be caught unawares."

Khafre and Snefru were amazed at this attention to detail and assumed that this must be a regular occurrence for him.

"Well, we've got it made hunting with you," Khafre declared.

Augustuskamoun never even answered, he had already struck out for a point on the map, which was said to be superb for their requirements, and that he had been informed of by an old explorer friend. The rest followed in unison with their men in tow. They had been marching for several hours in the direct sun, when some of the men began to cry out, they were about to drop.

"We need a rest!" one cried, and the word was passed back up the line.

"If we don't let them have a break, the men will be done for," Khafre said, in an insane moment of compassion. "But it also means that they won't be able to carry along all our equipment and supplies."

He and Snefru put their heads together and decided it is worth letting them have an hour off, where they can put down their heavy loads and re-energize. The men headed straight for the shade of the nearest palm trees, using the leaves to fan themselves. Khafre, Snefru, and Augustuskamoun followed from a distance, then parted ways and found their own place where they could rest a while, and recharge their batteries, a spot near to a river frequented by wildlife. As they approached, they saw the grass had been crushed by some huge animals, and they were scratching their heads as to what might have caused it.

Augustuskamoun volunteered, "It must have been an elephant, judging by the size of the patch."

They plumped themselves down in the centre of it, anyway, without giving much further thought. Within minutes a ghastly crashing of bushes and trees was heard, and they looked up in fear just in time to see an enormous, fully grown elephant bearing down on them, its trunk waggling, and its tusks raised high in the air, ready for attack.

Khafre pushed Augustuskamoun to one side, but didn't have time to shift his friend, Snefru. Before long, his body had been scooped up and gored, never to be seen again. The other two looked around aghast at what just happened, but he had vanished.

"It must have taken it off to its lair to dispose of," Khafre said.

Augustuskamoun replied, "Don't be stupid, you'll never see him again. But at least his head won't be hurting anymore!"

Khafre looked at the pharaoh in chilling silence and Augustuskamoun had the grace to look contrite. The men began to pack up and prepare for the off, the pharaohs not yet having communicated the information of Snefru's death to the men.

"You ought to tell them," Khafre said. "Then we can do the honourable thing by his body."

Augustuskamoun saw sense, and that the respectable thing to do was to tell the men so they can perform a full funeral ceremony for Snefru. Even though most of the men hated him, he was their leader, and a lot felt he provided a sense of guidance.

One cried, "Without him who will look after us?" Another replied, "We can look after ourselves better."

The men were divided about this and fell to arguing, shouting, and bickering amongst themselves. Then Augustuskamoun gave a hearty cough, cracked a whip, and shouted for Khafre to round up the rowdier and more anarchistic elements. This Khafre did with joy, mounted upon a camel, one of their own.

He circled the group twice to bring it down to size, running out to pick up any would-be escapees. They were escorted back and fed into the group, again. Augustuskamoun had promised not a word of this was to be spread to any other pharaohs.

It had to remain a secret, he thought, desperately.

"We will give our own account of what has happened. Let's get our story straight, then we can give the most convincing version when we get back. We were out hunting, and Snefru was trampled, it's as simple as that," Khafre said.

Augustuskamoun nodded in reply. "Agreed", he said, and left it at that, which was the end of poor Snefru!

Upon returning to the pyramid the next day, Augustuskamoun began preparations for an elaborate funeral service.

"We don't have his body," he told Nitocris, "but we will give him the best send-off possible."

Nitocris was horrified at the story, always being one for superstitions, a believer in curses, and said so.

"Maybe it's because he'd taken that mummy back to England with him, just previously. We all know how fickle curses can be, one minute it's happy enough to simply ruin your life, and the next, it decides to end it." She shivered at the thought.

Augustuskamoun as ever wasn't one too let an old wife's tale get in the way of reality. Unless there was some form of political advantage that he could make out of it, of course. He said, "He was just unlucky, that's all there was to it."

"You'll always be a non-believer, you're far too much of a realist," Nitocris told him.

"Pah!" he exclaimed and scurried off to make further arrangements.

He wanted to get the word out to the rest of the pharaohs so that they might all be able to attend the funeral. He called for Nitocris to bring parchment and a quill.

"You can contact the pharaohs, one by one. Tell them that the service will happen in one weeks' time, and they are all expected to be there," Augustuskamoun told her.

She began jotting down other preparations that needed to be made, then went off to the administration office for a mail out to be done, so that all would-be attendees were informed by the end of the day. She left the palace and walked down a tunnel that connected the building to the pyramid; from there it was only minutes to where she wanted to be.

The air was thick with the smell of roasting meat, as she passed close to the kitchens before bursting straight through the door of a low-ceilinged room, where there was a constant whirring of cogs, and flywheels. In front of her there was a hollowed out concrete trough, it had a belt powered by a pulley that circulated to all the distant departments of the pyramid.

She spoke with one of the workers there. "Could you please pass on a message that an event will take place, and which they are obliged to participate in."

The worker inscribed a fragment of pottery and then deposited it onto the belt, where it rumbled off into the darkness. Nodding, he replied, "I will let you know if there is anybody who won't be able to make it".

Nitocris nodded and then was on her way back to Augustuskamoun, ruminating whether anything more could be done about his recently vanquished manhood, his ever-important breeding organs. *I have already sent him to have a further inspection, but they just agreed, not offering any help,* Nitocris thought. *I think he did it as an excuse to have himself examined in the groin area by two females, but what good has it done him anyway?*

As she arrived back, she planted a kiss on his flaky

forehead and asked, "Have there been any more notable signs of the curse that brought down Snefru?"

She was worried that it might have affected all three of them, and that the worst was still to come.

"This can touch on all aspects of your career, relationships, future dynasties, and kingdoms, not just the everyday people you rule," Nitocris declared.

Augustuskamoun grunted, "Like I really care about them, if they all catch cholera the country would end up far richer."

Nitocris thought it wasn't worth arguing and continued along more personal lines instead. "Think about yourself then, and how this could take its toll on your planned political and social activities for the country."

Augustuskamoun answered, "Yes, maybe you're right, this could be a crippling curse."

At that he went silent for a bit, he hadn't heard a word from Khafre for a while, not since they'd got back from their expedition, and he was curious to know if he was feeling anything amiss. He sent a messenger up to his tomb, where apparently on their return, he was informed he had retired for the day. Even this sounded faintly suspicious when it was reported back.

Augustuskamoun said, "What's wrong with him if he is so fatigued and low on energy?"

"Khafre told his men that he wasn't feeling right in the head, that he had been seeing and hearing things. Whilst in his tomb, he had been assailed by images of the trampling, in brutal detail, the squishing of organs, the screaming of banshees, and he had awoken in cold sweats. He fears that something has taken hold of his insides, since he was out with Snefru and Augustuskamoun the other day," the messenger replied.

At this news Augustuskamoun was quaking with fear, and when Nitocris next came upon him he had gone white as a sheet.

Nitocris said, "You don't have your normal red, ruddy faced, and healthy-looking complexion."

No words came from his mouth, but with gentle coaxing from Nitocris he began to explain further.

"One of Khafre's men said he is delirious and talking nonsense."

"It sounds like he might have got the curse, too," she told him, reluctantly.

"But does that mean it will spread to me also?" Augustuskamoun said with a gleam of terror in his eye.

Nitocris was well practised with curses. "There are no rules with the way curses operate, sometimes they can affect many people, other times just one."

With that she left him to his own devices. She had an errand of her own to run, she must go and collect the results of the mailout, to find out who will be attending. When she returned, she gave a full list to Augustuskamoun, who read the names out one by one.

Augustuskamoun said, "A healthy response, though it will be at their own peril if they disagree."

Nitocris changed the subject, her mind full of curses. "Do you feel in your right mind?"

"Of course," he shouted back gruffly, feeling miffed and out of sorts. "Are you insane! I have plans to open more test centres and to look at alternatives to the vaccine, such as offering the correct gift to the gods so that they will look more favourably upon you and your ailment."

Nitocris replied, "But isn't that only a thing that the pharaohs can afford?"

"Perhaps," he said, and in a muddled fug blithered on. "Just one other question," Augustuskamoun asked. "How will it affect me?"

"If Khafre's been experiencing mild hallucinations, then it's possible for you to suffer the same symptoms," she told him, deliberately not mentioning his groin.

Augustuskamoun gave a shudder. He couldn't think of anything worse, but as if to add insult to injury, he suddenly remembered the gaping hole in his groin.

"Maybe I'll be lucky, and the curse will counter out the oddity that has occurred, would that work? Is that even possible?"

Nitocris gave an uncertain murmur as she was lost in her thoughts, and they weren't of Augustuskamoun's groin!

Chapter Thirteen

They both went their separate ways, Nitocris back to her palace bedroom, and Augustuskamoun to his tomb in the Valley of the Kings. It was late before she got back, but she promised to call on Augustuskamoun first thing in the morning to see how he felt. He headed straight to his bed, but unable to sleep immediately, got up and set off out on a walk, thinking the fresh evening air would calm his nerves. He left the grounds of the pyramid and could hear the distant sound of monkeys chattering. *They are usually let loose in the main square around this time of night, when it is quiet,* he thought.

His ears were well trained to the various noises that one encountered on this walk, and he caught the murmur of a river gurgling past. He walked further and planned out what he must do tomorrow, and when he would see his aides again, but every time he tried to concentrate, his mind went blank when he thought about these things. *It feels like there is a fog clouding my brain, causing great confusion,* he thought. He stumbled back towards the pyramid and his tomb where he called for two slaves to wait on him, to stamp his authority on the whole matter more than anything else.

If I can pretend through controlling and manipulating other people's lives, that my own isn't in such a mess, then so be it, he thought. Through the after haze of wine, finely roasted meats, rich and luxuriously decadent desserts, puddings, sweets, and chocolates that he had demanded, he began to fall into a deep, food induced coma. *I'm not feeling as randy as I usually do, has that something to do with my latest diminishment?* was his last coherent thought.

Nitocris's voice came trilling through the air like an exotic bird, only lacking in melody, first thing the next morning. Augustuskamoun rubbed his eyes, picked his ear, then blew his nose before awakening fully. He pushed back the slab that laid over the tomb and poked his head out the top. He could see Nitocris, a tiny speck on the floor, waving to him. It was clear she wanted to tell him something; she was jumping up and down frantically. He called for a ladder to be pulled up and clambered down its length, struggling to squeeze his mammoth feet onto the tiny rungs.

"Can't you bring something more befitting of a king," he called out. "This is ludicrous."

A few men scrambled, then pushed a giant stone structure over, one that had stairs carved into it and which descended to the floor. With his full bodily grace, he negotiated the small step at the bottom, then he could see Nitocris bursting with excitement, ready to inform him of something worth hearing, he hoped.

She ran into his arms squealing, "How did you sleep last night, any strange signs that the curse might be developing?"

His mind took him directly back to the night before, struggling to sleep and be coherent over his own thoughts, and he answered, "Yes."

"That's it," she cried. "We are done for. Well, you are, anyway. Once it's done its worst on you, it can easily keep spreading through the lot of us, never mind catching cholera, this is what will bring us down."

At this cheery summary, Augustuskamoun raised his

eyes to the heavens.

"Well, at least the rest of the pharaohs will be able to keep on raising hell against the minions," he replied, meaning it to be a comfort, but not really finding any.

Ammon and Husain set off early in their pursuit to bring the Rosetta stone back to the rest of the group. They travelled many long and gruelling hours until they reached a familiar, elaborate network of tunnels. Negotiating their way through was difficult as they knew they had to remember the route, then follow it back again. Husain's sense of direction was bad, and as he was leading the way, they were continually lost, but when Ammon took over, they made up for all the lost time. He seemed to have a good nose for directions, recognizing familiar smells and scents along the way.

Before long, they were back in the huge cavern where they had seen the stone previously, and the pair of them were craning their necks to see if it was still where they left it.

"That thing hasn't moved for centuries," said Ammon.

Husain murmured in agreement, and they began scaling the wall, until they reached a central plateau on which the stone itself was located. Straightening up, they brushed themselves down, getting rid of the dust and cobwebs in their hair, they approached it at the same level. Ammon turned to his father and realised their next challenge.

"How are we supposed to remove this from the wall? You can see it's never been moved before."

Ammon looked frustratedly at his father.

"The only way to chip it away is with hammer and chisel," Husain replied.

"But we don't have either of those pieces of equipment with us now," Ammon said, rather obviously.

They rummaged through their bags and between them all they could find were dented and crushed pieces of cutlery.

"We will just have to use those," Husain said, and they both started chipping away at the mortar with their impromptu tools. The plaster in the walls was ancient and crumbled away easily enough once they got down to a deeper level, but to begin with it was hard going. They took turns to conserve energy, Ammon doing as much as he could because he saw his father tiring.

Husain was grateful for this, but said, "You don't need to make me feel like a cripple, I've got many more years get up and go in me."

Ammon agreed, and his father went back to it. After a while, the crevice they had been carving out became larger and they could both climb into it. They kept digging, and with time they managed to ease the stone from its tight cavity and heave it onto the floor below. A sheet of bound together hay had been found, laid out, and they were planning to pull it using this.

Between the two of them the journey back took twice the time, with the added weight of the stone. They were pulling quite slowly because if they were hasty, the stone would easily be damaged, and they took regular breaks as they were concerned about their backs. By the evening as the light began to wane, the shadows were getting longer, the temperature of the air dropping, and they saw landmarks they recognized. Then they passed the bar, and Ammon gave a cheer.

"This was where we met Keket, Femi, and Huda," he said.

This last sentiment seemed to spur Husain on, and with incredible strength he lumped the stone up onto his back, then lumbered back on his own without even stopping for a breath.

I can't believe he's lugging that great hefty load, Ammon thought, fretting with worry. *But it seems to be cheering him, so I won't say a word. We are only around the corner from the lodging house now.*

"Let's leave it outside," Ammon said, and they went back up to see Huda, Femi, and Keket.

Once upstairs, there was no trace of anyone, so they wandered back through the house, when the landlady saw them and told them, "Huda has gone out for a walk, not long since, and told me she will return soon. The other two, I saw them yesterday on their way in, but today I haven't seen hide nor hair of them the whole day."

Ammon and Husain decided to hang out with the landlady, the hour was late now, and it was safest for them to be indoors.

Ammon said, "It's much safer to be in here out of the way of slithering serpents, snapping camels and crocodiles, and mosquitoes that suck your blood."

The landlady was a kindly soul and said, "Why don't you stay for some food and drink, it looks like you have been travelling?"

"We will take up your offer gladly," replied Ammon. "We've spent most of the day collecting the stone. You look like one of us. We are involved in a plight to revolt against the pharaohs, as they are a common evil."

"Huda's the one to speak to," Husain proclaimed. "Make sure you sign her petition too, and you can join the forces as we make our uprising."

A few minutes later, Huda came waltzing in, and from the opposite end of the room saw Keket and Femi, they all had so much to talk about.

Ammon said, "But first, do please oblige this generous woman for feeding and reviving us, she wants to sign the petition, too."

They rested a while and took stock of their situation. Keket and Femi had been out for the whole night. Huda was talking animatedly with the landlady, and once they finished, she offered them all a room to sleep in for the night, but at no cost this time. They were up long after the landlady had gone to bed, discussing Ammon and Husain's trip to collect the stone, their own at the pagan festival, and how they learnt that a cat, a scarab beetle, a crocodile, and a serpent could be used in their own venture against the pharaohs, each having its own superior quality.

"It's just a case of calling upon it, by chanting or invoking its name," Keket told them.

Huda said, "I have heard of a curse that is rampantly and erratically coursing its way through the people, irrespective of class, gender, or any other boundaries. Its origins are out in the wilds, where it has brought down a pharaoh it came into company with, and they have passed away."

There was a cry of shock as some of them hadn't heard this news.

"Snefru, for all his faults, was considered as a good ruler by many," Femi carried on. "It is rumoured he took a mummy back to England and people are saying this is what triggered the whole thing. He was with Augustuskamoun and Khafre on a short hunting trip, and he was unlucky enough to be trampled by elephants."

More squeals of horror and some burst into tears.

"The curse spread with equal speed and force to Augustuskamoun and Khafre. Now people are saying that it has spread to his slaves, servants, and men." Femi fell silent.

Ammon asked, "How does the curse affect its hosts?"

Femi replied, "It has been causing hallucinations and more general feelings of fear, anxiety, and paranoia."

Huda intervened. "Those pharaohs deserve it; their consciences must be riddled with guilt anyway."

At that Keket gave a half-hearted cheer. Their enthusiasm was waning for the causes that Huda had been so vehemently ramming down other people's throats.

"What about us though? Our people, families, friends, women, too." Keket was keen to know. "Never mind their consciences, what about yours?" The question was directed at Huda, who looked shocked.

Femi nodded quietly in agreement.

"I'm doing this for you people, for all of us, so that we can have a better life, so that we don't need to be second class citizens to them anymore," Huda declared, with feeling. She was getting tearful herself now. "Haven't I made it so clear all the way along?"

Then Femi tugged at Keket's arm and said, "Don't you remember the people that we delivered flyers to, the woman who we met? She is an example of why things need to change, the way she is second in command to the man of the house."

They continued explaining this to Huda, and she listened, and they talked together for a long time, and finally resolved for nothing else to bring them down. Not even the actions of the other men, or of their friends.

"What do you know about the curse then?" Ammon asked Femi.

"It has already passed from one slave to another, and now it is bounding limitlessly towards us," Femi replied.

Husain was scratching his head in bewilderment at the whole thing. He had left school at an early age, never following up on any of his education, keener instead to begin work straight away. Keket, who had been listening attentively, explained it to him in layman's terms.

Husain's only comment was, "How's that going to make any difference to the plight we have been left in by the pandemic?"

Huda stepped in to answer that one. "Good point," she said. "That won't replace any of the dead, but siding with me, we can make some form of protest, we can rally together, we can collaborate, we can fight the pharaohs at their own game."

Husain gave a weary sigh, "I guess it's pointless me even trying to fight it," he said, and with a grimace of admission, he agreed.

"I know exactly what you can do, Husain, you, and

your son. You've done such a grand job of locating and bringing back the Rosetta stone. How do you fancy going out on another voyage of discovery?" Huda asked the old man brightly, hoping to put him into a more enthusiastic frame of mind.

Husain beamed proudly as he looked at Huda. Ammon could see that he was tapping his foot and sensed it was out of nervousness. Huda gave each of them a penetrating stare, as she waited for an answer.

"Sure," replied Ammon, shrugging. "What do you say, Father?"

Rising to the occasion, Husain agreed to be a part of it, as Huda began speaking again, telling them their mission.

"At the lost city of Aten, they say a fifteen-foot piece of papyrus exists. It includes texts of the Book of the Dead, a collection of spells, and rules that have been designed to help the deceased pass into the afterlife, and to stop the spread of cholera. If you can locate it and bring it back for us; we badly need those rules so that we can play the pharaohs at their own game. It's self-explanatory, each one is concerned with areas of daily life, and how they are to be obeyed by the masses."

"Give me an example?" said Husain, but Huda shook her head.

"I cannot, until you return. Passing the rules is like a green light into the afterlife, if people want to access the next life, they must do these things."

Husain quivered with bemusement and said, "I have seen enough nonsense, I am of an age where I don't care so much for what the others think, but at the same time I can see the importance of securing your position in the next life. If it means I must jump through a few more hoops for the pharaohs, what's wrong with that?"

Huda said, "You are entitled to your own views, of course."

Ammon grabbed his father's arm and rushed him to the lodging house where they were to spend another night. He agreed with the rest of the group that the two of them will leave in the morning, bright and early. They had no idea of where they were going, and his father said so.

With that, Ammon marched out of their room, only to return a few moments later with a medley of maps and compasses under his arm.

Oh, it's going to be one of those trips, his father thought, rolling his eyes. Ammon beckoned him to one side of the room, out of the direct sunlight.

"We are fools," Husain told his son. "We should have left long since, now the sun is high, and it will impede our way."

Ammon, who should have known better, could only find the excuse, "I slept long and hard, dreamt like a trooper."

Husain made a noise of exasperation and said, "Don't mind me," and set off.

Husain struck out into the desert with his long stick, which he used for walking, and to assist him as he had developed a limp in one of his legs. He knew Ammon was worried about his health, so he said nothing and told him nothing. Now, he simply gazed ahead, pretending to be in good health. Ammon knew he had a series of issues, and that he was classified as extra vulnerable in terms of the pandemic. It wasn't just his age though, he also had gout, high cholesterol, and a dodgy ticker, as well as a case of dead man's fingers through a punishing schedule of self-imposed drinking. This last condition meant that he couldn't even feel his way through a public space during the daytime, let alone at night. So, Ammon was rather glad they were setting off now, even though the sun was high, and it would impede the journey somewhat. He called to his father who was up ahead.

"Slow down, we've got a long way to go."

Husain didn't reply, so Ammon called again. "Father, Father!" and the volume of Ammon's voice increased with worry.

He feared the worst. *Where could he have got to? Only minutes before he had been leading the way as if there was no tomorrow. Now all I can hear is the echoing of silence, which in the desert feels even more isolating. The weather is fine, there hasn't been any reports of sandstorms or extreme climates,* Ammon thought. As he looked around him the land was parched with skeletons of trees dotting the landscape, small nests, and straggly branches hanging down.

Ammon called once again, but there was no reply. Just silence. Now he felt really lost and alone. He kept on pushing forward, putting his feet into Husain's footprints. *I can't tell if they are his but in some funny way it reassures me,* he thought, then suddenly the footprints disappeared, and he lost them. *It feels like groping in the dark again, my eyesight has never been bad, but now it is as if I have tunnel vision.*

Feeling his way along inch by inch, Ammon cursed, when suddenly, his peripheral vision cleared where his father's footprints ended, and he could see three hundred and sixty degrees again. Below him was a stone stairwell that dropped several fathoms to the depths of the earth's core. Ammon entered. It was so deep he felt the thermal warmth permeating from its walls, it wasn't just radiating from the sun above anymore.

Putting a hand on his head to protect him as he went under and using his other hand to steady himself, Ammon stepped onto a rickety rope ladder that descended to a greater depth. Plummeting into darker, duskier, and grimier conditions, he wiped his brow, and a furrow of black sweat was left deeply encased in the wrinkles of his forehead.

"Father," Ammon bleated.

There was no reply, only an eerie resonance of sound. To Ammon's ear it was like the dull clash of a symbol, or as if he had tinnitus. Bouncing for a millisecond in the pit of his ear canals, his hearing was as though it were tuned through a gramophone trumpet, but in reverse, so loud noises became far smaller, converted to minuscule, whereas quiet turned into ear-piercing sounds.

Ammon stumbled over rocks and falls, but suddenly, a familiar hand outstretched for him to steady himself by. He nearly took a nosedive, which could have been painful, but then he heard gravelly tones he recognized so well.

"Father, it's you!" Ammon exclaimed.

Husain pushed him and escorted him to one side, steadying him, then began to explain what he'd seen further down the passage.

"You won't believe it," he said. "It exists, exactly as

Huda told us about. No word of a lie."

"What?" Ammon said.

"The lost city of Aten," Husain said. "I saw a signpost that must lead up that way. I've heard of that place, it was a city that was abandoned as cholera struck, some rulers and citizens stayed put to prove that they couldn't be shifted by anything. Most people said they are imbeciles, and that their fate was sealed. The city supposedly has been left exactly as it was, it's like the Mary Celeste, so they say. Plazas, markets, roads, pavements, sphinx, pyramids, mosques, temples, statues, and catacombs all ringing with silence and decrepitude. Cholera sufferers on the street corners begging alms, crosses painted on doors to ward off the virus, the streets deserted, the only thing blowing through them is tumbleweed. Apparently, the rulers tried to keep as many people back as possible, they were trying every trick in the book, giving extra money, making promises to people that their belongings and property wouldn't be affected."

"Of course, it would have been," Ammon chimed in. "Then wasn't the whole city lost in a huge sandstorm, and we never saw anything of it ever again! I was gobsmacked when that happened, despite knowing how unreliable and what tyrants the pharaohs can be, but this took the biscuit, tricking people into staying in a city that was doomed with cholera!" He sighed.

"How low can they stoop?"

His voice was impassioned, and his father patted his shoulder in understanding. He knew how low they could stoop!

Husain said, "They told people there was no virus

206

there, then next minute it coursed through the veins of the city."

"It was outrageous," agreed Ammon.

They kept walking. "Well at least we know what kind of place to look out for," Husain said. "We are probably in the right place to encounter it, at this subterranean level."

Ammon nodded, and they pushed on down the tunnel as the path dropped like a ramp before them. As they went lower, the walls began to open out until they realised, they were in a huge cavern. The walls seemed to be lined with something, but it was difficult to tell exactly what until they got closer. Ammon pulled out a spoon from his pack and began scratching the wall, then suddenly he jumped back.

"I can see the outline of a body," Ammon said in fright.

He kept excavating it until the crevice around the shape became deep enough to get a knife into it, then began wedging the former out. Ammon hacked at the wall from all angles, then out popped the body, and dropped straight onto the floor of the cave.

"Gruesome," said Husain, coming closer.

Ammon peered in to examine it closer then realized the body had no intestines.

"Maybe they have been removed?" he said.

Husain volunteered, "Maybe they were taken out because it was a cholera sufferer and they have packed up from overuse, with that disease it runs your bowels to rack and ruin, plays havoc with your digestive system."

"Could be," said Ammon, and they both went into a

quiet and reflective mode.

"I am thinking about death," Husain said, after a while. "I'm getting older, so probably logical for me, but I don't want to go that way, for sure."

Ammon replied, "If you get the virus there's not much you can do about it. You might be lucky, and it will just treat you lightly, but overall, the medicines are not advanced enough yet."

"What about if you get it, Ammon? You're young, full of life. Maybe you want to start a family? Have meaningful experiences? Broaden your horizons? Even see some of the world?"

"Yes, to all of those things" Ammon told his father. "But I'm realistic. If I got the virus, and went onto recover, I wouldn't live as long. I know the numbers of years humans live is lower now than ever, and the virus has a large part to play in that, too."

Husain shuddered. "Try not to see it as depressing, though."

He looked at Ammon with a po-face and Ammon smiled, and thought, *Not think about death as depressing. My father is the only person I know who could view it optimistically!*

He looked at Husain with a mixture of respect and disbelief.

"Anyway, let's get on our way," he said, gathering his thoughts into more appropriate ones. "We've much to do. It's all on us, we can make an impact on the lives of the pharaohs, and hopefully people will see sense when they look at them, realize there is something better than that. It will be the beginning of the thaw for Huda, the seeds of a new society."

Chapter Fourteen

Sometime later, Ammon and Husain both decided to stop for a rest, they had no idea what time it was, usually the sun guided them, but today, they were sheltered from its barbaric rays. They found a place, a small alcove dug out of the plaster wall and stood there soaking up the coolness of its surface. They needed rehydration, but there wasn't even a small well to be found. They had lost a lot of fluids.

Ammon saw a small drip, glistening and trickling as it fell from the ceiling.

"I'm suspicious because I know we are under the desert, so where could such moisture and water spring from?" he pondered aloud.

Husain replied, "The only place it can emerge from would be an oasis."

"It's that or one of the Nile's tributaries," reasoned Ammon.

"Could it give us any idea as to the whereabouts of the lost city of Aten itself?" asked his father.

They both looked around and then at one another.

"Possibly," replied Ammon, and taking out his array of cutlery, he selected the most appropriate tool for the job. "But I'm not so worried about that as I am getting us some fluids. I'm going to try digging at this small crack here, where the drop of water is coming from, to see if I can make it any bigger and then we will have some water."

He had been digging for several hours, when suddenly, the drip became a gush and flowed out, soaking him. A steady stream of water sploshed around his ankles as he stood there laughing.

His laughter petered out when Husain gave a cry, "The whole wall is about to give way!"

The ceiling had sprung several more leaks in other places close to where Ammon had been hacking, and suddenly the whole thing collapsed as the pressure behind gradually became too much. They were both thrown to the ground and left swimming about in chest high water that was radiant and warm to the touch, and to the skin.

"This feels beautiful," Husain said. "Maybe these are the hot springs that used to exist at Aten?"

"Yes, I have heard about occurrences like this in the desert. They are rare, but a combination of the hot thermal rocks, and the presence of an oasis are usually the given features."

They swam until their feet hit rocks underwater, then they found that they could shimmy their way up onto the bank. They clambered out, up a sheer cliff face, and onto a rocky outcrop on top. The view was breathtaking from there, and as Ammon scanned the horizon, he saw what looked like huge cast iron signposts that arose menacingly from the surrounding water, each one announcing the old city limits.

"We've made it," said Ammon under his breath.

The two of them set off heading for the buildings in the distance, each rejoiced in the rejuvenating waters. They both felt like children again. The heat of the sun was drying their clothes, which now felt cleansed, as did their skin.

"This is amazing, it must be a miracle, not a curse,"

Husain said.

They strode on, reenergised from their soaking and swimming, feeling happier than they had earlier, but each of them also harboured an underlying feeling of unease and discontent. Neither could work out where it came from and it was only as they passed through the harbour arms themselves, they can make out grim and grisly reminders of where they had come to.

Each had on it towering and decaying columns of flesh, both covered with dissected organs that had been painstakingly pieced back together again. As they passed close by, they could see they were peppered with the virus, littered with germs, and hundreds of flies buzzed in clouds around each pillar, green geysers of gas shot out from the centre.

"But who could have done this?" cried Husain.

"Looks like the work of the pharaohs to me, who else would risk doing something of this scale, and who could get away with it?" asked Ammon.

"True," said Husain, "and they have access to all the mutilated parts they need. From the multiple mausoleums we see about us, now, everywhere, and they can get hold of cranes, pullies, gantries, and all the related construction equipment to build these monstrosities. It's quite plain to see that the bodies have all been affected by cholera too, so many that they are trying to get rid of the bodies, hide the numbers, conceal the figures. There is so many legal repositories for all this, so why the need to make another?"

Ammon was silent, and the two of them watched in awe as a war boat that had been requisitioned for different uses now, cruised idly up the river, its open hull piled high with bodies. Another hellish scene confronted them.

"Do you suppose its heading to Aten?" Husain said.

The boat vanished in minutes leaving the pair of them scratching their heads.

"Let's follow the boat," Ammon said.

"You're right, but how do we do that from here?" Husain replied. "This navigation is the only path into the city. All around us is an eternal gloaming that stretches to the ceiling of the cave, and to its furthest reaches in all directions of the compass."

"The light will be lost soon, too," Ammon said, looking upwards at the sky. "You will struggle to make out your own hand, let alone anything of importance, shortly."

Husain agreed but then came up with what he thought sounded like a good plan.

"Let's build our own contraption for sailing up the river, we can use any found objects we encounter, as well as planks, wood, tree trunks, roots, plus anything else float worthy that we might find enroute."

It was resolved and they set about searching the banks in the non-existent light. For Ammon and Husain to continue their upriver trip they must source materials, and build a craft, so they raced around searching for what might be feasible for its construction. Ammon ran off into the undergrowth, coming back with bushes, bracken and dried up sticks. Husain came back hauling a root over his shoulder.

"We can use this," he said.

Ammon wanted to know, "How?"

"It is simple, we just need to gather a few, bind them

together, then we can use them to build a raft."

Ammon found some lengths of sisal and began to lay them out, to untangle them.

"Soon we will be ready," he urged his father on as he could see he was flagging.

Husain lumbered a few more roots over, then he threw himself to the floor, and said, "I'm done".

Ammon stepped up and took over, laid out the pieces of wood, end to end, then lashed them together with the strings of sisal. Before long the craft was looking ready for launching.

"Do you think it will be watertight?" Husain said.

"I'm sure of it," boasted Ammon.

And with that the pair of them seized a corner each and lunged towards the river with the raft at their shoulders. They hit the water running, and as they got deeper the oncoming current hit them, almost sweeping them back with its ferocity. They were both powerful swimmers, but the tide got the better of them, and they were pushed into the middle of the river where they floated along, paddling to keep their heads out of the water.

"Ammon," Husain cried. "Are we done for?"

Ammon was kicking hard and with the gutsiness of youth, he didn't let the situation get the better of him. He struck out for a bank, tugged his father and the raft with him; he had the strength of an ox. Partly the thought of delivering his father to safety back home drove him, but also the goal of their mission which lay further upstream.

Gasping and panting the two dragged themselves from the murky depths. Ammon caught sight of a flailing tower of limbs above them, and now they looked up within its shadow, shivered partly with fright, the cold, and their teeth were chattering.

Ammon watched as his father's Adams apple dropped, and he went drip white. He felt a peculiar sensation that tingled over his body. They both looked up and this time the tower was formed of the dried-out corpses of cats, crocodiles, serpents, and scarabs. Creatures the pharaohs used for their own transition into the afterlife. It was wriggling like Medusa, with the incisors of a beetle, and the jaws of a crocodile that snapped away.

Husain said, "I don't want to get too much closer to that living and breathing skin."

"Its surface is of reptile scales, shiny and wet. Rotting and drenched cats fur runs around its fringes," gasped Ammon.

"Its body looks like that of a shelled invertebrate."

Each section moved and rotated as it stood over them.

"Is it trying to decide which of us to pick off first?" Ammon asked.

Husain gave no answer, his eyes were locked into the darkened voids of the creature's dull retinas as they darted about, trying to keep up with the flicker of tongues that came from several snakes.

Husain said. "Each looks more poisonous than a black mamba, our fate is sealed."

At that, the creature took its chance to seize the pair of them, and both were drawn up at the same time, one by its left-handed reptilian digit, the other by a padded and furry claw. Ammon winked to Husain, and they both gave a kick to its unprotected vulnerable underside, and the beast dropped them.

"This is our chance!" screamed Ammon. "Run like hell, towards the river!"

And they threw themselves headlong into the inky deep water. They submerged themselves and swam underwater back into the depths of the cave. For a minute or so, there wasn't even a gurgling of bubbles, then the sound of broken pants, as if somebody had burst from below, their lungs on fire. Ammon surfaced before Husain, and they were embracing each other despite the cold.

"I thought I'd never see you again," his father said.

"Let's go back to the source of the water," said Ammon, "then we can get out of the river again and stay underground. Remember, where we climbed onto a rock? There was some vegetation there that may afford us cover and keep us warm after our soaking!"

Agreeing, his father swam in the direction they had come, and eventually, they reached the underground rocky escarpment where they decided to rest for the night, to recuperate and to gauge their whereabouts, and how far they had to go to the city. They found some withered out palm fronds and threw them over the nearest low-lying trunk.

"This should make a half decent hammock," Husain said.

As they were underground it was difficult to tell the hour, and they dozed on and off for several hours, until they felt sufficiently replenished in energy.

"Not a single bloodsucker has tried to sink its fangs into us last night. I've heard stories of all manner of blood sucking creature, including leeches being around at this level," said Husain, thoughtfully.

Ammon murmured about how he was suffering with the lack of light. "We are both so used to being surrounded by the vivid and resplendent radiation of the sun. I feel like some burrowing creature, or as if I am going half blind."

Husain nodded, then proposed a plan that might get them to Aten within the next few hours.

"We can't stay underground. Why don't we make our way along the banks of the river this time, it should be far safer now. I suspect after we gave it a good kicking in its nether regions, that the wriggling creature will be gone."

His son agreed, and they made off, reaching an underground layer of the city before long.

As they walked through the streets Ammon said, "Its geography is the same as our own beloved Cairo. The avenues, plazas, squares, pyramids, everything is as if mirrored, but in total darkness, where normally throngs of life would stream the streets, here you can hear a pin drop."

"There is an eeriness, as if a pestilence has recently passed. The constant racket of millions of living and breathing mortals, whose time has been cut short. Red crosses are daubed on walls and blood splatted on fence posts; it is as if hand to hand combat has recently been carried out. Its inhabitants, the cholera sufferers against the survivors, and the cruel pharaohs overseeing the whole diabolical operation. It is very discomforting indeed," Husain agreed.

Ammon replied. "One can imagine them scrapping

in desperation for whatever odds and ends they can find, such as, food, water, or medication. The circumstances must have been dire indeed."

Ammon glanced at Husain for some sense of assurance and caught only the same draining of colour from his features.

"We can't leave," Ammon said. "We must go on; we must find this rule book."

They steadied one another as they negotiated their way down the street. An immense pyramid rose before them, usually its play of light fell across the steps, but now the shadows were foremost.

Husain said, as he craned his necks upwards, "I can't even see its tip."

"The scrolls' length is gargantuan," Ammon said. "Apparently, it's one of the longest ever recorded."

Husain gave a low whistle. "So, I guess we are looking for something with similar dimensions that it could be encased within, would it have been made from hard or soft stone? Could it have been chipped into the parchments surface?"

"Questions, questions," Ammon said, as they continued their perambulation.

"The further we walk down this street the more difficult it will be for us to know where to look." Husain was persistent. "We are screwed then, how are we supposed to know the best place to search?"

Ammon shrugged his shoulders and they both gazed about them. Then Ammon caught sight of something amiss, up to the left-hand side of a rockface. It looked like there was an opening, a crevice which led into the cliff.

"But why do you have the feeling that we should try up there?" asked Husain.

"If you hush and pay attention, you might get the strange premonition as I am," said his son, somewhat impatiently.

Husain listened, staring silently at the cliff before he replied. "I've got an inkling, and when you've been around for as long as I have you get to trust your inner voice. You're right! We should try up there!"

Ammon didn't need to answer, he knew his father in these situations. He was an ardent follower of his own instincts, who trusted his own orientation and ability to find his way out of a fix.

"Sometimes you can be so infuriating," he said, eventually. "So pig-headed. You're telling me something I already knew!"

But Husain was already up on the ledge, he hadn't even given his son time to catch up, when he offered Ammon his hand and pulled him up.

"Come on, slow coach," he blurted out.

Strange for him to make a comment like that, Ammon thought. *He's not usually that critical, or am I just being oversensitive?*

As Ammon came up onto the ledge, he glanced around checking his footing; rubble had slipped from under him, and he was worried if he would go tumbling down.

"I've got you!" Husain cried out.

"It's a good job I trust you," Ammon said, grinning at his father.

Husain was pulling lumps of stone from the face, as if it was an open quarry.

Now he threw down huge boulders, too.

"Duck!" Husain called.

And another came flying Ammon's way, narrowly missing him, as it went plummeting down.

"You are aiming for me!" he cried.

His father didn't hear a word of it. As he became buried him up to his waist in stones, a small cave was opening beneath. Ammon was amazed at his father's sixth sense, but didn't have long to conjecture, as he was beckoned from below, and skipped down to where his father now stood. It looked like a tunnel, and the walls were scrawled with hieroglyphics.

"We need to dig through to a lower level," Husain said. "But the floor is covered in centuries old dust that has been compacted through stamping and packing down, making it near impossible to break through."

Ammon went running off to see what he could find that might help them and came back with a rusty old piece of iron piping. It looked jagged, sharp, and as if it might be able to make a dent in the surface of the floor. Ammon ran up and launched himself at the floor with the full weight of the rusting hulk of metal above him. As they came together there was a loud crack and the floor below them seemed to split and rive into two. Husain was sheltering in a smaller cave, and at the almighty roar, he screamed out.

"I am deaf already!"

There was an echo as the din reverberated, bouncing in and out of hollows, and off vertical and horizontal walls.

The pair of them were silent for a moment as they waited for the dust to settle, then Husain said, "You've done a grand job there, as well as if you had a spear or an axe."

A gaping hole had opened beneath them, and they both peered down. It was difficult to see in the half-light, but they could just make out dim outlines of mummified bodies, human and animal. Masses of jars filled with various ointments, each with a cork stopper. There was also a multitude of funnels, pipes, tubes, and glass conical vessels.

"This stuff must be used for preparing peoples bodies, for their journeys to the far side," Husain said. "Pretty creepy all in all."

Ammon nodded in agreement, but the two of them were compelled to continue their discovery and persisted in their exploration of the cave below. They both dropped down through the hole, then Husain pulled out matches and a candlestick from his pack, to light up their way. Once lit, they saw the illumination reflected in the watchful faces of the surrounding sarcophagi, each had in its face two tiny red opal eyes, that gleamed.

"This makes me feel uncomfortable," Ammon said. "Down here, let's make our way along," and he shuffled through the barely lit space.

Husain gripped onto his arm and followed, trying his best not to stumble and fall. They continued along a short tunnel that then opened out into a larger cavity. Ammon looked up and saw a great block of stone that looked like it had been hand carved and weighed many tonnes.

"Let's climb up and investigate," Ammon said.

He was up there before Husain, and blew off the

dust, doing his best to wipe it. It was extremely long and covered in hieroglyphics. The deep grooves in the stone were filled with pockets of dust, mud, cobwebs, clay, and peppered with the bodies of small, mummified insects that lived in the earth.

"Judging by its length, I think we've found the parchment scroll," Ammon declared.

Husain was having a break, his lungs had been complaining of late, and now they were suffering with some new form of toxic mineral, that can only be found underground. He was coughing his guts up, and Ammon held his hand to steady him. As his father gradually composed himself, Ammon guided his eyes towards the bewildering list of rules and regulations carved into the stone.

"I haven't seen anything like this for years," Husain wheezed. "Not since the fourth cholera pandemic. The pharaohs at the time were going to great lengths to cover up their dirty work. There was corruption at every level, and they were trying every trick in the book to cover up their own actions, and how responsible they were for its whole mismanagement."

"Really!" said Ammon, and feigned shock.

Husain said to him, "Don't mock things you don't understand."

Instead of answering his father's rather puzzling statement, Ammon kept reading the letters. *My knowledge of ancient Egyptian is low, so it is difficult, but I'll do my best to take away from here what I can,* he thought. As Ammon puzzled away, Husain had a recollection.

"If you ever read out the words of the Book of the Dead aloud, a great echoing boom of truth will be heard

221

thereafter."

Husain laughed at the simplicity of it, then walked back over. He had a slight grasp of the language being a little older and knew a few verbs, consonants, nouns, and sounds. Husain read them at the top of his voice, and the ceiling above them began to crack, and then the pair of them started to run. The action of reading brought a force that ripped through the whole chamber, and now the words he had spoken were still hanging in the air.

Husain said, "People must obey the two-metre rule." There was an echoing of, "This was disobeyed by one who slapped a colleague over the back."

He called again. "People must follow quarantine rules coming back into the country." There was a ringing back of, "One got caught out by his own rules and had to self-isolate on the way back."

Once again, he shouted. "Everybody must wear masks." Another echo rattled forth, "Pharoah Augustuskamoun wasn't always wearing one."

The words stuttered above their heads, agitated, and bounced in and out of smaller craters and negative spaces.

"This is unbelievable!" Ammon cried, turning to his father. "Do you know what this means? We have proof of them breaking their own laws, and if we can report this back to Huda, Femi, and Keket, we can have some chance of overturning those miserable low life's. All they ever do is lie, cheat, run our people ragged, and go on killing sprees such as the one that's happening right now."

His father nodded, and they both made the choice to

head back to the rest of the group, where they would find safety and solace.

Chapter Fifteen

Tarek had been out the entire day at training; he had to go to a new site on the outskirts of Luxor. It was noon by the time he got there, and he arranged for a camel and its owner, who introduced himself as Mohammed, to come and pick him up. The pair arrived and the animal was wearing blinkers to protect its eyes from the glare of the sun, and had a scarf wrapped around its head to stop it from getting heat stroke.

As they pulled up, the camels' legs nearly gave way, it had been walking all morning as Mohammed was a cruel and evil man. He mostly ran camels about for the pharaohs and had gotten into the practise of treating them poorly. He always wanted to get the most out of them without having to feed, water, or let them sleep.

The poor beast was spitting globules of sand and dust, and its eyes were full of grit.

"Let the animals have a rest before we set off," shouted Tarek. "The poor creatures on its last legs!"

Mohammed looked over with a gleam of malice and said, "To hell with the rest, I'll use my whip to lash him instead."

Tarek, not being able to forgo the offer of transport over the dunes, merely nodded in a compliant way, and stepped up onto its back. There was a small flight of stairs with Arabian rugs that hung down on both sides. They were covered with geometrical designs and had gold tassels hanging low. As Tarek clambered aboard, the camel got on its feet and he lost his footing, going headlong into a dizzying array of bright red and yellow cushions. Tarek regained his position and his composure, then arranged his robe and scarf.

There were blinds made of wicker surrounding him that were pulled tight, and as he pulled one up, he got the full brunt of the sun's rays. It highlighted his outline, drawing a shadow up against the wall of the tiny shelter. Tarek snapped it shut, and he heard Mohammed violently giving retribution to the camel, urging it on until its last drop of energy was spent. They rose and fell in time with the landscape outside, until several hours later Tarek was awoken by a whistle from the door.

"It is your stop, and you must alight," Mohammed said.

Tarek plunged his hand into the darkness searching for his case full of equipment, then hastily left. He tipped Mohammed regardless of his cruel behaviour, as he knew he'd be struggling for a lift home, otherwise. He had been dropped at a large, tented structure that was surrounded by awnings hanging down, each one looked like a ventilation shaft.

Tarek pulled back one of the tent doors and entered, glad of the coolness within. His robe was snatched from him by an impatient set of hands waiting to avail him of his outfit, then they ushered him into a corner where a large rug lay over the sand. Tarek stared about him, taking in the other guests. There were two men and a woman. They were all there with the same intent, having travelled strictly for the workshop.

The woman leant over and said, "The man who runs the workshop, his name is Dakarai, and he is said to have a great reputation."

Then one of the men introduced himself saying, "I'm Ahmed and this Dakarai's a genius. He's worked for the pharaohs for many years and runs his own successful embalming business. We couldn't be in better hands."

At that there was a slow round of applause as people stood up, some were bowing and dropping to the floor to pay respects to him. *Dakarai must be good,* thought Tarek. There was a hush as Dakarai took centre stage, then began elaborating about his history and experience. Dakarai finished with a short speech about how, with this type of training, you could ascend the mythical gateway into work at the great pyramid.

"If anybody wants to further their calling in this area, please come and see me after," he told them all.

There was a rush of people wanting to shake and kiss his hand, then Tarek saw an opportunity to introduce himself. Dakarai was wearing a blue and white robe, with a thickly banded velvet cord that was loosely draped around his traditional headdress.

Tarek thrusted his hand forward and shook Dakarai's deeply tanned and muscular arm. He had nails that were shapely and clean, which he thought odd for somebody who spent so much time working with scented oils and resins.

"Could my name be put on the list of people who would like to take the training to a further level?" Tarek asked.

Dakarai agreed, then pulled out a long and graceful quill, which he licked the end of. Out of his robe he drew an old design of mirror case, into which he had put an ink pad.

"Sign here, my friend," Dakarai said, giving a weak

and thin smile.

Tarek signed, then went and sat down, consulting the notes he'd been making during the lecture. He compared them with the other guests and before long they were being shown to their seats, as it was nearly time for the evening meal.

Ahmed said, "We will adjourn to another room from which a full assortment of refreshments will be provided. There will be urns of mint tea, tahini and honey on bread, sesame bars, and fruit by the handful."

They all paraded through making space for Dakarai to come and join them. He sat in the centre and talked for many hours.

Ahmed said to Tarek, "He can talk the hindlegs off a donkey."

Tarek paid no attention, only to Dakarai, who he saw as being a great fountain of knowledge, and a leading light in his field. It was nearly midnight before the whole soirée finished, and the guests were led back out to the cool night air. Dakarai promised to contact Tarek again after he finished his examinations, and when he had some of his own samples to show him. *I must look Dakarai up in the future, but for now I must focus on becoming fully qualified,* he thought, before hollering for Mohammed to attend him.

The servant was in a nearby den of ill repute, playing dominoes and drinking rum. Now sufficiently sloshed, Mohammed was happy to saddle up and allowed his own drunken motion to guide the way. Leaping aboard his camel, he missed his footing, cursing the poor creature, and gave it another earful as he blamed it for his own stupidity.

Tarek sat below and let himself be borne back to the throbbing heart of Luxor; the darkened presence of countless pyramids guided them along their way. He had a constant pain in the back of his eyeballs from trying to block out the harsh light of the day. He arrived at Eshe's place, and after paying Mohammed, let himself in with a huge key that was kept under a rock in the street. Tarek heard the thundering of feet as Eshe came running up.

"Where have you been?" Eshe said.

"At my training, there was a talk that overran, I'm sorry for waking you on the way back in."

"Don't worry," she said. "Sit down, I want to bend your ear about something. Why don't I make you a tea?"

Tarek turned down the offer but went up with her to a small hollowed out space that made do for a balcony. Now, with the fresh night air it was a place to soak up the fragrances of the city's squares and gardens, and citrus fruit groves assaulted his senses. Eshe was talking but he only caught half of what she had to say.

"I want to let you know I spoke with the pharaohs and there has been an agreement for you to call in at Narmer's to pick up bodies from him, ones that they have been left over from the pandemic. Don't expect anything pretty," Eshe said, and broke off. "Is it even safe to be accepting such diseased and infected donations?"

Tarek snapped out of it and murmured, "Probably not, but do I have any other choice? Apart from yours, obviously, but you've got a long way to go."

Eshe laughed nervously. At that, the pair of them yawned and both made their excuses to go and sleep. She had to be up early for another day at the pyramid, and he wanted to get back to Cairo. The seminar he attended was the last one, and now he was free to go in search of alternative employment. Tarek planned to call in at Narmer's as soon as he got back, then he would send drawings of his samples via a messenger to Dakarai. After that, he could claim his final qualification and certificate. "Much to do," he uttered under his breath, and headed off to the upstairs room.

Tarek had strange dreams that night, combining thoughts of seeing Nour again, with embalming Eshe, and finding an occupation that was the continual source of his life's joy. *The three are peculiarly linked,* he thought. *If I have happiness through my life's works, then my wife will be content. Embalming the body of the woman who runs the lodging house will bring us great riches in the long run, again contributing to our overall happiness.*

Tarek's visions were tumultuous and erupting, and within hours he felt he was being rudely awoken. He heard a bang at the door, and then another, and then another. *It must be Eshe,* he thought, trying to regain consciousness. Tarek stumbled to his door and let her in.

He said, "Why are you so irately knocking?"

Eshe didn't give a full answer, preferring instead to waltz right into the room, and took up her position by the window. She wanted to gaze out at the street; there was an early morning rush of people from one place to the next.

Eshe said. "I can see the pharaoh's warriors, orderlies

off to hospital, priests on their way to temple, and on the steps of the pyramid, the worn figures of cholera sufferers, those whose bodies are wasting away from the disease. They look like the shadow of their former selves."

Tarek approached Eshe, asking, "What's wrong?" He joined her by the window, which had concrete awnings. They blocked out much of the sun. Even at this hour, the whole room was in shade.

Eshe burst into tears and seized him, grabbing him bodily. Tarek felt his insides jump. Ever since the pharaohs announced strict social distancing measures, he had never quite got his head around the idea. It was only when Tarek was with friends or family that he hadn't seen for a while, that he ever felt the urge to hug them. Eshe unclasped her body from Tarek, allowing him to breathe more easily, this time his heart was going ten to the dozen.

"I must set off for Cairo today," Tarek cried out as if to make his plans certain. "It's been weeks since I've last seen my beloved wife, Nour."

Tarek and Eshe left her dwelling around ten, after they'd had breakfast, and he'd packed. Tarek was planning to take the same route that he had taken by canal on his journey up to Luxor. This would be another ten-day long expedition fraught with danger. Before long, he left, promising Eshe that he would be back occasionally to check on her health, and to make sure that she still wanted the same burial arrangements. Until then, they would go on spending Eshe's money and improving their lives bit by bit.

Eshe accompanied Tarek to a spot on the outskirts of the city where the architectural rubble merged with the desert, and you had trouble telling where one ended, and another began. They were like carcasses that time had forgotten, every inch having become a pocket into which deep deposits of sand could be found, and its overall shape was difficult to distinguish.

As they bade each other farewell, he buried the snack that she made him, deep within the lining of his robe. Tarek had arranged for a camel to pick him up, and it was long overdue now. Shaking his headdress to remove any sand and adjusting the straps on his sandals, he retired to a more shaded, secluded spot.

The sun beat tirelessly into his eyes, and the seed of a headache was taking root. *Not again,* he thought. As Tarek stared into the shimmering distance, not sure if his eyes were playing tricks on him, the shadow of a huge beast fell upon him. It jerked up, all pointy angles, knee bones, long gangly legs, and topped with a flagged structure. The driver's finger beckoned to him, and Tarek happy to be out of the sun, scaled the shaky ladder and went through the curtained entrance. His camel taxi had arrived!

Once inside, Tarek fell upon the upholstery that had been covered with rugs, glad of its cool interior, and darkened surroundings. The gentle motion of the journey rocked him into a deep coma like sleep, from which he was awoken several hours later by a worried and frightened voice.

"Sir! We've run into a sandstorm," it said.

Tarek, a well-seasoned traveller of the region, knew what to do and saw sense, jumping up to baton down all the hatches, crying for the driver. "Come inside and take cover!"

As the man struggled in, he made conversation, and both began exchanging stories more designed to frighten one another, than anything else.

He said, "I remember seeing a camel being stripped of every inch of its skin by a particularly harsh storm that passed."

Tarek listened and his jaw dropped. "I can't tell you anything as fear inspiring, only a lame tale about a storm that begins and ends within the hour."

The driver laughed out loud, "If you'd been attending on some of the trips I've had to make, you wouldn't survive a minute in the job."

Tarek, not realizing that this was an opportunity to better oneself against the other's inadequacies, piped down, resolving that he might be better off in silence. The minutes ticked by, and the tent became even darker as the storm pressed on, the driver suddenly deciding that this was the correct moment to go and attend to his beast.

Tarek yelled, "You're mad to go out there!" But the sound of his voice was carried away by the battling winds.

As the driver climbed down to the ground level, he saw for the first time that the poor animal was completely undercover, every inch of its body concealed by sand, "Will it even be able to breathe?" he said.

Accustomed to such circumstances and having a flagon of water at his belt, he wet a cloth, then wrapped it around where he thought its muzzle and snout might be. He dug around to find their exact location, though, gave the camel a reassuring pat on its bony head, then retired back to the tent as the storm had long to go.

The driver and Tarek sat in silence; both mortified with fear at the reality that they might become vulture food. There was a sound of gulping as if somebody was struggling to breathe. It was the driver; he looked like a fish out of water; his throat parched with panic.

Tarek had a bottle of water tucked down the side of the seat, and he pulled it out to relieve the poor man; after that they became firm friends. By the next morning, the storm had passed, and they dared to venture off again, on their way. They pushed on with a gentle wind to encourage them, making good time, and before they knew it, they were back close to Cairo.

The driver dropped Tarek off right outside the bakery, near the dig where he knew Nour would be. Tarek wanted to sneak in, surprise her, and swamp her with news of his travels, but at the last moment, he thought better of it.

'I don't want to alarm her,' he decided.

So, he made his way around to the front of the building where access could be gained to the basement room. There was a gaping hole in the wall which afforded some ventilation to the bakery, and from there he called her name.

"Nour!"

She was in the middle of baking but heard this distant cry, which sounded so familiar.

"I know that voice," she shouted, and ran at top speed towards the window.

Upon seeing one another, they embraced for what

seemed like an age, then burst into floods of tears of anger and joy.

"Such confusion," Tarek said. "Has it really been that long since we saw one another? Has that much happened?"

Nour pushed him into a chair and shoved a table in front of him, forcing a crust of Saboob into his hand. "Tell me your news?"

Tarek took a while to get his breath back, but once he was composed and after sharing innumerable monotonous details, went on to tell her his jubilant news.

"I've completed my training," he said. "Now I'm just awaiting my certificate, before long I will be a fully-fledged mummification workshop leader."

On hearing this, again Nour was in floods of tears. "We've waited so long for this, and the bakery is right on the brink of ruin. Since you left, we've had barely a customer and been inundated with bad luck due to a curse."

"A curse!" Tarek said. "I don't know anything about that?"

Nour said, "I encountered it on the train one afternoon, and since then I've been snowed under with bad luck. I tried to arrange for somebody to come and perform a counter spell but couldn't find anybody suitable. Nobody wanted to volunteer for the role as they are worried the curse might be passed onto them."

Tarek said, "I'm not surprised business has been so bad, what with this new lockdown and people dropping like flies with cholera. Who's going to eat bread when you've got a hole in your bowels the size of a sinkhole?"

Nour nodded in grim agreement and the two of them reasoned on.

"Eshe has promised to leave her body, and she has bequeathed treasure on us already, courtesy of the pharaohs," Tarek told his wife.

At this news, she was cheering to her hearts content, yelling with delight. Her enthusiasm gripped him too, and he grabbed her by the waist and threw her into the air.

"You know what, I think everything is going to be okay," she said.

"What impact is cholera having? How are the pharaohs doing governing the whole thing?" Tarek wanted to know.

"They've launched test centres, they have plans to find a vaccine," Nour told him.

"They are always trying to cover up for their own mistakes and greediness, the rising death count, and to show that they are not the ones to be held accountable. If I ever must go and work for them again, let it be a cold day in hell. Working at the kitchens was the worst experience I've ever had."

Nour replied, "You still won't get out of it, you will be as dependent on them as the rest of us are, when you start your new job. You'll just be a bit higher up in the pecking order. Less likely to get pushed out of the equation because they are more reliant on your services."

"Maybe not a bad thing," Tarek said.

"I heard about a party that took place, and in the ensuing scandal, I lost any shred of respect I had for them at the time."

"And to speak of corruption, you'd have thought we are in the dark ages. If they can reduce their own chances of getting it in the neck, they will, favours from a friend, money laundering, profiteering, racketeering, you name it they've done it." Tarek's voice was filled with bitterness.

Nour was thoughtful for a little while, then said, "Let's go to sleep, hopefully events will look brighter in the morning."

They took Nephi and the three of them went to bed. Tarek always woke up regular as clockwork at the same time and today was no different. He rolled out of bed, but Nour was long since gone, even the warm patch had gone bitterly cold. He went down to the bakery and helped himself to a flatbread that was lying on the side; it was still warm, and the crumb was soft and springy.

He pulled himself out a small saucepan and put it onto the stove to make a coffee, kicked back his feet onto the tabletop and took loud slurps of his fresh brew. He tore off lumps of flatbread absentmindedly, dunked them into his drink, and deliberated upon his movements for the day.

Tarek promised to Nour that he would give her a hand getting the flour in, but then after that he would be free to head to Narmer's place. He wanted to go and pick up some bodies that he could practise on. Then he heard a cry from below. Tarek jumped, all thoughts evaporated from his head, then he made haste to the kitchen below. Within minutes he was slugging twenty-five-kilogram sacks through the door, no different than any other day. The sweat poured down his neck and back, even though they were in the basement, which was usually cool. Groaning and moaning, he tried to get his plans straight for the day, but all he could think of was the brutal force of manual labour.

"This is not much better than working for the pharaohs," Tarek complained out loud, but the words were lost on Nour, she didn't hear a thing.

When they were all done, Tarek hastened towards the steps. He wanted to escape before Nour noticed he was gone. Nephi the cat was sitting on the ledge sunning itself and gave a yowl as if to alert Nour to his departure. *Caught in the act,* Tarek thought.

Nour came rushing over and hugged him; she had been perspiring heavily in the kitchen and her brow and hair were wet through. She had been throwing great loaves upon paddles into an open fire, and had tossed the tools to one side, in her haste to run up to see him off. Nephi entwined itself around their legs to trip them over, then decided to curl up on his foot in protest of his leaving. Tarek shook his leg, and the cat went flying.

"I've got to get off," he said, watching the cat as he gave Nour a peck on the cheek.

"Goodbye and take care." Nour replied.

Tarek took off to catch the train that ran into the centre. There were rumours that the storm might rise again, and he wanted to be at Narmer's before there was no chance of finding his way. Narmer's palace lay at the junction of two ancient tracks, and there was a huge expanse of desolate and arid territory before them.

As Tarek drew closer, he saw huge fortifications that rose from the wasteland. There was no other opportunity to make his entry unnoticed here. He had to keep circulating the grounds until he found an entrance. He was walking in the shade of the walls, trying to keep as close to the wall as possible, tucked away so that the guards above won't see him. He didn't want to risk being fired at, a flurry of arrows coming his way, or a bubbling cauldron of oil to come plummeting down upon him.

He continued along his way until he saw a collection of men gazing out into the horizon and ruminating. They were sat atop camels. He decided to go and make himself known. As soon as they saw him, they took him for a cholera sufferer and wouldn't let him near.

"How can we trust you?" One said.

Tarek used his quick reactions and called back, "I am one of Nefertiti's servants, I have come a long way, and I have an urgent message for Narmer."

The men mocked Tarek and still wouldn't let him any nearer, taunting him and throwing meagre bits of food. To his disgrace he stooped and picked it up, giving them more fuel for their harassment.

"Look at this poor soul," said another, "he will eat from the ground even, what a pauper."

They kept on ridiculing him, and another joined in. "With a bit of luck, he won't last long in that fierce sunshine."

At that minute the men all clammed up and were silent, it appeared that Narmer was out doing a patrol, and what he saw pleased him greatly.

"Who's this low life?" Narmer shouted over.

One of the men replied, "It is a wretch from the local village."

"Well don't let him in, we've got enough trouble with

those types," Narmer said, and the men began again with their abusive treatment.

Tarek realized he needed a new tactic if he was to be able to gain access as required. *These men believe I am less than the lowest caste possible, I am merely a stain on the undersole of their foot,* he thought. With quick wits, he changed his story hoping to appease the men.

"If you let me in, I promise to cross your palms with silver."

At this the men went quiet, and one beckoned for him to step over. Tarek thought, *Nour will not be happy, but if she knows it is for my salvation, she might get over it.* The men eyed him suspiciously until he produced some form of payment, then thrusting it deep into their own pockets, they stepped away and let him pass.

"You did not see a thing," one uttered. "Do not say a word to Narmer."

Tarek continued into the grounds glancing about nervously, after his run in with the men. He was still visibly shaking. He headed towards a huge pyramid that dominated the landscape, rising to a height of three hundred hands. Its tip was concealed from view, enveloped in the gloom of an oncoming storm, billowing clouds of dust and sand hung menacingly over.

The weight of the air became apparent, and Tarek struggled to make out any forms apart from that of a huge tomb. *That must be Narmer's,* he thought. He was surprised he had managed to get this far without being obstructed again.

"I must have been lucky," he muttered to himself. Narmer hastened straight back to his resting place, as he had an urgent direction from Augustuskamoun about the future of the current lockdown, and new guidelines that had to be written. Tarek heard rustling of leaves and sticks, as small eddies of air were disturbed by the portly figure of Narmer, who struggled to pull himself up. Using its marble walls to prop himself against, he popped his head over and hearkened towards Tarek's voice.

As he came closer, Narmer cried out, "Identify yourself?"

Tarek was quiet for a minute, then went on to make out his plight.

"Eshe told me I could come here to collect bodies for my mummification workshops, regardless of what state they are in."

Narmer remembered the occasion with Khufu and Khafre, and how one had tried his best to work his evil charms upon her.

"It was when we were sitting in the great pyramid," he said to Tarek now. "Yes, I remember the promise well."

With that he gave a click of his fingers, and slaves ran from all four corners of the room dragging human bodies in their wake. Most were unclothed, still naked, not spared an ounce of decency, and especially not in the way they were thrown bodily down. Narmer gave a command, and the slaves bolted back into the recesses of the darkened room.

Tarek ran forward and cried, "These will be perfect for my needs. Would you be able to spare the use of a slave, for me to get them safely back to my dwelling before nightfall?"

Narmer agreed, and once the exchange was done and a few pounds thrown into his coffers, they both stole away. Tarek had a homemade contraption on his back where two bodies could be stored, and his borrowed slave carried the same again.

They headed back to Tarek's place and before dawn they arrived. On the prevailing breeze the stench hit Nour's delicate nostrils before she even saw what was coming, and she was repulsed.

"It smells like a morgue," Nour declared, as Tarek walked through the back doors, having dumped the offending items in the back yard. "If anybody gets wind of this, I could lose customers," she berated him.

"True," Tarek said, and looked thoughtfully into the distance. *She didn't have that many customers, anyway,* he thought, but then turned his mind to how his newly acquired cadavers could assist them in the future. His mind raced ahead.

"Just think of the orders from wealthy folk, not just the pharaohs, but their direct descendants, the royal dynastic families. Once they get wind of what a wonderful job, I am doing in preparing peoples bodies for that transition, and then seeing them off into the after world, then this world will be our oyster!"

Nour went quiet, she was well impressed, and the thought of the manual labour of the bakery suddenly began to evaporate from her mind.

"You mean we could rest easy?" she said, although she knew full well that she would never be able to sit still.

Tarek nodded, "I will still be working for the pharaohs, but this time the situation would be far more balanced in our favour, rather than theirs. I must get an early night; I need to be up early in the morning to go and conduct my first workshop. It's been booked in with a distant relative of Augustuskamoun. I'm feeling confident of my abilities now and putting them into practise tomorrow will make all the difference."

Chapter Sixteen

Several hours later Husain and Ammon reached the lodging house. The rest of the group; Huda, Keket, and Femi were already there, and welcomed them in with open arms, after having been away for so long. They were keen to fill the others in with news of their travels. They all sat around in reverential silence, drank tea, and listened to Husain and Ammon's tales. The audience was awestruck as they recalled various details from its entirety and finished with the legendary discovery of the fifteen-foot-long papyrus scroll.

"When we stumbled across that," Ammon said, "we were overwhelmed by the fact that this could be a realistic solution, to turn our fate in the war against the pharaohs."

"Explain more about how?" Huda said, curiously.

Husain took over at this point, "Halfway there I am assailed with this clarification of memory, it is as if I am seeing through a magnifying glass, my thoughts are focused and clear. I remember that you will always get an echo of truth after reading every inscription on the scroll."

Ammon interrupted him. "When we encountered the scroll itself much later, it is exactly as my father recalls. There are rules carved into its surface, that once uttered, an exact replica of them comes rattling forthwith, but with a correction of how the pharaohs slipped up in their ways."

"But how can this assist us though?" carried on Huda. "We know what lies the Pharaohs tell, their aptitude for corruption on a mammoth scale, and what low lives they are, this comes as nothing new to me."

Ammon said, "We haven't thought about it beyond that, we were just set on getting back."

"Will there be a way to use this knowledge with the Rosetta stone?" Huda asked.

The group fell into silence followed by bouts of discussion, each bringing them closer to their aim. Then Ammon, who had learnt the most about it during their trip to bring it back, began to elaborate his own version of how this can work.

"I've been digesting weighty tomes and can conclude that there is a way that the stone can be used in our favour. Its power can be reversed by scrambling up its varied hieroglyphics and inscriptions. This can be done simply by the act of taking a hammer and chisel to the ancient words and re-carving them. We will leave the rules as they have been broken by the pharaohs, so that the public know for perpetuity their wrongdoings, and what not to do themselves."

"Here, here!" cried Femi and Keket. "That sounds like a plan worth putting into action."

They fell into excited chatter then Huda took them to one side and gave each one a specified role.

"You will be responsible for recarving the stone," she said to Husain and Ammon. "Keket and Femi, you must go off and contact Kissa and Karim, tell them about what you learnt when you went to the pagan festival, and how that can contribute to their work. They might think it's a long shot, but it's worth a try."

Keket said, "Sounds plausible, we will do our best to accommodate. What about you, Huda?"

"I will stay here for now and make sure negotiations are kept running between us all. Once we have the power of the Rosetta stone, it will give us a psychological advantage. The pharaohs have been struggling anyway, I hear. Their leader, plus at least one other, has succumbed to a curse after a hunting trip, and rumour has it that it has put paid to his dark and dastardly sexual ways.

Femi said, "It's true about the curse, hearing this has increased my positivity, now I believe we are really in a place to sock it to the pharaohs. How else will society be changed?"

"There will be no more parties of decadence, hedonistic and erotically charged gatherings, especially not at our expense! Their plan with the love spells to conquer and bring all women under their power will be a thing of the past, there will be no more exploitation, and we will finally be on the path to liberation," cried Huda.

As they went their separate ways, Femi confided, "This pep talk with Huda has really inspired me; I believe we can do this."

"Me too, I'm feeling in a revolutionary mood," Keket replied.

The pair carried along on their way, back towards the neighbourhood where Karim and Kissa had set up their laboratory. It was a three hour walk across the city, and at this hour, the sun in the sky was like a burning rock, its core about to crack and split, spilling boiling hot magma upon the unsuspecting inhabitants of Cairo. It fell in red hot rays upon the backs of Femi and Keket as they meandered through the back streets.

All conversation dried up and they merely focused their efforts on putting one foot in front of another. When they began, they had urged each other on with rousing cries to build up their excitement. But now they could afford for no distractions, their goal was to make it before dusk. They pushed on, and as they came closer, they saw palm and date trees through the haze. Tubes, funnels, and long armed apparatus poked though the leafy foliage. Below was an open window where they were able to peer through, and found there were rows upon rows of stands, test tubes, and conical flasks inside.

"This must be the dwelling of Karim and Kissa," Femi said.

They hurried towards the house partly to escape the heat, and more so as they were eager to be reunited with old friends. It had been months since they had last cast eyes upon each other, and they all had a lot to share, not just upon the subject of the revolution. The pair had made a heroic effort in their quest to make beds and tests for the multitudes. Kissa marched into the street and greeted them; she motioned for them to follow her into the property.

"Come on in," said Kissa. "Come down to the basement where I witnessed multiple experimentations being carried out, concluding on so many occasions that we are almost there, but then, alas, Karim came trudging back upstairs with a crestfallen look upon his face."

Karim came running over, shouting out, "So close,

so many times but always beaten to the finish line by another possibility, a new hypothesis to try out, and always racing against the clock."

Kissa gave him a look combined of adoration and admiration; she had stars in her eyes. Keket and Femi were silent and listened before they broke down into tears, overcome with emotion.

"You've come so far," they replied in unison.

Femi tugged at Keket's robe. "Tell them about the spiritual animals we discovered at the pagan festival."

Keket took the hint and began recalling their adventurous trip.

"We witnessed a crocodile being hoisted from the waters of the Nile by a congenial villager. We asked him to run back in and get us another crocodile, which he did. After we went on to track down and bring back a scarab beetle, a serpent, and a cat too. Each creature has its associated magical powers, and it is hoped that merely by being in the presence of them, individual lives can be saved, and the mortality rate can be brought down. Some form of normality can be arrived at for the blighted people of this land."

Karim and Kissa had been listening with bated breath, but when they responded, it was with an air of caution.

"You can't trust these superstitious beliefs," Kissa told them, blowing the air out of their sails. They had been so hopeful of playing their part in the war on cholera.

"But what will we do with the animals now?" Femi asked, in a dispirited voice.

Keket groaned in appreciation but kept focused on

the more scientific approach offered by the pair.

"I guess we can let them back out into the wild," she said. "Either that or eat them. I don't fancy eating a beetle, though."

It was getting late, and Kissa invited them to stay overnight in their small outhouse.

"You can set off refreshed in the morning, Karim and I have much to do with regards to setting up new anti-cholera stations that will be responsible for the swift dispersal of all elements of the virus. We have ambitious plans and want to prove to the pharaohs that there is a far more humane way to go about with its management. They've made a total pig's ear of it," Kissa said, with emphasis.

Femi agreed. "I know four who've come a cropper to it, so with the rest of us, that makes sixteen!"

Keket, who had been listening, piped up, "Tell us more?"

Karim continued. "As well as a highly efficient system for coping with the rise in fatalities we want to have places where people can go to die in peace and dignity, these will work in the same way as elephant graveyards. People who know they are on their way out will be encouraged to go to these designated points, which will mostly be on the outskirts of the desert, and at a handful of locations by the sea. No other people will ever travel there and so the human bones will remain clean, pure, and untouched, gradually accruing in number until there is enough to build vast bone chapels. The dying will be given the task of constructing these huge architectural structures, which will be there for posterity and to preserve the will of the people.

They will serve as a poignant reminder of the pandemic and will arise shining and white from the steely hot sand, and in the full glare of the sun."

At this Femi said, "Won't they fall if the bones are about to disintegrate?"

Karim, who was in full flow, answered but off the point. "Even if people are suffering from cholera, they will be less likely to catch it because the bones are clean and free from any shred of the disease."

The more Karim spoke, the more Keket worried. "This doesn't sound like a realistic and scientifically sound way of dealing with the problem," she said. "If anything, it's not much better than the pharaohs with their mass cremation facilities. They put them up on the outskirts of the city where only the poor live, that gives the creeps to anyone."

Femi murmured in ascent, before coming out with, "If the people are as spiritual as they seem, tell them it's a place they can't avoid on the way to the afterlife, that its part of their beliefs, whatever they might be. If you can start spreading the word in temples and mosques, then it can blaze out of control, but all corners of society will get to hear about it."

Kissa was listening more avidly than Karim, and she said, "That's a great idea, but how do we go about pushing this forward? It's all well and good that the dog works been done in terms of developing new methods for fighting the disease, but how to go on?"

Then Keket, who was deep in thought for the last few minutes, cried out, "Why don't you come and join the revolution that Huda is initiating? That way you can be a part of resolving the problem first, then be in place at an early stage to offer your new system of management?"

Karim and Kissa answered together, "That might just work, you know."

"Huda wants to crush the pharaohs and put into play a whole new government. That will include immigration, defence, education, employment, as well as all the other departments. With your forward thinking, you would be an ideal nomination for health," Keket told the eager pair.

There was a silence as the four of them marvelled at this grand picture.

"Put in a good word for us next time you see Huda, tell her we want to be signed up, too," said Karim.

Keket and Femi left early the next day before the heat became an issue. They had a long journey, and much to tell Huda when they get back. They left Karim and Kissa to their own devices; they had much to be getting on with. The journey back to the lodging house took them through the city centre, and Keket wanted to stop at the market for supplies. Most of the traders had gone but there was a lone figure in the depths of the gloom who had a small pushcart, in front of them.

Keket called to Femi who was following behind, and the pair of them approached. The trader had fresh fruit, coconuts, dried biscuits, camels' milk, and they bought a bottle which they guzzled greedily. They were standing around making conversation.

Femi asked, "How has your business been of late?

The trader said, "I've been suffering badly, but this morning one visitor stands out far more than the rest.

She has the air of somebody dignified and haughty, but at the same time she is warm and friendly. She asks about my family and how the pandemic has affected us all, then she leaves giving me a huge tip."

"Maybe it was one of the pharaohs wives, though they don't usually shop on their own, they'll usually have at least one slave in tow, so you know who they are."

He continued his description of her, and as they puzzled over various people that it might be, Nitocris herself came waltzing past.

"That's her," cried the vendor and Nitocris halted within good social distancing, then began to relate tales of her newfound distrust with Augustuskamoun.

"His infidelity is even worse now," she said. "He recently suffered the loss of his manhood and used it as an excuse to be examined in the nether regions, by a young tart. I don't trust him a bit."

Femi was aghast, but Keket was more worldly and had heard tales about Eshe's experience from Huda. She knew their wicked ways.

"Nitocris, why don't you come and join a peaceful revolution to turn back the clocks on the ever-growing wall of masculine authority? We feel there is a more balanced society that can be formed, and we can be the seeds for its germination. Why not come and join us?" Keket said.

Nitocris stopped in shock. She hadn't known anything else, having been brought up for generations in the best families that were around. But then regained her senses quickly and snapped out of it.

Keket continued. "The pharaohs have been grinding

their axe over our species for too long now, and it's not just women, it's all the other disadvantaged groups. Different races, religions, sexual orientations, immigrants, as well as anyone who works directly for them, such as slaves or servants, you name it, the list is endless. Will you promise to pass on the word to the other pharaoh's wives?"

"Oh, do you mean Twosret and Cleopatra? Of course, I'll make sure it gets to them, but I can't see them making the change, they've been too far indoctrinated now, for many years. They're used to being treated as second class citizens, being the playthings of the rich. Centre of attention until they get married off, then pushed into the background, as more shapely and comely offerings bring themselves to the fore." Nitocris was scathing.

They wound the conversation up and the three of them went on their way, escorting Nitocris to the lodging house to meet Huda. The heat was merciless now, and they could only cover short distances out of the shadows, having to use parasols to barrage the full brunt of the sun. Their pace was slow, but they still had time to discuss Augustuskamoun's condition, and how he was doing with the curse.

"It's making its way through his whole body," Nitocris said. "Rendering all limbs, organs, cells, and tissues lifeless as it passes through. The diagnosis has been terminal so far from the latest priests and spiritual doctors he's sought solace with."

There was a sigh of relief from Keket and Femi, and they made a mental note to inform Huda when they saw her.

Nitocris carried on. "One of the doctors suggests that it might be a wise idea for him to get his books straightened up, though we all know that this will be an endless task. He might also do well to have his last rites read to him, or to seek the services of somebody dependable to mummify his huge and grossly overweight form."

The pair of them both scratched their heads, then Keket remembered Tarek. She had met him several times before and knew that he had recently changed his trade.

"Tarek! He would be ideal. If we could get him to come over and carry out this mammoth task, that would be the answer," she said.

As they continued along their way, Nitocris came back to the subject of a peaceful revolution.

"How will that work?"

"Huda has it all planned out," Keket said. "She wants to bring the pharaohs down one by one using the curse. It's already torn its way through two of them and shouldn't take much longer to bring the whole rotten order down. Once that is done, we will be in with a chance of taking eventual control."

They kept pushing on, the streets were silent now as they passed through, not a soul about, most locked up either sleeping or social distancing.

"Strange and eerie times," Femi was heard to say in the background.

It wasn't as if they ignored her, but they were too engrossed trying to navigate so they didn't get lost. They wanted to be back at the lodging house before sunset, and were chasing endless shadows down streets, each one getting longer as the hours slipped away. They passed the familiar towering statues of Anubis and Osiris. Then they looked up and saw an immense pyramid, down one edge thronged millions of cockroaches, crickets, and scorpions.

Femi said, "That should bring us luck."

As they continued walking, Nitocris was happy to talk about her relationships with Twosret and Cleopatra and the effect the pandemic had on all of them.

"None of us have struggled that badly, for obvious reasons. Their partners, Ramses and Pepi, after they got involved in the party at the test centre, we never saw them again. Pepi's sordid fling is a national shame and almost ruined his marriage and reputation, but in the end, they rank him more highly for his mischievous ways, which they just see as good-humoured male japery. Ramses isn't much better, he got involved in trying to brainwash the population back into shopping again."

They were so engrossed in their conversation that they didn't notice they were almost at their destination, and as they turned the corner, a sight greeted them that they knew well. The overhanging cranes and telegraph poles of the festival sprouted high above various tents and marquees that had been erected at short notice.

Keket said in a lowered voice, "Be quiet as we approach the house, it is getting late, we don't want to disturb the neighbours."

She gave them a hush, and all three members sailed through into the main room. Huda sat at a table on her own, doling out instructions.

"Husain and Ammon, go to the basement to work on the stone, it's such a messy job."

It was the first time that Huda had met Nitocris, and for a minute she was agog, not recognizing this well-dressed person, so well-spoken too. *She must be related to the pharaohs,* she thought.

Keket stepped in and gave formal introductions explaining how they met, and Nitocris' recent change of attitude.

"Nitocris has been through much pain and heartache," she explained, "after having to deal with the pharaohs and their wives for so long. Now she has come over to our side and she wants to assist us in any way she can. She's well connected and can help us with the many different plans and programs the pharaohs have lined up for us."

Huda was extremely impressed to see this woman who had been through so much, *Most would never come across to our way of thinking, it means they must give up the good life,* she thought.

Nitocris wanted to speak to Huda on a personal level, so Keket and Femi arranged to go down and see how Husain and Ammon were getting on. They stumbled down the stairs and were greeted by clouds of billowing dust, and the constant smashing of hammer and chisel.

"What are you two up to?" Keket said. "It sounds as if you're trying to rewrite history"

"Not far off," said Ammon. "We've been asked to remove all traces of the original inscriptions and for it to be replaced by a common Egyptian script, something that can be read by the masses and misleads no one."

"What did it say before then?" said Femi.

Ammon replied, "We only know this because Husain recalls a small amount of ancient Egyptian dialect, otherwise we would have been completely in the dark."

"Husain?" he called.

A tiny voice piped up, restricted beneath the heavy breathing that was taking its best out of him.

"They are plain instructions of how individuals should live, work, play, educate, and govern themselves, but in a heavily oppressive way, of course. This would probably have been one of the first tablets of learning for the pharaohs, and all deeper studies will have stemmed from that," Husain told the others.

"Or what we might call regressive knowledge," laughed Keket.

Meanwhile, upstairs, Nitocris was having a heart to heart with Huda, and the two women were now resolved in their attitudes and had forged an alliance. Nitocris thought, *we are both from radically different backgrounds, but we each have a deep reverential respect for the others position. Huda is a strong and independently minded feminist, and I am a proud and defiant ancestor of centuries of wisdom and honour. But no… this is what I am trying to escape!* And she hoped by speaking to Huda that she could learn and improve her outlook. She wanted the rest of the group to take her onboard, so that they would marvel at her progress in bringing those barriers down and achieve a new mutual level.

"Huda," Nitocris said. "Will you sign me up? I've been through such pains with Augustuskamoun, I can't be part of a society which is perpetually looking backwards. The pharaohs have no respect for anyone, not even when Twosret, Cleopatra and I got married to them. We were hoping for monogamous ways, but no such luck."

Huda looked up with an expression of tenderness and said with pity, "This is the only way we can teach the pharaohs. It has been passed down to me for many generations that the only way to fight them is with fire."

"Keket tells me this will be a peaceful revolution though," Nitocris said.

"It will be," came Huda's reply. "We are just waiting for the curse to do its work, as it rampantly travels between them, quicker than any virus can travel."

"How else can I help?" Nitocris asked.

Huda allocated Nitocris the role of being a messenger. "It's imperative that we can communicate well in these times, and that means that you will need to be fleet of foot. Quick and cunning, able to dart like an arrow, whether on the battlefields, on urban terrain, the desert, or underground at a subterranean level. Over sand you must fly without coming a cropper and falling to your peril or tripping and tumbling to your knees."

Nitocris nodded fervently, she wished to show her allegiance to the cause.

Huda took her to one side and said, "We believe in you and have no reason to suspect you might try to upset the finely tuned balance that we have been trying to ascertain."

Then they hugged to show their newfound trust in one another.

Huda whispered in her ear. "Can you deliver a message to the pharaohs? That we have our eye on them; tell them to look out for the curse and the damage it may reap."

Nitocris nodded and went on her way. Meanwhile the rest of the group came bumbling back upstairs.

Femi blurted out, "We learnt so much from Ammon about the stone, but how are we going to get it out into the public, so we can raise public awareness?"

"By recarving the text, we will make the stone more accessible to many groups, and we will improve our understanding tenfold. Through this we will know what they've done wrong, and how best for us to proceed. We will learn the best way to protect our own tribes of people, rather than having to rely on their shoddy government," Huda replied.

"Here, here!" cried Femi.

Nitocris was knocked back by the heat and the noise of the street. Constant pushing and shoving as she went through the market, now the lockdown had been lifted. *So stressful,* she thought. She was heading for the pyramid again, to warn the pharaohs that their reign was soon to be terminated, and they had to make short shrift of it.

She bumped into Narmer and Nefertiti and passed on the news, but as soon as they saw her, they began ridiculing her. When she told them she had given up her claim to the throne and the dynasty, they cackled and threw taunts at her.

"Your stupidity is incredible!" Narmer shouted.

Nitocris hit back because those accusations were stinging, and with the loss of trust that she had just suffered, she was in no place to argue her cause.

"You pair are cruel harbingers of the law," she said.

They both kept laughing manically, and as they ran

off, Nitocris screamed behind them. "Go spread the word about the curse to the rest of the pharaohs; your whole race will soon come tumbling down. The love spells have had their day, now it's the time of the curse to bring about the halt of the empire."

Nitocris didn't expect to receive an answer. *They will have been on their way back to the central pyramid,* she thought. She was right, they were on their way back, and when they arrived, the first person they saw was the transparent looking apparition of Augustuskamoun himself. He had less than a shadow of his normal booming voice, it was as if a cancer had been eating away at his insides. Nefertiti prodded Narmer in the stomach with her elbow and mentioned.

"He doesn't look a ruddy cheeked picture of health, does he?"

Narmer agreed, and as the pair kept walking, they told all they saw of the curse. As they rounded a corner, they bumped into Djoser and Snefru, who were looking in even worse shape than Augustuskamoun. Djoser tried to speak but his voice was a mere shadow of its normal self, his strength had gone completely and now he could hardly hold himself upright. Snefru came to his aid offering his hand, and a place to sit on the ground nearby.

"The curse has fallen both of us," he said. "Ever since that eventful hunting trip. I blame it on our leader, nothing positive came out of that one."

"True," said Djoser in a thinning voice.

Snefru looked gloomy, almost defeated, as he said,

"To begin with I had high hopes for us, but things have gone from bad to worse. Now we have nothing, not even our health and ability to reproduce!" His voice sounded hoarse. Was he going to cry?

Djoser was silent. "I think he's just slipped away," said Snefru, sorrowfully. "Narmer and Nefertiti, I'll probably be next."

And he tried to grapple with the full gravity of the situation; tried to understand that things of great importance were always difficult on your own. So, when Snefru saw the rest of the pharaohs coming around the corner, he began pleading and begging for them to save his soul, and to pass on the morbid conundrum that they all faced.

Ramses was heading up the rest of the group as they went from tomb to tomb, and tried to deliberate the cause of the curse, and whether there was a way to stop its insidious path. Nefertiti doubled back and was just in time to see Djoser's eyes close, and what she thought might be his spirit ascend to the heavens.

"Well, I hope I'm treated the same way," she cried out.

Narmer and Khafre laughed politely, remembered tales of how badly she taught her own constituents, as well as those of her colleagues. The rest of the group had now caught up; they had been ambling along behind. A small entourage of slaves who were carrying feather fans were in attendance, and threw down palm leaves as they walked, so they won't damage their delicate feet. Pepi and Seti were among them, and they began berating the death of Djoser, then beating furiously at their chests as if to trying to drive the anger from themselves.

"What if we are next?" Pepi said.

"We are set to be," cried Nefertiti, and her eyes blazed with fear.

Ramses tried to step in to calm the situation, he could see that people were seriously worried about this. Narmer didn't seem to be bothered and said, "I have a whole battalion of corpses at my palace, they can be used as currency to make sure I make it to the afterlife with the least possible concern."

Ramses and Khufu gave low whistles, impressed by his sheer hard-nosed business manner, then fell over themselves trying to ingratiate themselves with him.

Khufu said, "Maybe you can share yours, Narmer? And we can benefit in the same way. All pharaohs are capable of doing the most heinous of things, not one has a single shred of respect for themselves, or those around them. But what's the best way for us to proceed?"

Narmer's silence spoke volumes.

"This curse is likely to be our downfall," Ramses said.

He was met by puzzled expressions, partly of selfish concern, and looking blindly for solutions. Then Khafre asked, "Why don't we try a new direction, an alternative approach?"

"How would that work?" Seti answered.

"By removing our guilt from the equation," Khafre said, "then our conscience will be clear."

There was a murmur of disgruntlement from the other pharaohs who weren't happy with this idea.

Khafre went on, "Regardless of how many people fall to their deaths under our power, we will never be assailed by that feeling again."

He was booed down by the rest of the group, arguing

that they were better off with their original plan.

Then Nefertiti stepped forward and pledged to be their leader to the bitter end, "I will sacrifice myself for you all," she said.

"But what does that mean you will do?" Ramses asked.

Nefertiti replied, "I will guarantee your transition to the far side will be smooth. All you need to do is make sure you cross the palm of the ferryman with three gold doubloons. Then he will allow you to pass over to the other side."

There was a cry of rousing encouragement for Nefertiti, irrespective of her bullying ways.

"If we can trust her, then our future will be rest assured," Seti joined in. "How and when will this take place?"

Nefertiti replied, "Come and see me when you are at your lowest ebb, like Djoser, Augustuskamoun, and Snefru, when it feels like you are almost spent."

The remaining pharaohs began shouting to show their camaraderie, that this was a viable option.

Chapter Seventeen

It turned out that Tarek had already got wind of events, with regards to their national ruler. It was amazing how quickly news about the demise of Djoser, and the increasingly bad health of Snefru and Augustuskamoun, travelled. His first reaction was relief, shortly followed by a sense of anxiety for who will employ him when they were gone. *There's plenty of rich folk in this country, but they were to be my bread and butter,* he thought.

"Nour," he said, as he was preparing his bag to leave. "A number of the pharaohs have passed on, and I'm worried it might get in the way of what I am planning to do with the workshops."

"Don't be silly, with this recent windfall of Eshe's money, things won't be so bad after all," she told him, then said, "What will you do with the bodies that you've collected from Narmer's? Are they going to be left here?"

"I was aiming to use them for practise but never really got the opportunity last night. Maybe we can keep them in storage?"

Nour shuddered thinking about this and arranged for them to be buried by the slave, before sending him packing back off to the palace. Tarek had arranged to be at the central pyramid before noon, but he had a few errands to run on the way.

"I must pop in to pick up supplies of resin, date leaves, and the other ingredients I need from the herbarium," he said, before he left to go to his first official workshop, whistling a joyful tune.

The herbarium was a place that functioned as a small garden allotment, and the owners ran a shop over the weekends where people could pick up various homegrown and sourced Egyptian goods. It was on the way to the palace, and Tarek had to cross the centre of town. The temperature was soaring now, and he was forced to crawl at a sluggish pace.

His bag was soaked in sweat, and he mopped his brow. He felt beads of perspiration dripping down. *How can I carry on in this heat,* he thought, and pulled over under the shade of a towering statue of the deity, Ra. He was balancing a huge burning orb of solar powered energy in his hands, and it fizzled and spat.

Then Tarek felt each globe exploding in his wake, as if Ra was bombarding him for pleasure. He was pushed to great speeds by this and in no time, found himself at the bazaar. *This is where I can source the requirements for my recipe,* he mused and without further ado or hesitation, he plunged into the cool depths of the building.

Its walls were of bamboo and date palm leaves that had been knotted and woven together, and they allowed for some ventilation to pass through. There wasn't a breeze inside, and the atmosphere felt as if it could be pierced by a knife. He hollered into the darkness hoping for somebody to come, then heard the gruff voice of the vendor.

Enveloped in a cloud of cigarette smoke and seated at the head of a vast table, the vendor had spread before him innumerable herbs and spices, as well as dried and salted conserves. It was a veritable feast!

There were dates, raisins, figs, biscuits, and sacksful of sugar, cocoa, and flour. Huge jars of sweet treats, such as nuts soaked in honey, were towering above.

Right at the back behind the vendor were urns of syrup, and various oils, such as olive and peanut.

Tarek motioned for one and said, "Pass me sesame and resin, please?"

The vendor pulled out its glass stopper and began filling a small bag that Tarek proffered towards him.

"I must have extract of bullrushes too," Tarek said.

The vendor knew not to ask questions where no curiosity was invited. He didn't say a word, and the trade was made. He was a man of limited means, and he always held out for a hard bargain, not letting Tarek leave until a fair price had been arrived at. Tarek promised to drop several more items with him next time.

As he left the man, Tarek bade him farewell.

"Steer clear of the virus!"

The vendor looked back appreciatively and wished him the same for himself and his family. Tarek concealed the goods in his bags, where they were secure and would not fall out. Then, taking his stick, he struck out into the main street. The avenue was wide and to both sides' hoardings dangled from columns, each advertised regular usage of calcium that would do your bones good.

"I'm sick of these adverts," he said to himself.

To both sides, Sphinx reached as far as the eye could see. It was difficult to make out their individual outline and shape clearly, because of the haze and the shimmer of heat that pulsated from the ground. Tarek knew that by following this path he wouldn't get lost, and that around halfway along, a smaller passage bore left which took him down to a lower level, and gradually underground, through a long tunnel. He continued out of the shade of the sun for a while, other minerals sparkling in the stone above him. Tarek gazed up, transfixed by their beauty, then carried along on his way.

The tunnel burst out at ground level, then he was back on a busy highway, surrounded by carts, chariots, and wheeled wagons, people pushed them faster than he could walk. He was bustled from one side to another for a while, and people cried at him.

"Keep out the way!"

A cart passed. Its passenger sat in a tomb that protected them from all sides. A rough window had been hewn from the stone at the front, to the top there was a system of tubes and glass funnels for assisted breathing. As Tarek gazed about, he saw others race by, one wore a suit of fine linen that covered his person. Another had a huge sheet that covered his body making him look like a cocoon, with piping passing between his nose and mouth.

Tarek saw a rectangular structure with sharpened rods of bamboo at its corners. A long roll off linen had been wrapped around the canes so it wouldn't come free. As he peered into this vehicle as it passed, he could only make out the fuzzy outline of a figure concealed behind it. All the makeshift vehicles around him were travelling in the same direction, heading towards the palace. They all began to slow gradually and manoeuvre themselves into position around a huge square.

Each vehicle angled themselves so they could see into

the square, which for now was empty.

Shortly after that he heard the marching of tens of thousands of feet on the hardened mud. As he looked up, he saw a sea of slaves in battle formation each holding a shield to their sides and top. Either side huge pyramids rose with a towering entrance, that had been cut from the stone and lined with mud bricks. There was a great fanfare of trumpets, these were usually only played on military exercises to intimidate enemies, or to signal for other troops. Tarek looked about, fearful that an arrow or an axe might whistle passed his ear, but was reassured by a diligent audience of structures, standing tall, each within its protective device.

Tarek tried to speak to the one next to him but received no answer. *If there is anybody in there, I bet they can't even hear?* he thought. There was a warrior stood to one side whipping a young slave, and Tarek called over to intervene. The pair went on without saying a word, then once they had finished, the warrior addressed him more officially.

"What do you want?"

"I want to know what the solemn occasion is for. Why the melancholic blowing of trumpets and sombre beating of tambourines?" asked Tarek.

"The great Augustuskamoun has passed away," came the warrior's reply. "Did you not hear the latest news?"

"I'm not surprised, judging by what I've heard about his failing health. There have been rumours of him being brought down by a curse, too, that's going about. Now I realize it's not strictly gossip."

Tarek looked about him, and the great clouds of dust and sand which were billowing up already, there was talk of a storm on its way. *Those in their protective suits will be fine,* he thought, *but the rest of us are going to be engulfed.*

The pyramids were already lost to view, only their entrances could be seen. Suddenly, the central procession began to snake its way towards the coastline. Tarek got up onto his tiptoes and could just about see an immense tomb, laden with various flowers, garlands, and other small gifts that had been left for his highness.

Tarek thought, *People have left sacred mummified creatures all over: bulls, crocodiles, cats, falcons, scarabs, and ibises. They are more princely and will escort him in his swift departure to the next life. There are no domestic creatures such as monkeys, dogs, cats, or geese to be seen. These are all pets which are favourable and much loved by the people. That doesn't surprise me, Augustuskamoun was never really known for his human touch, let alone towards animals.* He craned his neck and just about made out the tail end of the funeral parade disappearing. *Where will they take him next?*

Now the crowds had died down, Tarek continued along his way, into the sultry streets nearby. The sun beat down on the opposite plane of the pyramid, and he was afforded a brief respite of coolness as he climbed its steps, stopping to speak with a cholera sufferer. The poor devil was surrounded by flies and a void of silence.

The man cried as he left. "The pharaohs are an insufferable bunch; many lives could have been saved!"

"How do you mean?" Tarek said, as he slowed up.

"They made no effort to save any lives, so anyone who survived is considered a small miracle. Even the high priests and elders at the temple are affected. They have been snowed under with people praying and throwing themselves at their feet."

"Did it make any difference?" Tarek asked.

"Not one iota," the man sighed. "We are all left to our own devices, and they put their own salvation first."

Tarek moved on, he flew like the wind, his satchel was full to overflowing so he didn't need to make any more stops along the way. He took a left and a right, then he was passing through a huge square with a ceiling of tightly interlaced palms, the lull in the temperature was welcome, so he stopped to gather his thoughts happy in the knowledge he wouldn't get lost.

He knew he was only five minutes away, and once he had taken a breather, he proceeded on the rest of the journey and it was not long before he was yelling through an open window into an enormous room, dug out from the sandstone. It had a framework of scaffolding which was walled by mud bricks. As Tarek peered around, a commanding voice told him to step with good grace into the back of the building, and Tarek obeyed, treading with a light foot. It was a distant cousin of Augustuskamoun, who introduced himself cordially, but with an air of mistrust.

Tarek saw a mischievous and deviant glint in the cousin's eye, as he peered to see beneath the brim of the fine linen parasol. He was trying to keep himself under its shade, and he had to raise his voice for Tarek to hear properly.

"Why are you here?"

Tarek offered his satchel as proof for his visit, and seeing the requisite ingredients that were required for embalming, the man stepped to one side and let him in.

"We have a corpse for you to operate on," he said with a thin laugh. "It's been kept in the basement, so it won't start to putrefy," and he beckoned to Tarek with a gnarled and bony finger.

Tarek gulped with fear; he was paranoid and afraid. *This man can push me down the stairs, throttle me, then use my body in any way he pleases,* he thought. He stepped lightly to quieten his descent into the lower room. It opened out in front of him, the walls were hung with huge rolled up scrolls of parchment, upon each were symbols and hieroglyphics. There were small columns and on top of each one was a treasure box with a tightly clasped lid. There were hangings that draped down from the ceiling with instructions for the correct praising of Osiris.

Tarek stepped forward and read with difficulty, gradually summonsing the god from his slumber.

"I am about to conduct an embalming," he told Osiris, when questioned as to why he had been awoken.

Osiris rolled off a platform nearby and buried his face in his hands, then went on wailing and tried to summon up the darkest spirits of the underworld.

Osiris called, "Hatayw," into the air, and a marble platform rolled across, revealing the long since dead ruler of Tutankhamun, one of Augustuskamoun's distant cousins. Then a tongue of flame came from the mouth of the figure and its arms elevated to both sides. There was a hellish din and Tarek quaked with fear, as he cowered in a corner next to a boulder. He was partly sheltered there but not when the cries of Diablos began, and the evil serpents beat their blackened wings, leaving great sooty marks all about the room.

"This is the body of the great Augustuskamoun," the shivering voice of Osiris cried out, "this is the cadaver that you must embalm."

Tarek took the cue and hastened for his bag, then pulled the relevant equipment together.

"For this I will need one of these, one of those, and one of those," said Tarek assembling all the necessary items.

Then he broke into a long sigh, it was more of a dirge if the truth be told, and it was to assure that the body had passed away. Tarek knew this was the great ruler and approached his vast frame, his pure and sacrosanct form. He started digging about under the skin of the body, the start of the whole gruesome process that he needed to undergo, that was to be his ordeal. Scratching its sensitive surface began to raise light particles, cells and shreds of skin went billowing up into the air like a feather cushion recently burst.

Suddenly the whole room was covered in the tissue of the virus, and it floated about infecting every crevice, nook, and cranny. Tarek realised what it was and grabbed his nose, and mouth, running for cover.

He shouted, "I'm not likely to catch cholera, I've done so well up until now."

Tarek pulled a scarf up over his face to his eyeballs. *I can't leave yet; my work is unfinished. I must stay and finish what I've started,* he thought. He had heard stories about the first unwrapping that occurred, and he assumed that this must be similar. He didn't understand that Augustuskamoun's misshapen form and grinning skull full of dentures, will be emblazoned upon his memory banks for perpetuity.

He pulled out his knife and worked it around the edges of his body, and not blood and organs ran out, but clouds of dust and thick cobwebs that fell to the floor. *This man must have been dead for many years,* he thought, *still, I must carry on.* He pulled out his bag and took up a bowl that was lying nearby, then began pouring quantities of salt into it, grabbed a nearby brush, and worked it into the seams and wrinkles of the obese and flabby form.

Once he had finished, he left the body to preserve, sealing up the eyes, the nostrils, and the mouth, before departing from the basement. As he passed through the house, he bade the servants farewell and informed them that he would be back in a few weeks.

"It's best for you to leave the room, as it is my belief that there's a huge cholera count in the air, it must have escaped whilst I was working on the body. When I return the salt will have done its work in curing his body, and it will be ready for the next step," Tarek told them.

A servant saw him off and Tarek stumbled out into the harsh, bright sunlight, adjusting his eyes after so long underground. He was making his way along one of the central walkways that wound up in the centre, when suddenly he heard a friendly and familiar voice from behind, which he recognized instantly. *It's that of my wife, Nour,* he thought. *She must be with Femi, Keket, Huda, and the rest of the group.* As they pulled over it was as if she'd read his mind.

Nour said, "I bumped into them earlier, they were heading over to Karim and Kissa's place to build up their numbers. Huda hasn't even met that pair yet, so it will be a good opportunity for them to see if they can work together in some way," Nour confirmed to Tarek.

Tarek agreed to tag along for a while, but urged them to stop beforehand, as he had grave news for them.

"Augustuskamoun, our great leader, has passed away; I've seen it with my own eyes."

There were cries of joy, yelps of pleasure and happiness, and excited whistles, they were so happy to be rid of him. But Keket didn't believe him, so she asked Tarek to prove it.

Tarek said, "Trust me, I've just left his body, I was carrying out an embalming which I had been sent along for earlier on. I was working away when suddenly, there was a huge explosion of cholera molecules in the air. I kept working as the task had to be finished but rest assured that the God of massacre is dead."

"He must be telling the truth, why would he lie?" Femi asked.

Nour also offered support to her husband.

"In a few weeks I've got to go back to finish the embalming off, but until then we are pretty much free to do as we please." Tarek grinned.

"Apart from the rest of the pharaohs, that are still loose," cried Huda. "Only three have succumbed to the curse so far."

"So how do you propose to finish them off?" Keket asked.

"It's just a waiting game, is how I see it," she replied. "We need to go and park ourselves somewhere, settle in for the long haul. Once Nitocris gets back, she will have more updated news of how the pharaohs are coping, whether they are falling like flies, or if we need to up our game."

The rest of the group was quiet; nobody would argue with her wise words.

Tarek said, "Why don't you come with me to the place where Augustuskamoun's body is, then you can see for yourselves if it's still alive or not."

"There's no need for you to prove it," Femi cried.

The hour was still early, and so they departed with Tarek at their lead. He promised to call into a couple of places enroute, where they could pick up food for the next few days, as well as to top up his own supplies that were running low. They must pass through the Valley of the Kings to get there, and a small road ran through its centre. To the left and right, mammoth sandstone statues of each pharaoh stood towering eerily above them.

They all bore a golden symbol in their outstretched hands, which represented their subject: Ramses with a saucer of coins overflowing, Nefertiti with a stamp, Snefru held a winged wheel and a spoke from the axle of a chariot, Seti had a pile of bricks, Djoser a stethoscope, Narmer a pile of books, and Khafre a catapult.

Each glared menacingly at their opposite member, they were supposed to illustrate intellect, liberty, justice, all the great and endearing factors of the pharaohs. *That is debateable,* thought Tarek, as he wandered beneath. The group struck up a conversation as they walked, and as the temperatures were searing, they thought conversation would help to keep themselves awake and mentally alert.

Huda said, "What did Djoser ever do for us and the great cholera pandemic?"

"They set up test centres, sourced vaccines, and made sure we have the necessary equipment for doing tests. Really, we know they did nothing, all the budget that should have gone towards these things was frittered away on sending Khufu Robertson up and down the country to find places where they could escape too, if the lockdown got the better of them. In the end they never even followed up on his leads, he got caught in flagrante with some young dancing girl at an all-night party." Keket said, in disgust.

"Karim and Kissa have done as much as they have but on less than half the budget. They sourced the supplies they need by scavenging and relying on the assistance of goodwill from friends, and people who lent them a property to set up a laboratory. As for the rest of the pharaohs, when they stole off to have that party..." Femi's words petered out.

"You mean Augustuskamoun, Ramses, Seti, and Pepi, they were all involved in that. Nitocris told me that was one of the actions which pushed her over the edge, and made her yearn for an alternative society, where she wouldn't be in danger of encountering that type of behaviour anymore. We've always been at loggerheads with them, we're from two entirely different backgrounds but there must be common ground with politics," Keket replied.

"Not with the pharaohs though," shouted Huda. "They take their two penny's worth, and don't give back a dime."

Their voices reverberated from the vast rockfaces

surrounding them, echoing up into the quiet solitude of the afternoon.

Each member of the group tied their lip, and not a word more was spoken until they arrived at the other side of the vast plain of desert they had been traversing. As they ascended between boulders, stunted trees, and weathered and beaten thorny shrubs, they looked to Tarek for leadership.

"Tell us which way to go?" Femi said.

He beckoned to them to follow his lead, and he bolted down a small tunnel that came out by a rocky stairwell. From here, they followed him leaping from one stepping-stone to another, bringing them out at the opposite side of the valley.

Tarek answered, "We must head towards the top, over the ridge, then back down the ravine on the other side."

As they walked, they stumbled on the rocks and brought an avalanche of pebbles down behind them. They began to pass through an area which descended into pure white, everything had been bleached by the sun, including logs, stones and tree trunks that littered the sand. It was difficult to see so they used their hands to shade their eyes.

Keket said, "Do you think we've found the elephants graveyard?"

Femi joined in. "Karim and Kissa's plan to find a more humane solution for the ever-spiralling death toll from cholera, is a truly magnificent effort."

"It's a noble thing that they aspire to," said Tarek. "It's truly a problem, but I don't believe an elephants graveyard will solve it."

He continued walking along an ancient path, mostly composed of shells and bones that had been trampled flat over the years. As he looked up at the mountains around him, they were white with traces of various minerals running through them. In this white-hot atmosphere, they mingled like a rainbow spectrum of colours. He was lost in his own reflections and out of contact with the rest of the group for a while, then he heard them calling him back. Slowly he began coming back around, he heard Femi's incessant pleading.

"Tarek, Tarek, are you still with us?"

It seemed as if he stumbled and fell on the path, twisted his ankle. Femi drew out supplies of water from her bag and doused a little around his mouth, he slurped it up gratefully.

"I haven't had a drink for a while and I am beginning to hallucinate," he said. "The mountains around here have salt crystals in them; I must have ingested it into my skin and it's causing me to suffer from dehydration."

Then he grabbed the nearest two rocks and began chipping them against each other.

"I must collect more salt for the preservation of Augustuskamoun's body," Tarek said.

He was busy with this for a while before jumping back up to his feet and summoning the rest of the group to join him.

"Let's carry on along our way, we must make it back before sundown."

Then Femi said, "Why don't you buy a test when you get back to the centre? You said you think you might have been exposed to the virus recently."

Tarek agreed, "I don't mind testing."

They dropped down quickly, and before they knew it, they could see the ever-expanding metropolis of Cairo opening out before them, dotted with pyramids, temples, mosques, statues, and sphinx. They were almost at sea level again, though still a long way off.

The first ramshackle parade of huts they came across had a board in the window offering free cholera test kits, Tarek ran in and told the owner he would like to have one. She was a friendly soul, but had suffered badly with the virus, having lost half of her family. Tarek and she spoke for a while, he offered his best wishes to the woman and hoped that things would improve for her.

She passed him a test, and he thrust it into his bag, as he stepped back outside. It was nearing tea-time and the rest of the group though keen to get on, wanted to have a break for refreshments, before they made their way into the city. They cracked open the snacks and drinks they had with them and began talking about the events of that day, mostly whether Tarek might test positive for cholera. They talked in lowered voices and every time he looked around, they quietened down, paranoid that he might hear them.

"Why do we have to be so gossipy about this," said Femi. "Let's confront him, there's no point making him more edgy about the whole thing."

Then she went across to Tarek and demanded, "Give me an entire recollection of your movements, so that we can backtrack and assess all those you might have met and infected along the way?"

He was quiet for a moment as he tried to calculate

the numbers, but then he said, very quietly, "That would be you. You, and Huda, Keket and Nour."

Femi's reaction was of shock, and she said, "None of us have been infected by cholera to date, most have either been trying to keep away from it as if it's the plague, or otherwise, hoping that some form of herd immunity may happen. How could you expose us to the potential of the virus!"

Keket joined in, "Neither me nor Femi want to speak to you, Tarek."

Tarek thought, *this is totally unreasonable, how can it be my fault? Maybe it is because I came into close contact with a pharaoh?* Only Huda and Nour would speak to him.

"Huda, pass it onto the rest of the group to follow me, I will have to isolate, and if you've all been infected, you'll have to do the same. Why don't we go back down to the house where I was working on Augustuskamoun, then at least we can stay there until we test negative again?"

Keket replied, "That's stupid, if we are free of the virus, then if we follow you, we run the risk of becoming infected."

Femi agreed, and they make plans to find Ammon, Husain, Karim, and Kissa.

"If anybody wants to come with us, they can," Femi said.

Tarek with his head hung low made off on his own, Nour and Huda having ran off to join Femi and Keket. He continued along his way, counting the people he saw who he knew were cholera sufferers. You could usually tell by the dejection in the eye. Then he realized this was probably making him feel worse, so he lifted his gaze away from the people, and took in the landscape instead, something that always reassured him.

The gently elevating rise and fall of the mud brick structures they called home, the grandiose architecture of cultural institutions, libraries, temples, and mosques. The vain and grandiloquent monstrosities which functioned as the pharaoh's palaces came next, dotting the horizon in smaller numbers. He thought, *why do we have to be controlled by these cruel tyrants?*

Tarek took a left turn which ran him alongside a pyramid, which he knew of old. As far back as he remembered, stories had been handed down about the construction of these valiant structures. Vast armies of men had built these pantheons of power. They were controlled by the pharaohs, but the ordinary people were still proud of the part they played.

He tried to imagine each man standing his ground in the pyramid, supporting one another on their shoulders. He imagined he could hear the tumultuous sound of activity, followed by the buzzing of bees, it was as if each man worked the hive for its queen. Fetched and brought vital supplies of honey back and forth, then re-pollinated flowers and plants in the outside world.

It's not much different from the spreading of the viruses, then his thoughts came crashing back down to reality and he came back from his make believe world. *I must accept the justice that has been meted out on me by the gods of cholera, but I am only a mortal man. If I do my isolation as stipulated, I may never see the rest of the group again, including my Nour. The treasures endowed upon us by Eshe, mean at least she will have a better quality of life, irrespective of whether I ever manage to break the burden of my solitude and get to see the light of a new day.*

🛕

Chapter Eighteen

Once Ammon and Husain finished recarving the Rosetta stone, they sat back to admire their handiwork.

"I think we've done a good job of it," said Ammon.

His father was older and more reserved in his outlook and opinions, but he agreed.

"We've made it readable for future generations, as well as our own to understand," Husain said. "Now the rules each read as they should, telling of various laws set out by the pharaohs that they themselves have undermined. What's the next step then? As we never discussed this with the rest of the group."

Ammon replied, "I think we need to return it to its source, in the layer underground, or in a more prominent place, this time where more people can come across it."

"That's a brilliant idea," said Husain, "where exactly?"

They both racked their brains for a while and then Husain said, "Why don't we hoist it up onto the top of one of the pyramids, or the sphinx, deposit it at the souk? It must be a place that will really spit in the face of the pharaohs, make it obvious that there's been plenty of slip ups here."

"It must have optimum visibility," agreed Ammon. "Why don't we leave it in one of the larger squares in the centre."

His father said, "Done! Let's wrap it and make our way there now, then."

They both went off and packed the necessary

requirements for their journey, food, drink, fresh clothes, palm leaves, and plenty of rope to secure the stone as they were going to pull it again.

Husain said, "We can use trunks for this and roll it as we did before."

Ammon ran off with his saw to harvest several trees that could be used for wheels, then left them outside at the top of the stairs.

"Once we've pulled it up," he said, "we can manoeuvre it into position on the logs."

They spent the next hour puffing and panting, whilst they struggled to bring the stone up using lengths of wood laid out flat on the stairs, prising and pushing with additional bits of wood they used as levers. As they rounded the corner of the stairwell, they both gave a grunt, and raising it with all their might, threw it into place. Ammon took some leaves and folded them around its fragile front surface, emblazoned with the script. He tucked more leaves around the back and corners, for added protection.

"That'll do nicely," he said to himself. Husain was resting in the shade, preparing himself for the mammoth journey that was to follow, he knew it would take its toll on his body. He was telling himself that if he could finish his life by some kind and selfless act, then so much the better with his passing. His son enquired as to his mood and quiet mutterings and knew he must perk him up by changing the subject.

"Dad, you'll be fine. Think of why we are doing this, anyway."

"True, true," his father replied.

Once they both felt mentally and physically

composed, they grabbed their belongings, threw them into the tray they had created for carrying extra baggage.

"Courage!" Ammon shouted to Husain as he pushed up his arm. "In the name of the struggle against the pharaohs."

The pair of them were inspired and they both tugged with immense energy and a superhuman strength. They had to negotiate a tight corner that emerged out onto one of the city's main thoroughfares. Lockdown restrictions were still in place, but innumerable conveyances passed them by. One was carrying the recently dead, taking them out to one of the new elephant graveyards. They knew this because they can see huge lettering on its side, that it had been funded by an arm of Karim and Kissa's new organization.

"That's amazing," said Ammon. "They must have struck a deal with the pharaohs if they are allowing them to merge forces in this way. I wonder how they managed to fool them?"

Husain said, "Probably by not letting on that our aims are different."

The human traffic kept bustling past, and before long they found themselves at a small alcove in the adjacent wall. Columns rose from each corner, and a smaller plateau below was used for the sacrificing of mammals to the gods. They must make a turn there as it was the direction to the central pyramid, and then they were only a stone's throw to where they wanted to leave the stone.

They persevered and within minutes they were at the square, blinking to block out the harsh light. The trees were sparse, there was only a handful of them to afford any shade, amongst them rowan, mulberry, and a few pines. In its centre was an immense fountain that never had any water, only when the floods came twice a year. It was highly ornate with carvings of birds of prey that were revered by the pharaohs, falcon, eagle, and hawk.

Ammon tugged his father's arm, "This is the place, isn't it?"

"Yes." Husain nodded.

They shifted the stone into position and once they were happy with its overall location, they both stood to one side, and took it all in.

"I can see people coming from far and wide to see this," Ammon said.

Husain agreed. "I think we've done our bit, I'm happy to die in peace now. Even if the cholera takes me off."

"Don't be so morbid," Ammon said, worriedly.

As they were gazing around gathering their thoughts, they heard familiar voices.

"I recognize them!" Ammon said. "They sound like Karim and Kissa."

They rounded the corner and shortly after were followed by Huda, Keket, Femi, and Nour.

"Well, we've erected the stone as we want it," said Ammon. Huda was gleeful to the point of being ecstatic.

"This means that we have taken another small step in the direction of crushing the pharaohs spirit," Huda said. "I believe this will encourage the public to engage in new ways of thinking, that from the interior to the common people, all will assist in toppling the pharaohs, then, it's just left for us to remove them on a more physical basis. For this we need to look to the activities of Tarek, who we have seen recently. We left him in isolation working on the embalming of Augustuskamoun. He will be capable of working on all the pharaohs bodies, so they can pass through the all-important ferry of truth."

"Explain please?" said Ammon.

"For each pharaoh to travel to the afterlife, they must negotiate with Osiris who will weigh them with the feather of truth. If he decides that they acted in mistrustful and deceitful ways, their bodies will be cast into purgatory," Keket told him.

"None of them will have a chance," cried Husain.

Karim and Kissa had been standing in the background discussing how they were going to proceed.

Ammon interrupted, joyfully saying, "We saw your contraption earlier on, how great it is that you've managed to coordinate some form of arrangement."

Karim came over and stood at arm's length, answering, "Yes, we were very lucky that they agreed to collaborate. The pharaohs aren't renowned for this type of action."

"Don't ask us what we had to do to make this work," Kissa said.

Ammon asked. "Go on, what?"

"We agreed to make monthly payments directly into their trust. Promised as well that they can make regular checks of the graveyard to make sure nothing fishy is going on."

"How do you mean?" Ammon said.

"They are concerned that people might see it as a way to avoid the death tax, by arriving unannounced, and slipping off quietly with the other elephants."

"Do you think that might happen?" said Husain.

Karim answered, "Look, there's so many desperate people out there that nothing is out of the question as to what they might do."

"True, true," said Husain, and the group fell silent in front of the stone.

Nitocris was still out prowling for an update on how the pharaohs were doing. Nefertiti had given her a clear indication of the process that each one must pass through, and she had got the indication that they were heading for a fall. *There seems to be some universal madness going about,* she thought. *I've never seen them looking so ill at ease, usually they are more content with ruling the roost and making the lives of the minions a misery.*

Nefertiti herself approached Nitocris and said, "We know you're spying on us, Nitocris. So go and sling your hook, we can make your existence, or what's left of it, very ugly."

Nitocris hit back. "I've taken as much punishment as I want from this screwed up and stuck-up family. You've given a hard time without care, indiscriminately, to anyone who comes in your way. Now you'll be set for a fall," and she started cackling.

Nefertiti answered, with a false smile, "If you say so, how come?"

"Because your days are numbered," Nitocris said. "Huda has plans to take over from where you leave off, new systems, new heads of chair, and new elections.

Dealings will be more honest and transparent, no more back handers or corruption. The world will spin on a straight and true axle again. People will know what hour it is when they look at a sundial and won't expect it to have been tampered with by the pharaohs."

Nefertiti snarled and Nitocris narrowly missed slapping her in the face.

Nefertiti arched away and headed towards a place where she could recoup her losses.

"Much has gone already," she said, licking her wounds. "I've already lost three good men, Djoser, Snefru, and our handsome and lovable rogue of a ruler, Augustuskamoun. If I lose anymore to that curse, things have taken a twisted and hellish turn. Narmer, Khufu, and Ramses!"

She screamed for their attention and the three came scurrying over. They had been discussing the probability of falling victim to the curse, and were tallying up their money between them, trying to work out if there will be enough to pay off the ferry keeper.

"I think you've got it all wrong," Narmer said. "The ferry keeper has to be paid before, then we receive the gold coins after."

"What about the feather of truth?" Khufu said. "It seems that even we don't know our own mythology and just see any opportunity to give money away as beneficial for ourselves, so that we can ensure our future wellbeing in some way."

Nefertiti kept shouting louder and louder until they noticed steam streaming from her nostrils, then one of them stepped forward, and said, "Yes ma'am?"

Nefertiti was howling with rage by now, and said,

"Even my own flesh and blood mocks me," she screamed and with an echoing crash she went tumbling and hit the deck. Narmer, Ramses, and Khufu ran over to assist her, trying to save her dignity before she fell. But it was too late; the heels were up in the air and panties around the ankles. They all floundered around on the floor, attempting to pick her up with some form of decency. Nitocris who was crouching nearby and had a great view of all that went on, peered over noticing black voids in the crotches of all three men.

Another three fall to the curse, she thought. Making a mental note, she ducked under some bushes concealing herself for the next act. *They have suicidal tendencies; I can see that.*

They were fumbling about for a while before they managed to pick Nefertiti up and prop her back into her seat. Then she began blazing again, but this time about the stupidity of those that worked at the pyramid, one called Eshe, she knew well.

"That low life and her dirty immigrant husband," Nefertiti cried.

Nitocris gathered her latest comments were about race, making her blood boil. All those years working at the border had turned Nefertiti into a racist. Nefertiti was seething with anger, and she began rocking again, but this time, she rocked so violently, that she tumbled forwards and somersaulted embarrassingly towards Nitocris, who jumped up and tried to run, to escape but Nefertiti was upon her, all her pent-up rage being released.

Suddenly, the others were upon them. As Nitocris tried to slip away, Pepi, Seti and Khafre appeared and were summoned by Nefertiti to throw Nitocris to one side before making sure she was put back into her seat. Once Nefertiti was again installed on her seat, punches were thrown and kicks aimed mostly at Nitocris, who managed to extract herself from the flailing pile of limbs like a snake and taking great delight, while all this was going on, in noticing that another three crotches had fallen victims to the curse! She was delighted!

Keeping this to herself for the time being, Nitocris rolled away from the kerfuffle.

She could relax for a minute, take stock of her situation, lick her own wounds. She'd taken a beating and a grilling from Nefertiti, and she wouldn't stand for it anymore. *I'm pleased to see that the curse is spreading like wildfire between the pharaohs,* she thought. *It's no surprise though, they spend enough time in bed with each other. I'm surprised that crone Nefertiti hasn't got it herself, or its female counterpart, anyway. I guess that's why none of the rest of us have been touched either, Twosret, Cleopatra, or I.*

Nitocris counted on her fingers how many pharaohs altogether that made. Whilst she stood around, she tried to weigh up what the next best strategical move would be. She could either go back to the rest of the group, tell them what she's seen, and then they could take it from there. She looked up to keep an eye on any further developments between the pharaohs, but they were so intent on tangling horns with each other, they hardly noticed her disappear. Then she saw Khafre pop up, stumble about, grab hold of his testicles, and with a falsetto scream of false drama, he stuttered out, "I've lost the use of my testes and my innate ability to reproduce! The curse has worked its way through my whole being!"

Not another pharaoh listened, but then she saw another one step up and do the same, keeling over shortly after. Apparently, they all had the same issue, and it had spread like the clappers through their systems. She had heard of its toxicity and the rate its poison shot through the body, quicker than from the dart of an Amazon huntsman with a blow pipe. Now it was just a matter of time before it did its work, pulsing its way into the extremities of their fingers and toes, blood vessels in their feet, elbows, hands, and arms. Each one fell fast.

The commotion quietened down, and all was calm in the place they had been doing their best to defend for their second in command's honour. Only Nefertiti was left now, sitting proud and high above an arena of dead pharaohs. *They look like jack in the boxes,* Nitocris thought. *Twisted neck, tongue sticking out, eyes popping on springs. I don't think they can be any more resistant to this.* She glanced about uneasily, only now becoming aware of their location.

The clouds of dust and tireless screaming had nearly died down. She tried to estimate how long she had been gone, since she left the rest of the group. *They will worry,* she thought. She looked down and saw that she was visibly trembling, and her upper lip wouldn't stop quivering.

"Maybe I've developed one of those nervous ticks," Nitocris said to herself. Then realized she was speaking out loud, and resorted to a whisper, "That Nefertiti is still about."

She ducked her head down and ran like the wind, to

where she could find safety. She heard Nefertiti snarling and snapping like one of the hounds of hell, drooling with fury, like she might burst another blood vessel. *That can't be good for her heart,* Nitocris thought. And taking the image of Nefertiti about to keel over with a dodgy ticker and self-induced coronary disease, she went whistling along on her way.

I must get along, Nitocris thought, urging herself to hurry despite the weight of what she had just seen, the traumatic experience undergone. The shock of having witnessed the pharaohs dropping like flies, each missing their scrotum sacks, their ability to breed like bunnies, both amused and frightened her.

She shuddered at the thought, then began picturing all the awful ways that they had treated people and soon got over it. *The way they spread their seed without a care or a thought for where it ends up, they don't want to profligate it, they want it to be deposited as far as is humanly possible around the globe, and they don't care who gets embroiled within it. They spend years perfecting their technique of dominating situations. They were like control freaks. Another perfect example was during elections. They always tried to push that little bit further, to make another preposterous claim or try to push another outrageous bit of legislation, another update about lockdown restrictions, or how to handle safely the virus. As if by doing this they would increase their popularity, even though many more found themselves out of favour, their ideas outdated.*

She hummed to herself in a flat tone. *Huda proposes we will all have our roles, and each will be charged equally with their duties,* she thought, and realised it sounded idyllic. *All of us working as cogs, health, education, defence, immigration, plus all the other departments. Perfectly in time and in tune with each other.* Huda had really convinced her of the validity of their proposed society and how it would work. Nitocris was really impressed by its scope, breadth, and the ambition of a small outfit to go up against the weight of the current system.

Nitocris's blinding vision was shattered as she approached a group of people she knew well. She ran across and tapped the closest person to her.

"Keket, it's me, Nitocris."

Keket jumped back with fright, "Explain yourself?"

"I've been with the pharaohs; you'll never guess what? All the pharaohs apart from Nefertiti have succumbed to the curse, I've never spoken a more honest word."

Keket, to alleviate her sense of having to prove herself, offered a kind word.

"I believe you," she said.

"That's a relief, then," said Nitocris.

"That's some mind-boggling news," Keket replied.

And she tapped the nearest member of the group on the shoulder, spreading the news quickly between them. It reached Huda's ears at the front and there was a shout of elation which proceeded to swamp and damp out the rest of the group's ability to hear. They were all so excited, and each began to spread the gossip as they heard it. The core of it didn't change much, but the outer layer altered radically, each person spinning out their own version of it.

Huda manoeuvred herself into a position from which she could be heard and said, "With just one of them lurking about and her being on her last legs, I think we can safely say that this is the revolution. Also, Karim and Kissa have been putting their stamp on the world about us, already, ensuring none of us will ever have to live under their oppressive yoke, again."

Cries of jubilation went up into the air from the rest of the group.

A huge procession was to be carried out in honour of the pharaohs; it would take place from one temple and ran to another on the other side of the city. Their mummies would be transported in specialised carriages, featuring small pockets of air to cushion them, stop them from disintegrating further along the way.

Word had got about that Tarek had been taking care of the embalming of Augustuskamoun and was making a splendid job of it so far. He was called in to do the same for the rest of them, to put a golden tongue into each of their mouths, so they can speak to the lord of the underworld, Osiris. This was a typical request from the pharaohs.

The morning the march was to occur dawned, already broiling hot. The fan bearers were out in force; they had been posted at various points along the way and were to provide a constant source of ventilation for guests. Overall, there was a poor turn out, only a handful of visitors came along this time, unlike at Augustuskamoun's procession. He had many more crowds, though most of these only showed up out of fear that if they didn't attend, they might be seen as national traitors and be thrown to their deaths in grim and grisly ways.

The route circulated through the city and navigated

relevant places of religion, learning, and public veneration. They would pass through the public square where Ramses made his speech, trying to lure shoppers back to their daily business of buying, bartering, and selling. It would go through markets, bazaars, souks, and busy shopping streets, where all human traffic had been called to a halt.

At the Avenue of the Sphinx, they would stop and read a list of names out. These were of the other pharaohs who had passed away, for each there would be a blast on a trumpet. Not a single mention would be made for families who had died of cholera. Then the march would continue, circumnavigating cremation facilities, test centres, and other generous donations to society that had been made, such as the central pyramid where most of the governments administration was done.

It was their aim that the best possible send-off would be given, as well as ensuring that their reception would be assured through copious amounts of treasure being endowed upon them by various families of the pharaohs. After leaving this point, they would head up towards the central pyramid, where the bodies were to be removed from their caskets, then placed in their individual tombs.

Members of the public, including slaves and servants who they had grown close too, though these were very few, came to lay garlands of Egyptian flowers. There were poppies, lotus, and papyrus, amongst others. Once the necessary time of mourning had elapsed, they were to make official funeral arrangements.

The bodies had been worked on by Tarek, who

recovered from his bout of cholera and was feeling much better. He had been in attendance for at least a week at the embalming. They provided him with all the necessary equipment and arranged for him to be on constant call for any eventuality that might arise. He debated inviting Nour up to keep him company, for the duration, but decided the space for him to work in is too small. Its top window has shutters of wood and a crane operated by winches and a pulley on the outside wall.

The pharaohs were transported into the space using cradles and ropes. As each one came bouncing through the window, Tarek caught it, then threw it to the floor, where he began his morbid task of painting their faces up. He had no professional experience of decorating corpses in this way, but it wasn't such a difficult task. He just needed a good assortment of pigments and oils with which to mix his colours.

He complemented the traditional blues and golds of their headpieces, as well as rebuilding their beards if they were missing. He had a lot of work trying to make them look sincere and lovable, if anything, their sallow pallor and wrinkles of death just make them look even more unapproachable. Their furrowed brows had become deeper and more etched in, making them appear more critical.

When Tarek felt that they had been restored to their former glory, he sent them soaring through an open grate, where they encountered the burning flames of Hades. There was an intense burst of heat, light, and colour, as if magnesium was exploding, then it fizzled furiously like a stick of dynamite. Tarek peered through a curtain that was ajar a tiny bit, and he saw the coffin being consumed whole. *Well, that's a relief,* he thought, making a mental note to tell the rest of the group of this evidential occurrence.

Tarek heard loud pops as if a chemical reaction was going off in there, so he glanced around. He could only see one who seemed to be in a lot of pain. He heard them calling for help or somebody's name.

"Osiris!"

Then the voices died down. He had heard stories of the souls of the departed hovering or hanging over the bodies, because they were lost and didn't know which way to go to find the ferry keeper.

Osiris raised his hand; he wouldn't let anyone through until they had been judged with the feather of truth. A disembodied form floated towards him.

"Halt!" Osiris yelled. "You may go no further."

Eight or ten formless apparitions hovered in the air; they were merely the souls of the departed. Osiris motioned to the first one to follow him, and he proceeded to walk towards a pair of huge weighing scales of overly elaborate form. Its arms were columns of solid gold with built in fretwork beneath, and its chains were of delicate and fragile silver.

The whole structure shone like a magpie's nest and at one end of the scale was a tiny platform where a microscopic feather lay. As they looked at it, they could see this was no ordinary feather, this was one of extraordinary purity, you could see right through it, and it had no markings that suggest evil, or other discolouration's.

Osiris pointed at the other end of the scale, and the first disembodied form in the queue went and sat down upon it. There was a tiny creak to begin with, the noise built to a crescendo, then a din of chains came crashing down like the gates of hell. Osiris looked back and laughed, jerking his thumb down.

A bolt from the sky was heard, then the noble god of Amenti was upon them and stuck out its arm. At this signal, the trapdoor opened in the cloudlike floor beneath them, swallowed them up, and they were never seen again. The echo of a cry of angst was heard. The second form floated over and like clockwork the process happened over, their pitiful soul being thrown to the hounds of hell.

Osiris was on call for around an hour, until he reported back to his authorities that all who came for judgment had passed through. Then there was a muffled slam, and the cloud trapdoor shut, its whole surrounding woolly-like structure folded up and disappeared, too.

Chapter Nineteen

After Tarek had finished flushing the last of the pharaohs through the gate. And sending them to their fiery deaths. He looked out of the window to gauge the time by the suns position. *It must be nearly 3pm.,* he thought. *I must get back to Nour and the others.* He waited until the last of the embers had burnt out just to be on the safe side, as he didn't want to risk the place going up in flames. Then he flew like the wind back out into the stifling heat, and the thrum of the city hit him.

As he was stood there, he noticed that Nour was walking over to see him.

Tarek said, "Nour my dear, I never thought I'd see you again."

"Thank God it's you," Nour replied.

"Where are the others?"

"They are just around the corner," she said.

"What happened with the pharaohs was something else. I didn't exactly see it, but they were disappearing off somewhere."

"How do you mean?" Nour replied.

"The feather of truth transports you to the other side, no questions asked. Regardless of how guilty the pharaohs might have felt about their actions."

"Okay, that sounds believable," she replied.

A minute later Femi walked around the corner.

"What are you two doing around here?" She said.

"Not much," Nour replied, "I was talking with Tarek. What have you guys been up to?"

Femi said, "Debating our next move. Right now,

things are sweet with Karim and Kissa running the show. Apparently, Nefertiti is still about, she's female so the curse couldn't take her out."

"That's lousy," Tarek replied.

"Isn't that the truth," Femi said.

Tarek spoke over both. "How amazing would it be if we could make use of the trapdoor ourselves."

"But to do what though?" Femi said.

"Get out of here, escape the cholera pandemic and any danger of getting the curse."

Femi said, "That sounds like it would be a clever move. Even though its only really you, Ammon and Husain who are at risk of getting it, being male."

"True enough," he replied, "but for all of us it will improve our odds no end."

Nour was quiet for a minute.

Tarek nudged her in the ribs, "What's wrong with you, cat got your tongue?"

Nour replied, "Not really, I was deliberating the idea. But overall, I think it would be a sensible option. Will our continuing financial arrangement with Eshe carry on?"

"Of course," he said, "that's an ongoing deal."

"How about your business running the mummification workshops?"

Tarek said, "It depends where we end up, doesn't it. If we go to a place where they still need such a service, I'll be laughing - otherwise it'll be curtains for me. But Nour, your bakery will always keep running, I don't see a problem with that. People always need bread."

"True," she replied. "Okay. Let's not hesitate a minute longer, lead the way to this trapdoor you talked of."

"With pleasure," he said.

Tarek slunk off round the corner with Nour on his tail.

Tarek shouted out to Femi, "Go and tell the others that we have a plan, and for them to come and join us if they want. We'll wait here."

"Deal," she yelled.

She ran off. In two minutes, she'd found the others.

"He wants to try and follow the pharaohs," she blurted out to Keket.

Keket said, "How though? That sounds very far-fetched to me."

Femi replied, "I trust him on this one. He's got that mischievous look in his eye, as if he's planned the whole thing."

"Let's go then," Keket cried out, "anybody else coming to join us?"

Karim ran after her, then Kissa followed behind her love, seeing no other option.

"Are you coming as well?" Kissa said to Huda.

"If it will get us away from these stinking pharaohs, I don't see why not, it can only improve our situation."

And that was it, within a minute they were all gathered around Tarek. Who was stood by the trapdoor with a gleam in his eye.

"I can see what you mean," said Kissa to Nour. "If he told me that we'd all be transported to a place where we would all live forever, I'd believe him."

Tarek took them back into the building where he'd carried out the embalming and pointed at the fire grate.

Tarek said, "That's where I pushed the pharaohs to their fiery end. Now the fire's gone out so the passage should be a safe one for us."

"Good thing," Kissa replied, who was right by his side.

She ducked her head under the metal surrounding and lowered herself into the central part of the chamber where the burning took place. Tarek stood back and waved his arm for Nour and the others to pass through.

Nour was next, and Tarek planted a kiss on her forehead.

"If I never see you again, it'll be awful. But at least we will have known love for each other. And I've had an amazing existence living with you, our relationship has been wonderful."

Nour replied, "You're making me blush."

Then Nour ducked her head and followed Kissa.

One by the one the whole queue of them filed through, until it was just left for Tarek to go. He took a deep breath, wished himself luck and that they would all have a safe passage.

Kissa was at the front, and she groped about in the blackened confines of the furnace.

Tarek yelled from behind, "Follow your nose, it shouldn't be too much further."

"Right," she replied.

Kissa kept on walking, then she stumbled and fell into an open trapdoor.

Nour cried out, "Oh my God, she's disappeared!"

Then Nour's voice was lost in the upper part of the chimney, as she slipped through too. One by one they all took their turn to make the trip through the trapdoor.

A few moments later, Kissa popped back out into

another grimy oily furnace. She pulled herself to safety and waited for the others to arrive.

"Wow," said Kissa, "that was crazy. But where the hell are we now?"

"I've no idea," replied Tarek. "Let's go and explore."

Tarek pushed open the door, then led the whole group down the stairs two at a time. As they reached the bottom of the staircase, they found themselves on the ground floor of an immense building.

"What is this place?" Femi said.

"I've no idea," replied Nour.

Tarek was bravest and took the lead. Soon he was joined by Huda.

"Let's go," said Huda.

The pair of them ran off, and there was quiet from the rest of the group.

"Do you think we will be okay?" Keket said to Femi.

"I've no idea," she replied. "Let's follow them."

"Okay," Keket said.

After a while they discovered a hallway with an immense window that looked out over a street. Huda pulled the curtain back and peered her head out.

"It looks radically different to me here, where the hell have, we brought ourselves to?"

"What do you mean?" Tarek replied.

Huda grabbed his shoulders and jostled him into position so that he could see for himself.

"Wow," he said, "this place looks like nowhere I've ever been before."

Huda replied, "You're right on that one."

"Where's he brought us to?" Nour interrupted.

Huda gently nudged her into place.

As she gazed out of the window, she was suddenly confronted by a loud screech coming from high in the air.

"What the heck was that?" Nour said.

She looked up into the sky.

"Perhaps it was a giant bird," replied Huda.

"A big one, maybe it was prehistoric," said Tarek.

"Ha, ha," chuckled Nour, regaining her sense of humour.

A minute later there was another high-pitched deafening boom.

"That was even louder than last time," Tarek said, "what could it be?"

Tarek craned his head and neck out of the window so that he could view all the sky. Right then, a gigantic angel of steel came tearing down from the skies.

"Oh my God," cried out Tarek, and leapt to the floor, "we are all finished!"

Huda who was cooler, peeped her head out of the window to investigate further. "It looks like nothing I've seen before, but I've heard of such things being built. Leonardo da Vinci was a great artist who used to design flying machines."

"A flying machine," screamed Femi, delirious with fear and ducked below. She was far more superstitious. "I don't trust anything I've not seen with my own eyes before."

"Let's venture out into the street," Tarek said, "it looks like that hellish force has vanished."

"Good plan," replied Femi who was stood by his side. Tarek was the boldest, and tried the handle of the door, unlatching it, then checking in each direction, before heading out quiet as a mouse. The others followed in his footsteps. A minute later Tarek found himself at a vast span of grey. It seemed to stretch for miles.

"Is it a desert?" Femi said.

"I think so," replied Tarek, "but a dull and monotonous one. Let's venture out onto it."

He plunged his strappy sandal into the surface, but instead of sinking in as he'd expected, it was solid as a rock.

"I think I know what this is," he said, "it must be a flattened mountain range."

"Is that even possible?" She replied.

"I don't know but I'm willing to offer options as to what it might be."

"Let's cross it and find out then," Femi said, and stepped one foot onto the surface.

As she was about to take another step a high sided vehicle with many carriages came rattling passed, and she was knocked flying.

"Do you think it's a train?" Tarek said, who had leapt back himself, he was more familiar with those.

"It could be," replied Huda, in a serious tone, who was stood nearby.

"That thing was dangerous though; we can't risk trying to cross and being flattened." Tarek said, "but in that case how are we supposed to get across? We could wait for it to get dark, then perhaps it'll be easier."

"Good plan," replied Huda. "But we may have to wait a while."

The group sat down to rest a little and gather their

thoughts. Above them they could see endless shimmering lights trailing off into the distance.

"They are all tearing along," said Femi. "Pretty scary overall."

To their left and right they could see avenues of towering lampposts stretching away. Huge great monstrosities tore through the air, some with several floors.

Femi was laid on her back with her eyes agog and her mouth gaping open. Keket leaned over to her and said, "You don't want to do that, or you might end up catching flies."

And she nudged Femi.

"True enough," she replied.

"We need a plan of action," Tarek said, and he came to the aid of the group. "I can get us through this situation. I promise you all."

Nour had hearts in her eyes and waited politely for him to speak.

Tarek said, "Now we've found ourselves in this location, let's think about what we need to do. Who wants to go and find the pharaohs, is anybody up for that?"

There was a cheer, and a few hands went up in support of the idea.

"Come on then who's with me!"

"But what about the pharaohs?" Femi said.

"Nefertiti is still alive, and the others came through shortly after," replied Keket.

"Let's take stock and wait it out," said Nour, "with a bit of luck we'll soon be able to cross that vast expanse of concrete."

"Good plan," replied Tarek.

They got themselves comfortable, in their space, so they could sleep a little. Then in the middle of the night they were suddenly awoken by a furious panting.

"I know that sound," said Tarek, rubbing his eyes blearily.

Huda joined him, and the two of them sat in shocked silence as the whole group of pharaohs marched passed.

"Duck your head behind a rock," Tarek cried out, "we don't want to be seen."

"Good point," replied Huda, and she was gone in a flash.

They watched as the pharaohs led by Augustuskamoun and Nefertiti paraded by.

Nefertiti was stood next to Augustuskamoun, and she said slyly to him, "I thought that was it, once you'd lost your manhood, we'd never see you again."

"Me too," replied Augustuskamoun, "but how wrong I've been. Look, I'm all in one piece, albeit missing a vital part of my gonads still."

"I wouldn't say in one piece then," said Nefertiti.

"True enough."

Nefertiti stood there fuming and bellowing to the rest of the group. "I'm not sure where we've ended up coming to here, any ideas?"

Augustuskamoun replied, "Perhaps we've come to a new time, I know a thing or two about that. It happened to me not so long ago."

Ramses, who'd been keeping quiet, said, "He's got a good point, he brought us from another era, along with that cholera pandemic."

Twosret and Cleopatra both looked revitalised, and full of fight once again.

Twosret said, "What happened to Nitocris? has anybody seen her?"

"Not me," replied Augustuskamoun, "and she's my other half."

There was silence as they gathered their thoughts, then Nefertiti said, "I know where she's gone, she must be with Tarek, Nour, Femi, Keket, Huda, Karim and Kissa."

"But why would she do that?" Augustuskamoun said.

"I've no idea," she replied. "Maybe she wants to keep betraying us."

"Never mind that anyway," said Augustuskamoun. "Let's get along, we've much to do now we've crossed into this new world."

"Like what?" Seti said.

"Spreading the cholera virus and the curse, you buffoon," he replied.

"Of course."

They kept on with their discussion as they passed Tarek and his slumbering group.

"Let's make tracks then," said Augustuskamoun.

"Good plan," said Pepi. "But where to?"

"No idea, let's see what we mischief we can raise."

"I'm up for that," Seti said.

"Let's head for the nearest population hub," said Augustuskamoun, somewhat wearily. "Then hopefully we can find somebody who might be able to inform us where we are. And to enlighten us as to the events of the day."

Seti replied, "Okay," and fell into line behind Augustuskamoun.

The whole motley queue of pharaohs made their way along, with Augustuskamoun at the front. A short while later, they bumped into somebody who was taking an evening stroll. They were dressed in several layers of clothing, a scarf, woolly hat, and a bag with an umbrella tucked into it.

"Who is this guy?" Nefertiti said, "he must be a local, lets quiz him to find out what we need to know."

The group stopped for minute, just long enough for Augustuskamoun to address the poor shaking chap.

"Could you tell us where we are?" He said to the man.

The man looked up at him, then without fear in his voice, but constantly blowing his nose, coughing and spluttering, said, "You've found yourself in England where we are suffering from a Covid pandemic."

"Pandemic, Pandemic?" replied Augustuskamoun, "that sounds vaguely familiar."

The man took up his position a safe distance way, then continued their discussion.

"We are currently going through a lockdown; nobody may go within five feet of another."

"Wow, that's ingenious," said Seti, who had been stood nearby. "What a great way to solve a pandemic."

The man looked uncomfortable for a minute, then carried on. "Well, we are under the control of an absolute bunch of reprobates - The Elite party - have you heard of them?"

Seti replied, "No."

The man said, "They are a hard-nosed government. They won't let any of the minions even sneeze, let alone speak, or have their own thoughts."

"Who are the minions?"

The man said, "Don't ask daft questions. Where have you guys come from? Judging by your outfits another time."

Seti shifted from foot to foot, then in a hoarse voice said, "The 1900's, we were the ruling pharaohs from our time. And where have you come from just out of interest?"

The man replied, "This is London, and the year is 2020."

"Oh my God," said Seti, and a minute later Ramses had to assist him to the floor as he felt feint.

"Give the poor man time to recover," Ramses said, "then we'll continue our conversation. We would much love to find those meddling Elites and have it out with them."

"But I thought," said the man, "if anything you wanted to join forces, not war against them."

Seti replied, "Perhaps that's a better plan, but we need to find out where they reside. Could you give us an address?"

The man said, "Sure. They can usually be found at a gothic looking towering cathedral that stretches back from the river, it's only a mile or so from here. And he pointed his thumb over his shoulder.

"Thanks."

"Think nothing of it," said the man, politely whilst wondering if what he had seen was actually real. *Maybe one less gin and tonic tonight,* he thought. *Or perhaps I should just give up drinking altogether. I'm talking to a pharaoh, for goodness' sake!*

The light was falling fast now, and tiny little stars could be seen popping out, lighting up the sky, constellations and milky ways far away in the distance. thundering traffic and endless din of people tramping passed was incredible. The streets were filthy and grey.

"Where are we?" Seti asked.

The man said, "This is Lambeth, you're only a stone's throw away from Westminster."

"What is this Westminster?" Ramses replied.

"It's what the government calls home."

"Come on then," said Ramses, and the pharaohs rushed off, all high falutin' and full of themselves.

An hour later they arrived at a monstrous sprawling building, exactly as the man spoke of.

"This must be the place," Ramses said.

"Of course," replied Nefertiti, and gave a signal to the other pharaohs to follow her.

"Let's take this alleyway, and with a bit of luck it will bring us out into the main building," he said.

"Good plan," said Seti who was close by.

The group of them followed Ramses' lead, and before long they found themselves at a mammoth chamber through which they could hear a monotonous droning of voices. Seti cupped his hand and put it to his ear, up against the oak panelled door, so he could hear what they were saying.

"It sounds as if they are planning the next government," he said, "only in another language, it's not Egyptian at all though."

"How can you tell?" Ramses replied, who was next to him.

Seti said, "I've no idea. I must have some idea of how

it sounds when we give orders to the masses, hand out tiresomely long policies and they have no option but to listen."

"Good point," he replied, and he was lost in a bubble of thought, as he cast himself back to the times when then were ruling the roost back in Cairo.

Seti cried out, "Duck! It must be winding down."

And he pulled Ramses to the ground, who came thundering down.

Then a heavy bolt was unlatched, and the door creaked open. The pharaohs hid wherever they could to avoid being seen, and a minute later plummy English public schoolboy tones came filtering through.

"So crisp and clear," whispered Ramses from the floor.

The room was filled with the banter of the over privileged. All at the same time the pharaohs tried to communicate, but they were so self-possessed and only worried about their own concerns that there was little conversation between them, they were just talking to themselves. Then one who seemed to be the leader got up onto a pedestal and began to speak.

"The next crushing cull of the public will be delivered by 4pm, where the fate of another lockdown will be announced. As well as new restrictions that will hit everybody's pockets apart from our own."

"What's he saying," Ramses said.

Seti replied, "It all sounds garbled to me, an unintelligible mess."

"The same here," said Nefertiti. "I'll tell you what, why don't we go and see what carnage we can cause?

It's that or we ask them to team up."

"I vote for us to team up," Seti replied.

"Alright," Nefertiti said, "but how will they understand us?"

Ramses said, "The universal language of being an arrogant fool, who only sees the world from their own eyes."

"Good point," said Nefertiti. "Go on then."

And she pushed Ramses out from under his cover.

Ramses' head popped out, he was wearing his war necklaces, beads and all his finery. On the tip of his chin, he had a gold shimmering protrusion that stretched down. It made him look severe and awe inspiring. And within a minute of him stepping up, all the men in the room were cowering on the floor.

"Now I've got your attention," said Ramses in Egyptian, "I need to make a few things clear; we are here to be your friends, we want to team up so that we can wipe out the masses together."

Their leader who was a bumbling fool with blonde floppy hair spoke next. Whilst he did, he caught Ramses' attention.

"I can see that we are going to get on like a house on fire," he said.

Ramses understood nothing, but judging by the smile on his face, decided he must agree.

He looked at Augustuskamoun and Nefertiti, "Did they mean us not harm them, or do they want us to all be on the same side?"

"It's difficult to tell," said Seti, who was stood nearby, "but how can we be sure of their good intentions, and that they are not leading us astray?"

"Good point," said Ramses, and he gave another unintended smirk.

Their leader began coughing and spluttering as he had Covid himself, then sent out a huge spray of germs into the air.

"Oh my God," cried out Ramses, "duck for your life, unless you want to get another disease."

"He's right you know," said Seti, and leapt to the floor, then the pair of them wriggled about trying to cover their eyes, ears, mouths and noses. But sadly, to no avail.

Millions of tiny virus-like particles with curious shapes rained down gently all over the pair of them.

"Argh, that's it, now we are done for," Ramses said.

"Why don't we offer them something they can't refuse," Nefertiti said.

"Like what?" Augustuskamoun said.

"I know," she said, and looked at the gaping hole in his knackers.

"What a neat idea," he replied. "But how exactly?"

"You decide, you're the clever one."

Augustuskamoun scratched his head, then gave a whoop of joy, "I've got it." As he stepped towards their leader and shook him warmly by the hand, he took hold of his groin and gave it a huge squeeze. "That should do trick."

Their leader fell back towards the rest of his Elite party enclave. Unintelligible words were sprouting from his mouth. One of his fellow men, caught him as he felt to the floor. Then they all watched in horror as the curse did its dirty work. Leaving his privates in a less than desired state.

"Oh my God," cried out one of his fellow MPs. "What has become of our leader?"

Ramses walked over next, using hand signals and pulling faces. "He hasn't got much time left, in under an hour he'll be a goner. And it'll be the same for the rest of you, only the men though, of course!" And he gave a cheery wink. "And you will all come down with cholera too. Just to ram it home, just imagine having to deal with two pandemics. The public will be fine."

One of their Elite party MP friends stood up and said, "Well we've made a fine mess of handling one, so I'm sure it shouldn't be too difficult for us, and of course, as you rightly say, the public will be fine!" And he gave a hideous hysterical guffaw.

About the Author

Nicholas Vaughan is an artist with a varied practice from sculpture to drawing, mixed media to installation, often developing fictional texts for the illustration of his artwork. He received his degree in Sculpture from Wolverhampton University (2001) and an MA in Fine Art from Chelsea College of Art and Design (2002).

His work has been shown in shows throughout Europe, including at The Corner House Gallery in Manchester and Imperial College in London as well as at Gliwice Museum in Poland. He has work in public and private collections.

Provoco is delighted to be publishing Nicholas's debut novel, which he tells us was a labour of love, and which kept him busy and amused during lockdown! Nicholas has two other self-published novels currently available online and is in the process of writing further work for Provoco about climate change and the environment.

The Unwrapping is Nicholas's debut novel for Provoco, and we look forward to his next release, scheduled for winter 2026, or early 2027.